MISSION IMPOSSIBLE

MISSION IMPOSSIBLE

HOW LENNOX LEWIS UNIFIED THE WORLD HEAVYWEIGHT TITLE

JAMES LAWTON

FOREWORD BY TOMMY 'HITMAN' HEARNS

EDINBURGH AND LONDON

First published in Great Britain in 2000 by
MAINSTREAM PUBLISHING COMPANY (EDINBURGH) LTD
7 Albany Street
Edinburgh EH1 3UG

ISBN 1 84018 272 5

Photographs © Michael J. Brennan
Drawings © Graham Allen

A catalogue record for this book is available from the British Library

Typeset in Futurist and Berkeley Book
Printed and bound in Great Britain by Butler & Tanner Ltd

Contents

FOREWORD BY TOMMY 'HITMAN' HEARNS   7

INTRODUCTION   13

ONE	Fear in the Garden	23
TWO	The Crowning Glory	41
THREE	A Warrior's Pain	57
FOUR	Touch of Class	71
FIVE	The Sun – and the Shadow	87
SIX	Evander's Anvil	103
SEVEN	Failure in the Fifth	119
EIGHT	The Scent of Scandal	141
NINE	Rages of Indecision	157
TEN	A Crime of Folly	173
ELEVEN	King Flies Again	189
TWELVE	The Honest Nave	205

THIRTEEN	One Last Step	219
FOURTEEN	A Kind of Justice	231
FIFTEEN	Standing with Ali	247

Foreword

Lennox Lewis has reached the peak of boxing. He stands in the place of Joe Louis and Muhammad Ali and Mike Tyson. He is somewhere any fighter would dream of being. He is the undisputed heavyweight champion of the world and I saw him do it in New York and Las Vegas. He fought 24 rounds with Evander Holyfield, a three-time world heavyweight champion, a feat matched only by Ali – and each one of those rounds could have changed his life at any moment.

The big man has the world of boxing at his feet now. He is *the man*, the one everyone has to look up to. The whole point of boxing is to find out who is the best in the world; that's the goal that spurs everyone who first puts on the gloves. So Lennox Lewis sets the tone for all fighters now. Every big, tough young kid in the world wants to be where he is. Wants to know what it's like walking down the street in New York or London or Paris and have people shout, 'Hi, howya doin' champion?' Man, that is something, isn't it? Snap your fingers, and it's right there, a limo, a bottle of champagne, a beautiful lady. It all goes with the territory.

Lennox has gone the distance. He's had the good times and the bad. Now he can look in the mirror and say, 'I got there.' But he may want to ask himself a question, one that I have always asked and I'm sure men like Louis and Ali and even Mike Tyson did from time to time.

The question is this: how will I be remembered? Will I be thought of as just another champion? Or someone who for a little while made the world stop?

I believe he should ask himself this question and if he does he may realise he has to do something more. He has to fight to please not only himself but also the people. The ones who pay for the tickets and make the rewards of every successful fighter. When the fans go to a big fight they want to see something they will never forget. They want to step out of themselves and their normal lives. They want to remember the action. They want to say, 'Man, that was a fight – that was a real fight. That's something I ain't ever going to forget.'

No one can argue with Lennox Lewis about whether he deserves his status. He got there with his skill and his ability and anyone who has shown the courage to get into the ring has my respect. Lennox never ran for the shadows. He never ducked an opponent. He was in Riddick Bowe's face all those years. He took on anyone they put in front of him and because of this he is in his rightful place. He looks so perfect, so big and strong and he carries himself with the bearing of a champion.

But I do want more from Lennox Lewis and I know that his trainer and my friend, Emanuel Steward, also wants more. Emanuel and I worked together many years and though we had rows about certain issues and tactics and which fights we should take – and even today we have arguments about whether I should still fight – we both knew what we were chasing.

It wasn't just winning fights, even titles. It was getting

everything out. It was walking away from the ring knowing that you had used every scrap of all that you brought to the place; all the pain and the effort and the strength you get from living, day in, day out, as a fighter. Lennox says he knows how to win a fight and he doesn't want to take unnecessary chances, and to a point he is right. But sometimes you have to go beyond that if you want something more than a belt to wear around your waist.

At the age of 40 I still want to fight – and it is really about winning more titles. It is so deep in my nature. I have won my world titles and people say I should just look back at my career with pride. But I still feel the urge to fight even though I have such a good life now, a big house, fancy cars, including a Rolls-Royce, and I see my eldest boy playing basketball in college and with maybe a future in the pros. But once fighting is in your blood it is difficult to shake away from it.

I suppose these feelings run so strong because nothing has come into my life which makes me feel so good as working out every day and knowing that there is a point to it, that I will be getting in the ring again and just letting everything hang out. After I take my youngest boy to school I go straight to the gym and I work and then when it is over I feel like running down the street and shouting, 'Man, I'm alive – I'm still alive.' Of course there is a lot to enjoy outside the ring. There is the pleasure of your friends. There is the joy of watching your child grow strong and right. But the ring is something different, something separate. Maybe you have to go in it to really understand why some men keep wanting to go back to it, men who don't just need the money, and why when they look at fights they are very hard to satisfy.

It touches me a lot when people say to me, 'Don't do it, Tommy. Don't go back in the ring.' That tells me they love me enough, and remember my great fights enough, to try to make the effort to influence me and get me to just sit back and enjoy the good life. But I tell them all, old good friends and guys I meet in the street,

'This is in my blood. This is what I do – and I can still do it.' Maybe I'm right, maybe I'm wrong, but that's how I am – an old fighting man.

Manny Steward doesn't want Lennox Lewis to be remembered just as the undisputed heavyweight champion of the world. He raves about his talent. He swears it is the greatest he has seen since Ali. He wants the world to see more than the fact that he has finished owning all the heavyweight belts. There is a lot of honour in that, I know. I speak as someone who spent a lot of his life winning titles. In all I've won six world titles at different weights from welter to cruiser but the heavyweight title, the most prestigious of all, was a little beyond my reach physically.

Lennox is a fine natural heavyweight with all the gifts but as he stands now he cannot expect to go down as one of the great champions. For that he has to take another step. He has to listen to Manny, and he has to know that being champion of the world, undisputed, out there on your own, is something that demands some special kind of payback.

Everything depends on how Lennox Lewis sees himself from here on in. If he is content to rest on what he has achieved, to win fights in the easiest way he can, he will go down as a very capable champion. But there comes a time when every man must find the best he has in himself. He has to go for broke.

If he finally does that they will speak of him as they did Muhammad Ali, the greatest champion, *the* man of all our boxing days, or as they think of the fighter Lennox beat, Evander Holyfield, and the man Holyfield beat, Mike Tyson. They might not like everything about Mike Tyson, but they know he is a fighter who is prepared to go to the limit. That he has a few times gone beyond it is another matter, and his big problem.

But for the kind of recognition I'm talking about you have to go to a bad place, you have to take risks in the belief that you will go down there and scuffle and battle and come back with the biggest prize of all, the knowledge that you have asked from yourself all you have and produced it when it mattered most.

Lennox Lewis may have done that a few times in his career but I cannot say he did it when he took the undisputed heavyweight title. In my opinion he showed Holyfield too much respect. I believe he can go beyond that. When I fought Marvin Hagler I knew I had to go to my limit. I had to gamble. But when I lost the gamble I didn't have any regrets. I made an honest decision about my best chance of winning, and winning well. Maybe I should have stayed away from him more, used my reach, tried to outbox him. But I knew how strong he was, how he would keep coming at me, and I decided I would go for him. I would hang out there, on the edge.

Man, that was a night. I'd worked so hard for the fight. When I got into the ring my legs felt so tired I didn't believe I could go 12 rounds with a fighter as strong as Hagler. I felt I had to get him out of there. I don't blame Manny – we had our rows but they were never about how good he was at his job. Lennox is sure about Manny's ability and he should be. He tried to rein me in against Hagler. But you can't get your time back. I can't, Lennox can't, but if I could I wouldn't fight Hagler in the same way. I would have trusted my legs a little more, fought through that feeling of tiredness. I would box him, use my reach, attempt to drive him crazy with frustration. That was always going to be the strategy and I'd fought it a thousand times in my head. But then the bell rings and you are in reality.

The reality that night was heavy, the crowd was going mad, there was a huge flag hanging down the side of Caesar's Palace and so what do you do when your legs feel like lead and all that frenzy is building up around you? You hit the guy as many times as you can.

People still tell me that was the greatest fight they ever saw, even though it went less than three rounds, and that they will remember it when they forget my other fights against such men as

Sugar Ray Leonard and Wilfred Benitez and Roberto Duran – all great fighters.

I want Lewis to be remembered for more than the way he beat Holyfield, even though he fought very professionally, and with a lot of control over what he was doing.

It is important for boxing that there is an undisputed heavyweight champion of the world. Lennox Lewis has done the sport a great service by fighting his way to the top of the game and by behaving so well, with such dignity. Now there is another step to take and he must do it. He owes it to himself and the game he now dominates. Boxing needs a man to push back the borders of fighting again. That is the last challenge for Lennox Lewis. He has the title he has been fighting for all his life. He has the money and the fame. Now he goes for the last prize and the most important one of all. Now he goes to win the hearts of the people.

A lot of us are remembered when we are gone, sure. But there are different ways of being remembered. The best way for a fighter to be remembered is that he was never afraid to go to the edge. That's what I hope they will always say about me and for his sake, after all the work he has done and all he has gone through, that they will say the same of Lewis.

Boxing needs a great heavyweight champion, always has, always will. We know that Lennox Lewis has the talent to meet the challenge. Now we have to see if he has the will.

Tommy 'Hitman' Hearns, 2000

Introduction

At last, and officially, Lennox Lewis had beaten Evander Holyfield and been declared the one and only heavyweight champion of the world. He stood in the ring big and amiable and so happy he might have been your son tearing at the Christmas wrappings.

But you had to wonder where he had been all this time that the random skulduggeries of the game he had first survived and then triumphed over had left him so whole, so resistant to the worst of its cynicism and brutality. When his sport had been getting so shopworn. When the question in the minds of those who loved it, and the growing number who despised it, had not been whether Lewis could win it all but if boxing could endure just one more descent into the gutter.

He was in victory as he had always been. Separate from the business he had finally come to dominate. Guileless except in the matter of tactics in the ring but indefatigable in his self-belief, he was rooted now in historic achievement. But in a strange way it was still as though he didn't belong in this place at this time. He had been sidetracked, cheated and derided but it had all skimmed off the smooth surface of his resolve without a hint of lasting damage.

They say that justice delayed is justice denied, but they never said it to Lewis. At least not in so many words. They simply worked the concept so hard it was as frayed as the cuff of a 'silk' fallen on hard times. But much depends on the resilience of the victim. He has two choices. He can subside before the weight of his difficulties. He can work out a compromise, 'cop a plea' as they say in America. Or he can stay the course. He can quietly curse his fate and seek to reverse it.

This had been the unswerving approach of Lewis and vindication had come now with a thunderclap of fireworks and a flutter of ticker tape at the Thomas and Mack Centre in Las Vegas on this night of 13 November 1999. Lewis was unanimously declared undisputed heavyweight champion of the world – the first for seven years, and the only Briton of the twentieth century to claim the richest prize in sport. The Cornish-born Bob Fitzsimmons, who had decamped for New Zealand as a nine-year-old, had last done it in 1897 when he beat Gentleman Jim Corbett in Carson City, Nevada. Fitzsimmons had set a standard beyond the scope of the best of British heavyweights until the arrival of Lewis.

Tommy Farr provoked bonfires in the Welsh valleys when he went 15 rounds with Joe Louis, the Brown Bomber, but he was fighting for honour rather than a serious chance of victory. Farr was the high watermark of British heavyweight achievement since Fitzsimmons. Bruce Woodcock, the hope of Yorkshire, subsided against Lee Savold when the American opened a huge cut over his eye in the fourth round. Don Cockell, fleshy but skilful, was consumed by the violent, unscrupulous force of Rocky Marciano. Brian London of Blackpool fought haplessly against both Floyd Patterson and Muhammad Ali. Henry Cooper, the most beloved of British heavyweights, landed a left hook on the head of

Muhammad Ali in a non-title fight but his brave assault was a gesture of momentary significance and he paid for his impertinence both in that fight and a subsequent, uneven battle for the title. Joe Bugner exceeded expectations against Joe Frazier, but reverted to his role as a mechanical man when he faced Ali in Kuala Lumpur. Frank Bruno was the creation of British boxing's Dr Frankenstein, the knowing Mickey Duff, and in his second fight against Mike Tyson the best you could say was that somehow he worked up enough nerve to enter the ring.

It is not a tradition to thrill a patriotic soul and down the years it has inspired outright contempt among American sportswriters, with one of the most celebrated, the late Jim Murray of the *Los Angeles Times*, referring to the British habit of quitting 'on the stool'. He was tweaked about this on a golf course by a British colleague, the veteran Ken Jones, who reminded him Britain alone engaged the centre of the ring against Hitler in 1939. Murray took the point, but the legend of the horizontal British heavyweight is not easily dismissed.

Lennox Lewis has risen patiently, inexorably above such mediocrity and his achievement is two-fold. He beat Holyfield, arguably the most improbable but insistent warrior in the history of heavyweight boxing. Lewis also beat Don King. He beat the most brilliant, most cynical manipulator the murky game had ever known and he had done it with decency and an unshakeable belief that if you are strong enough, constant enough, in your self-belief and your ambition, you can get there in the end. You can make delayed justice as sweet as the liberation of the Bastille. You can take on the odds and when the battle is over, and however labyrinthine it became, there will be the moment when you raise your arms up to the sky and declare, 'I'm the man, I'm the undisputed heavyweight champion of the world.' When Lewis did this King's face was drained. A small, ironical smile played on his lips. But his eyes were as cold as a mortuary.

Eight months earlier in New York King had shrugged off the pressure which inevitably came upon him when the first Lewis–Holyfield fight was declared, to the disbelief and then the horror of most who saw it, a draw. Lewis wept briefly when the reality finally sank in. But within a few minutes he was standing beside King and a bruised and pain-racked Holyfield as the world railed against his fate. As Richard Giachetti, an old King foot soldier who once trained the greatly undervalued champion Larry Holmes and a Mike Tyson going through one of his first seismic shifts of personality, handed me a piece of hotel stationery on which he had scored the fight. It said Lewis had won by a margin of eight rounds. I looked back at Giachetti. He rolled his eyes and shook his head. As Roy Jones, light-heavyweight champion of the world and in the opinion of many the world's best pound-for-pound fighter, told a vast TV audience, 'Tonight I feel ashamed to be an American.' As the *New York Post* and the *New York Daily News* dashed out front-page splash headlines of 'It Stinks' and 'It's Robbery'. As the mayor of New York City and the governor of New York State ordered investigations into the scoring of the fight – particularly that of Eugenia Williams, a ledger clerk from Atlantic City, a friend of the head of the International Boxing Federation, a former policeman named Bob Lee who was already under Federal investigation for suspected racketeering.

As the controversy exploded around him, as some wondered whether the old Fulton Street fish market had been relocated at Madison Square Garden because such was the aroma, Lewis headed off to the long black limo which would carry him uptown to his hotel suite above Fifth Avenue, saying, 'I worried what they would do to me here, but now I know I'm more determined than ever.' At his moments of fiercest reflection, Lewis goes sonorously into the third person. He added, 'Lennox Lewis will be back. He will complete his mission.'

It was bitingly cold when you walked on to 33rd Street. You thought of how it should have been. How Lewis's limo should have resembled more the pink cadillac so beloved of Sugar Ray Robinson, how it should have carried him to Harlem for sweet celebration, sweet jazz, sweet, honeyed celebration.

In fact when Lewis finally triumphed, when the scorecards were read out in the Thomas and Mack Centre and were more generous in their measurement of his victory than even his most committed fans could have hoped, he returned to his big penthouse suite in the shining new Vegas casino palace of the Mandalay Bay, took several electrolyte drinks and fell fast asleep, watched over by his fiercely protective, single-parent mother Violet. When justice, rough and imprecise but still demonstrably just, finally came it wasn't so much sweet as emptying. In the bright desert morning Lewis would savour and talk up his triumph. But now he would sleep like a baby. He had pulled off his Impossible Mission. He would not be surprised that some of his reviews were less than dazzling.

In America he had been relentlessly dismissed and even after the conquest of Holyfield there would be echoes of the old derision. Randy Harvey, a sports gossip columnist of the *Los Angeles Times*, not always conspicuous at the big fights, observed, 'If Lennox Lewis had fought 25 years earlier I would rank him no higher than eighth in the heavyweight division behind Muhammad Ali, Joe Frazier, George Foreman, Ken Norton, Jerry Quarry, Earnie Shavers and Ron Lyle. Forget Ali, I'd be happy if Lewis were as charismatic as Larry Holmes.' A ragbag of opinion, this. In the pantheon of champions, Holmes ranks high; of his contemporaries only Ali, Frazier and Foreman could claim a more consistent and formidable body of work, and if personality is the question Lewis's is open and generous and that of Holmes is a vertiginous mix of envy and resentment and is accompanied by a tongue so vicious a rattlesnake's might by comparison seem benign. Harvey's barb was in fact mild enough. Ron Borges of the *Boston Globe* once wrote that Lewis had a broad yellow streak running down his back.

When Lewis rose from his slumbers he engaged the issues of popularity and acceptance with a practised shrug. He had, after all, taken it all for ten years, the courtroom hassles and the dirty politics, the schemings of Don King and all the doubts and the sneers about his true allegiances, even his sexuality, but it wasn't important now. As the afternoon sun made a crimson splash over the Sierra Nevada, Lewis stretched out on the big sofa in the suite overlooking the desert and said, 'It doesn't really matter to me how people see me. Everyone has an opinion. They expect this and they expect that. They say I'm too cautious, I think too much and fight on the edge too little. They say someone who plays chess can't be a warrior.

'But I've only one reaction to such opinions now. I say, "I'm Lennox Lewis, undisputed heavyweight champion of the world." I think that says a lot. When I'm gone I'm not worried about my place in boxing history, how I'm compared to the great champions.

'I know who I am, what I am and what I've achieved. I'll be happy enough if they just say, "He was a man who could get the job done. He believed in himself and he didn't quit until he was where he wanted to be."'

He knew he had made it now. The next day he was a guest on the Jay Leno show in Los Angeles – an instant trip to the apex of American celebrity. Leno, a withering critic of American life and particularly the nation's president, took an immediate liking to Lewis when he appeared on the show in the hype that preceded the first fight in New York. Leno, whose normal diet is supplied by Hollywood, was taken with the way Lewis carried himself – and the conviction that came into his voice when he said that one day he would claim the richest prize in sport. Now Leno would embrace Lewis before his vast audience. He would quiz him about his sexual abstinence before a big fight. 'Three months,' said Lewis. 'It's like being in prison.' Leno frowned and then asked about Lewis's weight. He concluded, 'It's just great that there's someone out there who is 245 pounds and isn't dating the president of the United States.'

After more than a decade of Tyson, Lewis provoked a memory of other days. Days when to be world heavyweight champion was not to star in a violent freak show. When the idea was not to bite ears and serve time and mutter obscenities, when Rocky Marciano or Joe Louis or, ultimately, Muhammad Ali could bring the traffic grinding to a halt on Seventh Avenue, New York, because both in themselves and their office they had become so much larger than ordinary life. Here at the dawn of his reign, Lewis was asked, 'Do you realise you will have to be more visible?' Said Lewis, 'I've always been visible. You just need to know where to look.'

It was a classic Lewis response. It was his way of saying that he wasn't about to play anyone's role but his own. But, yes, he saw the need for a certain 'visibility'. Heavyweight champions, especially undisputed ones, shouldn't really lurk in the shadows. He planned to fly home to England as soon as his American television bosses Home Box Office released him from the promotional whirl planned to exploit his triumph.

Inevitably, there were criticisms of his latest performance. He was too clinical, too bloodless in his attempt to control the violent initiatives of Holyfield, some critics said. *Sports Illustrated* said it was a triumph for timidity. An extraordinary phrase, this one bannered across two pages. Beneath the headline, Richard Hoffer wrote, 'Inasmuch as the result provoked no congressional hearings, you might say it was a great night for boxing. The fix wasn't in, the performers were good sportsmen, and there was no obvious malfeasance at ringside, where the scoring is often so perverse that not even incompetence is a sufficiently implausible explanation.'

Hoffer moved relentlessly to the conclusion that all Lewis's positives added up to a negative for boxing. Having lauded the dangerous style of Holyfield, one born out of a chronic necessity to get inside the reach of bigger men, and citing his quote, 'I don't have what you call a convenient type job,' Hoffer decided, 'It may be that Lewis, for all his gifts, prefers a convenient type job.

'This may prove exasperating to some. Yet isn't it even more frustrating that for all the shame he has brought to the sport, Mike Tyson remains boxing's most mesmerising presence. It's not that he is so fearsome anymore – Holyfield beat him twice and Lewis (whom Tyson has skilfully avoided) would certainly outpoint him. It's not that he's beloved; he's probably more despised than any other athlete this century. It's that Tyson understands the public's appetite for shattering spectacle. Risks must be faced, odds overcome; somebody needs to be knocked out of his senses.'

So there at his moment of supreme triumph was the latest cavil against Lennox Lewis's right to call himself the best heavyweight on earth. He didn't fight Holyfield's fight. He didn't surrender his own advantages for the sake of a few explosive passages, which would thrill the crowd and give Holyfield his one chance of wrecking Lewis's life's work. No matter, apparently, that in the seventh round – at the end of which the crowd rose to their feet and roared their approval of the action – Lewis was obliged to dig into his resources simply for survival after a perfectly thrown Holyfield left hook scrambled his senses; that Lewis's response was not to cower but to deliver a series of uppercuts which almost certainly would have stopped anyone less than the remorseless Holyfield.

Lewis, as he had done in New York, had fought from a logical, practical script – but it was one which did not permit a moment of climactic power. Holyfield took a lot of heavy punches, but once again he chose not to submit to their effects. In the big sunlit suite you had to wonder if the fact that his trainer Emanuel

20

Steward echoed some of the complaints cut deeply. 'No, Manny's great. He says what's on his mind, and you know I am my own worst critic,' said Lewis. 'I wanted to knock out Evander Holyfield. I wanted to please the people, but I'm the one who is in the ring. I know what is expected of me and I try to deliver – but not at the expense of leaving myself open, not at the risk of throwing away the fight. I learned a lot from Holyfield over two fights – and one of the main things is that sometimes when someone throws a left hook he might be finding a way to use his head.'

The main charge against Lewis is that his nature is too passive for the savage imperatives of the ring. Yet after just two rounds of the second fight Nevada Athletic Commission doctor Flip Homansky turned to Lewis's manager Frank Maloney and said, 'If Lennox goes on hitting him like that he's going to knock his head off.'

The fact is nobody knocks Holyfield's head off and Homansky's tribute was a rare acknowledgement of Lewis's capacity for serious aggression. 'People say, oh just go and knock Holyfield out – you're big enough, you're strong enough,' Lewis sighed. 'But you have to be in the ring with him to know what this involves.' It means putting at risk the right to call yourself the best heavyweight in the world. For Lennox Lewis, number-one fighting citizen of the world, this was for the shining moment simply not negotiable.

Fear in the Garden

Angst is endemic in boxing. It accumulates like bacteria in a slipshod kitchen. Strange, you might think, to say this of a sport which demands a high order of courage from the least of its participants. But then perhaps you didn't see the look on the face of Michael Spinks that tumultuous night in Atlantic City in 1988.

Fear, some of it subtle, some of it raw, gets everywhere at fight time. It touches almost everyone to some degree as it rises up from the canvas and spreads into the corners of even the most obscure halls. It grips the fighters, the cornermen, however practised, the gamblers and all but the most brutalised fans.

Spinks, a fine champion, once told me that he wrapped himself in a ball and moaned with fear in the lonely nights before a big fight, and while I was sceptical at the time I knew it was true when he stepped into the ring with Mike Tyson. His eyes were wide and filled with alarm and you could see that he had been disabled utterly by sheer apprehension.

Someone counted the number of times Frank Bruno crossed

himself when he went to the ring to fight Tyson for a second time. The counting stopped at 17. Another Tyson victim, Bruce Seldon, was encountered in a Las Vegas restaurant a few nights before the biggest fight of his life. He was surrounded by friends and hangers-on, including the gnarled old daredevil Evel Knieval, and he told anyone who cared to listen how he was going to further erode the myth of Iron Mike. He looked relaxed enough when he stepped through the ropes. But when Tyson threw a wild punch which sailed over its target, Seldon fell to the canvas. Suddenly, his terror was so palpable you could reach out and touch it.

Cesar Soto, a featherweight champion of the world who had never been knocked down in 62 fights and who had first fought professionally, for the price of a packet of chewing gum and a few groceries for his mother and 11 siblings, in his native Durango at the age of 13, confided before colliding with Naseem Hamed in the Joe Louis Arena in Detroit, 'Hombre, I always feel fear; before every fight it sits on your shoulders, but then the bell rings and you are all right.'

Fear touches the bravest people in sport as a matter of routine, and if you care for one of them in any particular way it can be as infectious as the measles. Still, I should have been calmer taking my seat at ringside at Madison Square Garden on Saturday night, 13 March 1999, to watch Lennox Lewis and Evander Holyfield fight for the undisputed world heavyweight title. I shouldn't have walked away from the yellow cab without collecting at least some of my change. I should have sauntered in like an old hand. I should have joined in the banter of seasoned colleagues and friends.

It was not as though I didn't know the place well enough. I had covered a number of fights there, and they had run the full spectrum of the business, all the way from the epic to the derisory. My deadline was all of 12 hours away – or a full ashtray and several pots of room-service coffee – and it was in this town many years before that one of the idols of my youth, Frank McGhee of the *Daily Mirror*, had offered the invaluable advice, 'Son, if you can't write a good story on time, do a bad one.' Dapper, self-assured but with a concern for an untested young colleague I find touching now when I think back to that more companionable time, he came into my room at the old Statler Hilton across the road from the Garden. Here, Glenn Miller had composed one of his more memorable tunes and taken the title from the hotel telephone number, Pennsylvania 65000. My own work in progress was less advanced on that jumpy post-fight morning.

Now, though, the time had been served and the good advice taken and I had lost count of the big fights I had covered and written at ringside and in hotel rooms across this vast land, mostly in Las Vegas and Atlantic City, but also in other places like Tulsa, Atlanta, Sacramento, New Orleans, Philadelphia, Reno, Lake Tahoe, Washington DC, Houston and San Antonio, where boxing periodically reappears like some blowsy old vaudeville show trying to revive a dying trade. Yet I still felt a little tremor of dread this night. The fear of impending disaster, maybe; mine, Lennox Lewis's, I couldn't really say.

But then it is also true that a big fight is like nothing else in sport. An Olympic 100 metres final, the showdown of a World Cup, the decisive shots of a Ryder Cup, the action of the horses when they hit the rising ground at Epsom, the Tour de France when it reaches the mountains, all have their own power to move the spirit. The fight, however, is quite separate. The fight engages all of the emotions, not least fear – the fear of unravelling, of revulsion, of the dismembering of the pride if not the body of someone you have come to admire. Sometimes when the fight is big enough, when the atmosphere reflects not cheap hype but the certainty of a real and important collision, you worry that you will not even begin to capture the edge and the bite of the night.

Frenetically you write notes as you wait for the arrival of the gladiators with their glistening faces which sometimes give a hint of the course of the drama about to unfold. The notes are discarded soon enough, and you are left with a concern that, while small against the challenge of the men who duck into the ring, can be weighty in your own mind. It provokes the question: how will *you* perform? How well will you read the action, how truly and with what degree of detachment will you report it?

Now such apprehension was upon me in the Garden, and it didn't matter that I knew a little of my way around the heightened passion that had long been a staple here at 33rd Street. Twenty-two years earlier I had seen here the last of the best of Muhammad Ali, weathering so bravely the withering assaults of Earnie Shavers, the Acorn man from Ohio, and then fighting back so brilliantly, so atavistically, older, more experienced observers had tears in their eyes as they rose to their feet and the building seemed to shudder with the fury of the punches and the howls of the crowd. A few days before the fight I had been let into Ali's dressing-room after a work-out and had babbled a question or two and Angelo Dundee, the great sorcerer cornerman, had touched me on the sleeve and whispered, 'No, buddy, around this guy it's better just to look and to listen.' In those days it seemed you just couldn't get enough good advice.

In 1993 there was a fight which some feared had ruined the prospects of the old game at its most famous venue. It involved Michael Dokes, a former champion who once came into the ring with his hair pomaded and with roses to throw to the ladies but was now raddled by drugs and booze. His decline was so alarming that at a pre-fight press conference he seemed to have difficulty negotiating his way around a bright standard lamp and was later found devouring spare ribs in a Broadway restaurant. He was consumed by Riddick Bowe in less than a round. It was as disgusting as it was pitiable.

More recently Lewis had kept his ambitions alive here despite a ferocious ambush launched by Ray Mercer, a tough, durable pro who knew that this was his last chance to check a slide into the wilderness of small halls and negligible purses. Yes, there was a degree of familiarity with this fabled Garden, which now left me dry-mouthed and edgy.

Perspective should not have been so elusive in this place. After all, in its various relocations and resurrections it had produced the fight of the century, Ali–Frazier, 1971, and also the murder, Harry K. Thaw over Stanford White, by gunfire, 1906. White was one of America's most flamboyant celebrities. A leading architect, he had designed the first reincarnation of the Garden when it moved from Madison Square in downtown Manhattan, where it was founded in 1879, to 26th Street and Madison Avenue. In its first life the Garden had been a home for dog and horse shows and the fighters, including the great heavyweight John L. Sullivan, had been brought in almost as an afterthought to help the running costs.

White had more extravagant plans. He wanted the Garden to be a place of circus and cabaret as well as prize-fighting and animal shows. He created a penthouse floor which included a cabaret room and his own apartment, a place that was known quickly enough as the Love Nest. For a while the Garden thrived as New York's most vibrant centre of public entertainment. It featured Lily Langtree, the actress who won the heart of America, and Colonel 'Buffalo' Bill Cody and his wild west show. But White's world dissolved when Harry Thaw walked into the cabaret room carrying a gun. White had been conducting a well-publicised affair with Evelyn Nesbitt, a darling of Broadway known as the 'The Girl on the Velvet Swing'. She also happened to be Harry Thaw's wife. Thaw shot White through the head. A sympathetic jury sent him to a mental institution rather than a place of execution. But if it was the end of White, it was in many ways the start of the Garden. It would make two more moves, to

Eighth Avenue at 50th Street in 1925 and to its present home above Pennsylvania Station at Seventh Avenue and 33rd Street, in 1967. There would be a fabulous cast of fighters, but also some stunning support acts, including six-day bikers, ferocious ice-hockey players and Marilyn Monroe singing 'Happy Birthday, Mr President' to John F. Kennedy.

Even though so much of the juice of this city had flowed through these premises by 13 March 1999, its capacity to produce an aura of pure tension was still high. Now it left me prematurely drained, as nervous, in fact, as on that first Ali night back in October 1977 when even with my scant experience I knew I was watching the beginning of the end of something quite magnificent, something unique in the life of our century. As we waited for Lewis and Holyfield, as Jack Nicholson and Donald Trump and a division of minor showbiz celebrities preened themselves in their good seats, Ali–Shavers came back so vividly. It was an extraordinarily thrilling yet disturbing fight and later it provoked from the Garden match-maker Teddy Brenner the sobering comment, 'I never thought I'd live to see the day when Muhummad Ali's best asset was his ability to take a punch.'

Back in the dressing-room, Ali screamed. He screamed for them to turn off the lights, which he said were sending needles into his brain. His physician, Ferdie Pacheco, said solemnly, 'This should be the end for Ali. I've told him he's taking punishment everywhere now, to his brain, his kidneys, even his bowels. It can't go on.'

You wondered then if boxing could survive the demise of Muhammad Ali, and the hard edge of that speculation concerned the prospect of this wonderfully luminous man, this athlete and sage and catalyst for changes in the thinking and the aspirations of people all over the world, shuffling off into the half light of a catastrophically bruised retirement. He had come out of that torture chamber of a dressing-room with all the usual defiance and a touch of whimsy. 'He hit me so hard,' said Ali, 'my kinfolk in Africa felt the punches.' There was a ripple of laughter, but it was thin. There were so many ghosts in the Garden, and it was as though the meaning of Lewis–Holyfield had awakened us to their presence.

Boxing had indeed survived the fall of Ali. A new generation of welterweights and middleweights, Sugar Ray Leonard, Tommy 'Hitman' Hearns, Roberto 'Hands of Stone' Duran and Marvellous Marvin Hagler had issued a dramatic joint communiqué at the dawn of the eighties. It said that if the aura of Ali was beyond any one of them, if the grace and energy and the courage he had brought to the ring would always stand alone, among them they could supply the fight game with a new focus. They could bring the old sense that there were still men around who knew what it meant to be a champion, who could fight with such nerve and accomplishment that their efforts could take their places, seamlessly, in the best traditions of a sport which had always hovered between glory and brutal disillusionment.

These men also inhabited my thoughts on the countdown to Lewis–Holyfield. As the preliminaries unwound, their images imposed themselves on the ring. I remembered the day leading to the first of those great fights, Leonard–Duran for the welterweight title in the Olympic stadium in Montreal. Earlier, I had watched Jack Nicklaus, who still had major titles to win, playing in a rainstorm at the Canadian Open. You were reminded then of the cerebal nature of a golf champion, the relative stillness of his world, but also the majesty of his bearing, the thrill of his presence when he came over the brow of a fairway, the expectant hush as he addressed the ball. Then, on another planet it seemed, there was the tumult of the ring, the visceral force of Duran, the showy brilliance of Leonard, who for days had been taunted viciously by the coal-eyed man from Panama. 'Maracon – fairy,' he spat whenever Leonard was within earshot. It was a calculated assault on Leonard's pride. He sneered at Leonard's manhood, his wife, even, by implication, his race. It was cynicism without principle or an ounce of care or respect for his opponent, an Olympic champion of soaring reputation, but it worked to perfection. Leonard surrendered his advantages of speed and skill, and he went inside and battled with Duran as though they were drunken sailors wrecking a bar in the Canal Zone. The scoring was close but Duran had created irrepressible momentum and at the end of the fight he was appalled to see Leonard raise his hands to claim the fight. Duran conjured the most contemptuous gesture. He strode across the ring and kicked Leonard's backside.

Later in 1980 Leonard exacted exquisite revenge in New Orleans and after Duran had raised his hand and gestured *No Mas, No Mas* – he later confirmed that he would rather have been shot than mocked – I confessed sheepishly to Hugh McIlvanney of *The Observer*, that in my preview I had picked Duran, 'the implacable warrior'. It is possible his volcanic chortle was heard all the way across the Mississippi. With tears of laughter streaming down his face, McIlvanney declared, 'The bottom has fallen out of the implacability business.'

Here in the Garden, as the tension rose, as the seats filled and back in their dressing-rooms Lewis and Holyfield stole glances at the clock, there was another reason to recall that time. On the eve of the fight the great American sportswriter Red Smith had been in expansive form over his vodka and tonic. He warned younger men about the dangers of emotional attachment at ringside and at the track, though allowing he had always fancied Willie Shoemaker on a good thing and recalled how 'The Shoe' brought in one winner so serenely he might have been a 'Bluepoint oyster sitting up on the half shell'. But it was best, he said, to have a hard head and a cold heart when assessing professional matters, and if the rule could not be written in stone – once he had half raised himself to his feet when Jake La Motta was punished by Sugar Ray Robinson

30

in Chicago, 'because I just couldn't get it out of my head that it was said Jake had recently pushed his pregnant wife downstairs' – it made things a lot easier on both the judgement and the emotions.

Here in the Garden you could see Smith's point. After several decades of covering the great events of sport, it was odd to feel such anxiety before a fight. There could be little mystery about its source, however. The truth, as I saw it, was that this was more than another big fight. It was the potential validation of certain important principles, of constancy and honesty and, perhaps most of all, endurance. Lewis, as so many of his critics alleged, no doubt had a patchy performance record. There had been times when he had looked quite awesome, confirming with his savagely marshalled power the claim of Emanuel Steward, that in natural gifts he was maybe the most blessed heavyweight since the rise of Ali.

On other occasions, most notably when being punched to his only defeat by the erratic Oliver McCall and lagging behind Frank Bruno on a cold, wet early morning in Cardiff, he had been stolid, irresolute and, indeed, amateurish. No significant heavyweight had perhaps produced such a mingling of power and vacillation. But, still, Lewis always had the means of redemption in both his big right hand and his competitive nature. He had never run before the dangers of an opponent perceived to carry menace and this, of course, was ultimately true of tonight's adversary, Holyfield. With Mike Tyson long discredited, and now languishing in prison, there was no doubt that these were the best heavyweights still active and, wonder upon wonder, in a little time they would be disputing the unchallenged right to call themselves, in the fashion of Joe Louis and Rocky Marciano, Jack Dempsey and Ali, the one and only heavyweight champion of the world.

That was the sharp edge of this night at Madison Square Garden. It was, hopefully, an affirmation of the most compelling point of prize-fighting. It was to be an examination of who was indeed the best, the most resourceful, the most courageous.

Thus the animation of the ghosts of boxing, a sense of retrieved continuity and one's own extreme of nervous excitement flowed back like a current to those days of the eighties, when you took the great fights rather as a matter of course than some epic surge in the boxing cycle. They were such fights. If Duran and Leonard had drawn up a standard – especially in Montreal – it would be one relentlessly surpassed. If this fight here in New York exceeded all expectations, even if Lewis summoned all his power, Holyfield all his warrior instinct, we couldn't be sure it would be better than Leonard–Hearns I, Hagler–Hearns or Hagler–Leonard.

What we needed this night was confirmation that boxing could reassert some of its best values, that at the very least we would have a decent fight between the world's best two heavyweights and that when we spilled out into the early-morning, icy canyons of Manhattan we would be carrying at least a little evidence that the old sweet science had not soured beyond redemption.

Back in the eighties such pious hopes were redundant. We went, we saw, and we were ravished by the action. Leonard joined up a wondrous circle in the spring of 1987 when he beat Hagler in a fight which in its context was hardly less startling than Ali's invasion of the rough certainties of George Foreman in Zaire in 1974. Some feared for Leonard's very life before his collision with the apparently indestructible Hagler, just as seven years earlier they had worried for the health of his opponent, Hearns, on another Las Vegas backlot.

Leonard–Hearns I was a violent symphony. Hearns dominated each crescendo. Surprisingly for someone known as the Hitman, he did it with an insistent, elegant jab and wonderful movement about the ring. Leonard's patience was eroded by the sheer volume of Hearns's punches. He looked increasingly desperate and as the punishment accumulated his wife, Juanita, sitting on the fringe of the ring's apron, began to cry into the night. After one fierce exchange, from which Hearns again emerged the stronger, she jumped to her feet and yelled, 'No more, baby, oh, no more, baby.' But there would be so much more, and it would go beyond both the marriage and the concern that when Leonard fought Hagler he was playing recklessly with his eyesight if not his life. Somehow, Leonard found hidden reserves with which to rescue the Hearns fight. Above all, it was a supreme act of will. The technique which had made him a dazzling Olympic champion, and a surefire professional property, was shelved. Tactics were put aside. Leonard simply went down to the very basics of survival. He attacked, how he attacked. Hearns was coasting to victory one minute and in the next he was wrecked. There are many surviving images but the most pervasive is of Hearns being carried from the ring, his legs limp, his feet trailing in the dust. It was the picture of a man beaten after producing the fight of his life.

Against Hagler, Leonard was larcenous. But as thieves work in the night, no one ever did it with more touch and accomplishment than Leonard. Some judges will always swear this was the fight he stole rather than won. Hagler fought his usual fight, strong, progressive, but he was subject to blinding counter-attacks from Leonard. They generally did not last too long, they were flurries rather than assaults, but it was magical defiance. The strongest images of this fight are of Leonard fighting his way out of a corner with flashing combinations – and of Hagler mounting one huge barrage of punches which pinned Leonard into a corner for the best part of a minute and which seemed sure to end with the intervention of the referee. But again Leonard, whose career had been threatened so deeply when he suffered a detached retina whilst training for a fight against the obscure Roger Stafford, slipped out of trouble. The corners of the ring formed his *querencia*, that part of the disputed terrain where a wounded bull is most dangerous. The pattern was unbroken. Hagler dominated much of a round, Leonard stole back into it with a flutter of his feet and a beautiful combination.

Some were stunned when the points decision went to Leonard. Others exulted. I thought of the time, several years earlier, when I had seen Leonard in the shadows of the build-up to the Hagler–Hearns fight. He was officially retired under the weight of medical evidence that if he fought again he would endanger his eyesight. But when he stood in the corner of a big room in a casino hotel and watched the clamour around two fighters, one of whom he had beaten in such imperishable circumstances, he looked distant, haunted. I asked him if he would ever fight again and it was no great surprise that his answer was equivocal. 'I would be lying,' he said, 'if I told you I didn't envy those men right now. There is a lot you don't miss in boxing. You don't miss the road work while the rest of the world is sleeping, you don't miss all the hype, all the promotion, you don't miss running and rushing here and there to meet some commitment or other. But you do miss moments like these. You miss the feeling that for a little time the whole world is looking at you and the guy you are fighting, that for a few days you're at the dead centre of the world. We all do different things. I happen to be a fighter. It is the thing I do best. The answer to your question is that I'm retired – that's official. But in my life I've learned to never say never.'

If Leonard felt like a moth drawn to the light, there was no argument that the fight which worked so strongly on his imagination fulfilled all of its promise. Hagler–Hearns was brief in the way of an earth tremor, or the progress of a shooting star across the sky. It lasted less than three rounds, but it couldn't have gone on any longer than that. It was too intense, too disembowelling to permit any lengthier life. The first round was convulsive, riotous. Old men said they had seen nothing like it since Jack Dempsey and Luis Angel Firpo fought at the Polo Grounds in New York in 1923, when Dempsey put down the 'Wild Bull of the Pampas' seven times in the first round before completing his destruction in the second. The difference, and it was an amazing one, was that neither Hagler nor Hearns went down in that first torrent of action. Hearns hit Hagler with a bombardment of superbly delivered punches and for a while he hid his dismay that they achieved no more than a small cut on Hagler's forehead. Hagler was Hagler, the tough product of Philadelphia when it was by some distance America's hardest fight town. He bore in as the punches rained on his shorn head. Hearns, tall, skinny and with his fine-boned face framed by a mop of wiry hair, looked like some proud Ethiopian warrior. I shall never forget the sight of him, pushed back against the ropes but pounding at the head of Hagler.

Later, Budd Schulburg, author of *On the Waterfront* and *What Makes Sammy Run*, stood at my workdesk at ringside and shook his head slowly. He said the ferocity of the fight had made him tremble. He added, 'I never expected to see anything so intense in peace or war.' Schulburg knew something of the pain and the glory of life. As a young Hollywood writer, he had been a colleague and companion of the great Scott Fitzgerald and had watched him slip into a fog of alcoholism. That was a slow, dispiriting decline. Here on this desert night in Las Vegas we had seen a great fighter dwindle in almost the blink of an eye. It happened in the third round, so swiftly, so irrevocably, it was upon you even as you still fought to keep track of the astonishing action. Hearns's legs suddenly went. One moment they were carrying him smoothly to the point of attack, the next they were like reeds in the wind. Recently, while waiting to see his friend Tom Jones backstage at a Vegas casino, Hearns admitted to me that he had fought the wrong fight. He had worried about Hagler's strength, his capacity to wear him down over the long course, so he had elected to go for broke. It was a losing gamble, but he had no regrets because he had made an honest decision and fought an honest fight.

We could only hope for such commitment this night in the Garden, for echoes of the greatest heavyweight fight this arena had ever seen, the gargantuan battle of wills between Ali and Joe Frazier in 1971. Above all, we had to believe in the capacity of Lewis and Holyfield to repair at least some of the damage that had been brought to the game in general and this most lucrative heavyweight division in particular.

We had to move at least a little beyond the evasions and missed opportunities of Bowe, the spent and now disordered savagery of Tyson. We had to have the real fight which had been so long in coming. We had to have a fight between the world's best two heavyweights so that when it was over we could say, well, here at last was something that didn't reek of compromise or manipulation, here was a collison which was faithful to the point of this sport which at no time in its history had been clear of one suspicion or another but from time to time had erupted into action so compelling it would live for ever.

The point of Lewis–Holyfield, whatever you thought of the relative ability of these two fighters, was that it was transparently legitimate. Fate had conspired on this occasion to deliver into the ring the two men most deserving of the chance to fight for the richest prize in sport. This was such a rarity you had to go back seven years for a comparison. Holyfield was also involved then at the Thomas and Mack Arena in Las Vegas, late in 1992. He fought Bowe for the World Boxing Council, the World Boxing Association and the International Boxing Federation titles. It was a stupendous fight, one of the best anyone could remember.

Lennox Lewis was at ringside and he relished every moment of action which swelled into a superb crescendo in the tenth round, when Holyfield, who had been slipping out of the contest against waves of aggression from the bigger, younger, superbly conditioned Bowe, fought back with a fury, a majestic defiance which moved every witness to his or her feet. Holyfield gave

36

everything in that round, and inevitably his effort ebbed in the last two rounds. But not before he had reminded us, as all the great ones had at some point in their careers, what it is to be a warrior champion, a man who fought with every fibre of his body and every ounce of will. Bowe got the verdict and no one, not even Holyfield, could raise a whisper of complaint. Bowe was a gifted, exciting young champion and a few feet away from the ropes was the man who had a letter in his pocket from Holyfield promising a title chance in the event of his victory.

Bowe, whom Lewis had beaten for a gold medal in the Seoul Olympics four years earlier, had given no such commitment but this did not overly concern the number-one challenger. Bowe's manager Rock Newman had long railed against the rigging of boxing ranking lists and the contrived title fights they had produced. I had heard his favourite speech at least half a dozen times. He had been particularly heated after Holyfield had defended against old Larry Holmes, a fine former champion but who in his dotage had produced a challenge of absolute cynicism, a clutching, grabbing parody of a fight for the big prize. 'A disgrace, an absolute disgrace,' thundered Newman. 'Boxing has lost all integrity. It is alongside the World Wrestling Federation now. It's a bad joke.' Bowe, of course, nodded and waited for his chance.

When it came he had proved more than equal to the challenge. For once in his life he had done the hard work under the prompting of his great trainer Eddie Futch, who in his youth had sparred with Joe Louis and who had played a key role in the careers of such formidable champions as Joe Frazier, Holmes and Michael Spinks. Bowe was not Ali, who could be that? But he was a champion of great potential. He could bring class to a division which for so long had been turned into the violent playground of the anarchic and finally unmanageable Tyson. Iron Mike was doing time for rape now and no one seriously doubted that the

37

best of him as a fighter had gone with his freedom. So here was a redeemer, a young man of talent and humour – Bowe charmed boxing writers in Seoul with his deadly impersonation of President Reagan – and, as an extra gift, here too was an opponent against whom his promise could be properly measured.

Lewis was a real opponent, one who brought his own solid credentials. He was an Olympic champion and just a few weeks earlier he had demolished Donovan 'Razor' Ruddock at Earl's Court in London. Many in boxing had said that Lewis had been crazy to take the Ruddock fight. There were any number of profitable, easier pay nights available and the match with Bowe was inevitable at some point. But Lewis took the fight and won it with great power and conviction. If one had formed an attachment to Lewis, if indeed I had perhaps made too many excuses for him before this night in New York, as some of my colleagues had claimed, it had most likely been formed that night in Earl's Court. It was a night when Lewis was the victim of some astonishing revisionism by much of the boxing *cognoscenti*. Before the fight Ruddock was a dangerous opponent, one who had threatened Tyson in two eviscerating fights in Las Vegas, one of them ending controversially when some said referee Richard Steele stepped in too quickly to separate the fighters. But now, as he retreated to his dressing-room a broken man, Ruddock had really only been a shell. Tyson had not only beaten him twice, he had destroyed him.

Whatever the true weight of Lewis's victory, he had gone to Las Vegas in the best of spirits. He praised Bowe's triumph and said that he looked forward to stepping into the ring with a genuine champion. Bowe's reaction was a series of insults. He called Lewis a 'fag'. He said, 'Get out of here, man, my sister could whup your ass.' A little later Bowe threw the WBC belt, for which Lewis was the number-one contender, into a rubbish bin. Ali had once worn that belt but the new redeemer of boxing threw it into the garbage anyway. It was the better option, he reckoned, than fighting Lewis.

So who would Bowe fight? Newman, without so much as a blink of an eye, announced that the first defence would be against Dokes in Madison Square Garden. Bowe, the boy from the same streets in Brooklyn which had nourished the fighting instincts of Tyson, would take the title home. It was a travesty, a betrayal and Dokes, as we said, could only compound the scandal with his demeanour before the fight and his wretched performance when the bell rang.

Earlier that night farce had intruded into the Garden. Ray Mercer, so programmed when he fought Lewis a few years later, was on the undercard against the most leaden of journeymen, Jesse Ferguson. The Newman plan was for Mercer formally to defeat Ferguson and be announced as Bowe's next opponent. The problem was that Mercer considered Ferguson no more highly than the rest of boxing. Clearly unfit, he fought a sluggard's fight. This was both unfortunate for the image of the Bowe camp, and of some niggling expense. Bowe–Mercer publicity material had already been printed. Bowe–Ferguson at Washington's RFK stadium was an extension of the Bowe–Dokes joke. Bowe swept him aside with contempt. Old Eddie Futch was not conspicuous in his celebration of another triumph for the fighter he had whipped into shape for that great test against Evander Holyfield. Already Bowe was slipping out of shape, and why not? He could beat the likes of Dokes and Ferguson on his way to the fridge.

Meanwhile, Lewis beat Tony Tucker in Las Vegas and was crowned WBC champion. He said he wouldn't rest until he owned the undisputed championship of the world. He never swerved from that resolve. He had had good fights and bad, and one great disaster, but he always said – and so often that boxing writers looking for original copy groaned when he said it – that his mission was to be the best in the world, to have it unchallenged and with the underpinning of all three title belts.

He had behaved honourably and with some feeling for the sport which had transformed his life and that of his mother Violet, who had left the steamy poverty of Port Antonio, Jamaica, to make a better life working double shifts in an East End of London hospital. And now he came to fight for his rights in Madison Square Garden. It was a misson he had pursued with a decency that had been as rare as it was consistent.

Red Smith said how important it was to stay detached, and now I knew precisely what he meant as Jimmy Lennon Junior, the rasping ring announcer at Madison Square Garden, reached for the mike.

The Crowning Glory

Absurdly, and briefly gut-wrenchingly, Lennox Lewis was delayed on his way to the ring. He stood bewildered for a moment and then his face flashed first with exasperation, then anger. The pre-fight rituals are woven deep into a fighter's experience. Like the dressing of a matador in his suit of lights, they demand a seamless routine.

The issue was the carrying of a Union flag. A steward pointed out to Lewis's brother Dennis that Madison Square Garden regulations forbade such shows of nationalism, and for a little while – scarcely a minute, but in the circumstances it seemed like an age – there was an impasse. Lewis, who had looked particularly calm as he started his walk from the dressing-room, frowned thunderously. 'What now?' he later recalled thinking to himself, but soon enough his entourage was winding around the ring with the flags of Britain and his mother's native Jamaica.

The stall at the steps to the ring proved inconsequential enough but in the fevered atmosphere of the Garden this night it carried a symbolic hint of dread. This, after all, was the fight which had threatened to die of old age, of television contractual wrangle, of shifting opportunism and – there was at least a suspicion – of Holyfield's lack of enthusiasm. Could some bizarre eruption of stadium bureaucracy, small print lodged in City Hall, bring down this most delicate of arrangements to fight for the undisputed heavyweight championship of the world? The fear was maybe irrational but this was boxing, this was a Don King show and who cast webs of intrigue as elaborately as this electric-haired Machiavelli of the ring?

Negotiations had stretched down the months. King, beleaguered by a Federal trial for wire fraud and his disintegrating relationship with his great meal ticket, Mike Tyson, had finally pulled it all together late in 1998. He had been cleared of fiddling the expenses of his fighter Julio Cesar Chavez at the expense of Lloyd's of London – and promply sent the jury off to a fishing and shopping spree in the Bahamas. Shamelessly, he announced he was simply celebrating the checks and balances of the American legal system. He persuaded Showtime TV to step aside from their contractual hold on his fighters and thus award the fight, the only significant heavyweight asset in a collapsing market, to their fierce rivals Home Box Office television. It was formidable sleight of hand that King announced when, against all odds, I called his New York hotel to find that his line was free. 'You have called at a wonderful, propitious moment, Mr Lawton,' said King. 'Evander Holyfield and his attorney Jim Thomas are here with me now and I can tell you the ink is not yet dry on the contract. Evander Holyfield has signed to fight Lennox Lewis. Praise the Lord. The great historic heavyweight fight has been made.'

Thomas confirmed the signature and Holyfield said, 'How could anyone seriously say I was running from Lennox Lewis? Did I ever run from anyone? Why would I run from Lewis? I pay him due respect, he is a good heavyweight, but I'm going to whup him. I was always going to whup him.' King could be heard chortling in the background. Boxing had never known a more relentless manipulator and at 68, with chronic blood pressure and constant attention from Federal investigators, with Tyson launching a $100 million law suit after an angry, physically threatening break-up in the shining lobby of the Beverly Hills hotel, he was still clearly the great puppet master of the business.

In the hype-filled week before this fight he had been in quite masterful form. He knew that this fight had sold itself, rather as the great Ali–Frazier collision of 28 years earlier had done. This was not to compare either Holyfied or Lewis with the sublime Ali or the withering puncher Joe Frazier but this fight, like the one in 1971, had a compelling *raison d'être*. It was to settle the question which in boxing would always be most relevant to the public interest. Who was the best heavyweight in the world? The man who could claim to be that, unfettered by the pronouncements of squabbling organisations, still carried an unrivalled cachet into the ring.

It is an enduring tragedy of boxing that the most crucial limits on a fighter's talent are so often defined not in the ring but in the womb. Sugar Ray Robinson, an astonishing welterweight and later a middleweight of the deepest artistry and ingenuity, Willie Pep and Salvatore Sanchez, featherweights of beautiful balance, Henry Armstrong, a fighter of extraordinary will and talent, who held the world title at featherweight, welterweight and lightweight, were inhibited only by their genes. They couldn't dream of aspiring to the greatest prize in sport, no more than, practically, could the light-heavyweight champion of today, Roy Jones, a performer capable of entrancing any audience with his timing and his skill.

But Lewis and Holyfield could. Lewis, particularly, had the physical dimensions and the range of talent. Holyfield had an aura unique among all his peers. And now King rode these certainties with a relish peculiar to his showman's panache and his survivor's understanding that once again he had repelled the worst of his demons. More than anyone in the Garden King had cause to reflect on the extraordinary course of his life in boxing, how he had come to graduate from prison garb in an Ohio State penitentiary to a tuxedo and the centre of the stage yet again.

When the first Ali–Frazier fight was made, King was still scrabbling on the edges of the fight scene. He had done his time for kicking to death an ailing numbers runner on the streets of his native Cleveland – 'I'll get you the money, Don,' were the victim's last words – and consumed Shakespeare and Voltaire in the prison library. Captivated by Ali's ability to storm across all frontiers of class and prejudice, King's genius was to look beyond the old limits of boxing. He could wield the aura of an Ali and dazzle not only television executives but governments, and his great breakthrough would be to convince the reviled despot Mobutu of Zaire to sponsor the Rumble in the Jungle of Foreman and Ali. No one had ever been more transparent in his ambition and his greed than Don King. He was with his champions, 'win or draw', and classically travelled to the Foreman–Frazier fight in Kingston, Jamaica, in Frazier's limousine. When Frazier was dismantled by the power punching of Foreman, King shamelessly stepped over his prone figure and embraced Foreman. Naturally, he left the fight at the head of Foreman's entourage.

Here in New York he inevitably declared for Holyfield. He had promotional rights to Holyfield. Lewis, on the other hand, had long resisted the lure of the King empire, once checking out of a hotel at speed when he heard that the promoter had arrived at the local airport. When King promoted Lewis's first title fight against Tony Tucker in Las Vegas in 1993 he had paid, for once, through his nose, winning the purse bid with an offer of $7 million – an outlay which would leave King with a loss of around $3 million. But King saw that as seed money. Didn't money always work in the end? Not, though, in the case of Lewis.

Still, King had billowed on like some preposterous galleon, but all the time so knowing, so cunning, prising Tyson away from his managerial team after bombarding him with limousines and jewels and girls, and through Tyson he had gained the rights to Holyfield. Now, King insisted, Holyfield would deliver to him all three heavyweight title belts.

He was exultant about the prospects. Every ticket for the Garden had gone. Pay-per-view sales, HBO reported, would comfortably clear a million. 'It is not a time,' he said, 'for promotional "trickeration."' It was simply time to make the harvest of a great fight. 'The buzz is on,' he announced. 'On Saturday you will think Hollywood has come to New York. The world will stop for a few hours – even the war in the Balkans. This is just like putting a plant to grow and agronomy is my business. This fight was conceived in bitterness. The naysayers said we would sell no more than 700,000 but now records could be broken. We could break the all-time high of 1.85 million for Tyson–Holyfield I. I'm in the lemon-doctoring business. I have made lemonade here – and it's getting sweeter and sweeter and sweeter.'

Certainly the fight was confirming the old theory of Ali that in the public mind few events are more compelling than a title fight of genuine intrigue. Some years after his own glory had passed, but before he entered the dark valley ordained by a combination of Parkinson's disease and gross punishment in the ring, he declared, 'There is nothing like a fight to stop the world for a little while. The whole world wants to know, "who's gonna win, who's gonna win?" It's like chasing a pretty woman. It's the only thing you can think of. You slap on the cologne and you go chasing and then when it's over the world carries on.'

At the final press conference in Madison Square Garden King had the bearing of someone who could not be touched. He was heckled by the gnarled old fight man Lou Duva, a trainer of champions and patriarch of the family of promoters, led by his sons, the late Dan and Dino, who had controlled much of the career of Holyfield and held the American rights to Lewis. Dino challenged King's claims on behalf of Holyfield, pointing out that he had been as enthusiastic for Tyson before his first fight with Holyfield, when Tyson's entourage claimed that his victim would be flown out of Las Vegas in a coffin. 'Man, I was wrong,' said King. 'Holyfield is my man, he's made a believer of me.'

Such is King, boxing's ultimate existentialist. I was once in his company when disgraceful scenes erupted at a promotional breakfast in one of the big Las Vegas banqueting suites. Photographers put down their plates of scrambled eggs and pancakes and rushed to the stage where fighters and managers were embroiled in a violent scrum. King, resplendent in a velvet suit and a huge, diamond-encrusted crucifix, wore the most benign of expressions and his shoulders heaved a little with the beginnings of mirth. 'Don,' I said, 'you seem less than appalled by this wretched scene.' His eyes sparkled and he declared, 'Brother, my heart is jumping for joy.' Of course what he saw was not grown, in some cases elderly, men, writhing on the carpet, straining to get leverage for one decent punch, yelling and cursing. He saw lively footage for the afternoon news slots. He saw a little more fight ink in the morning papers. He saw more tickets sold.

An American writer Tom Archdeacon recalls how King nearly choked to death on a fishbone in a Cleveland restuarant. There was a conspicuous lack of rescue action on behalf of King. But he survived and after a dreadful bout of coughing he gathered himself to his full dignity, smiled beatifically, and uttered the phrase most commonly used in America when a great event has nearly come to pass. 'Close, gentlemen,' said King, 'but no cigar.'

On the eve of the Leonard–Duran King promotion in New Orleans in 1980 writers were suddenly summoned to a press conference. They assumed some dramatic news development; perhaps Duran, edgy all week, had erupted and put the fight in jeopardy.

No, it was the weekend of the fire disaster at the MGM Grand in Las Vegas and King wanted to tell us that he had sponsored a shipment of 'magically healing' water. 'I'm doing this in the service of humanity,' intoned King. From the back of the room a disgruntled hack declared, 'It would be an even greater service if you tied yourself to a wheel of the aircraft.' King chuckled indulgently.

No man in sport has ever generated so much money for individual fighters and yet provoked so much bitterness and scorn – and law suits. The former world heavyweight champion Larry Holmes has a particularly harsh verdict. 'Deep down, I think King hates all fighters. He envies them their recognition by the public. He wants to dominate everything but when the bell rings he has to leave the ring.' But then even Holmes gives to the dark Caesar of boxing what is his. When King was inducted into Boxing's Hall of Fame in 1997, Holmes grudgingly conceded, 'I've criticised Don King more than anybody, but he made me a millionaire – he gave me all the good things, made me secure for the rest of my life.'

Tim Witherspoon, another former world champion, could not say the same – but then as King points out, some men are easier to help than others. Witherspoon received a legally enforced settlement from King for over $100,000, but within months it was gone – a dismaying percentage of it assigned to telephone bills.

King controlled his empire for so long as rigorously as the KGB did that of the Kremlin. He probed the character of his charges, identified their weaknesses and exploited them quite effortlessly. Muhammad Ali was bedazzled by the sight of large amounts of money. Thus a large brown envelope containing new banknotes was a guarantee of settlement of a dispute which might cost the promoter far more were it processed through lawyers and accountants. Tyson liked cars and girls and jewellery, and they were relentlessly supplied by King. But Tyson was ultimately beyond all discipline, all blandishment. Even the wily, endlessly resourceful

King knew that one day he would fly beyond all control.

When it happened in Tyson's second fight with Holyfield in 1997, when Tyson spat out parts of Holyfield's ear, King launched himself into full-scale damage control. He hired a public relations firm which had served President Ronald Reagan, surely the apotheosis of spin doctoring and image projection. He sent honeyed messages to the Nevada Athletic Commission, who had taken away Tyson's licence and would not consider an appeal until the summer of 1998. But at the start of that year King's grasp on the world of boxing had never been under so much pressure. Tyson was no longer the pliant figure King had laid siege to when the fighter's relationship with Bill Caton, who had taken sole control over Tyson's career with the death of his partner Jimmy Jacobs, broke down irreparably. King was also having problems with his other main fighter, the Puerto Rican welterweight champion Felix Trinidad.

Dominating everything, though, when I arrived at King's headquarters in Deerfield Beach, Florida, early in January was the possibility that King would be in prison before the end of the year. The FBI, after years of pursuit, were convinced they had their man. My assignment was to secure an interview with Mike Tyson – the first full one since the outrage against Holyfield. But inevitably I was sucked into the drama of King's wider crisis.

You do not need a map to find King's HQ. You just collect a car at Miami airport and drive north to Fort Lauderdale. Then, soon enough you pick out huge flags flapping in the sea breeze. One carries the King trademarked legend, 'Only in America'. Another bears the Stars and Stripes. The third is decorated with the yellow crown of King Productions.

I spent three days at King HQ, mostly in the company of his veteran public relations man, the former fight manager Bobby Goodman. A superb old pro, Goodman regaled me with fight talk and coffee – would I like some takeaway pasta? – and when I got restive he assured me that King was doing all he could to set up something with Tyson, and when time permitted I would be ushered into the lavishly upholstered command centre on the second floor. King worked a long, hard shift. He drove himself to the office in his black Mercedes before eight each morning. Invariably, he was working the phones for at least another 12 hours. His staff brought in huge mounds of pasta and chicken. And when King left, invariably deep into the evening, it would not be for the lavish home he shares with his wife Henrietta on a nearby island but some local hostelry and a working dinner with a fightman who had flown in from Los Angeles or New York. When King left the office his staff, more than 80 of them, sat back at their desks like exhausted fighters on their stools. Their boss was both a workaholic and a control freak. Typed messages of command tattooed the walls – even the toilet. 'Consider your workmates,' ordered King. 'Make sure you wash up after using the toilet.' How disorienting, you thought as you adjusted your flies, such fastidiousness at the heart of the evil empire.

King's waiting-room was filled from dawn to dusk. On one cigarette break in the palm-fringed carpark I noticed a beat-up Chevy in a shady corner. It was filled with young children being fed fast food by their harassed mother. Her husband, a local fighter, had been waiting for hours to see King about the possibility of signing a contract. The fighter would have to return the following day, he told me later, glumly. But he wouldn't quit. His mates at the gym in Miami's Latino quarter laughed at his plan, but the fighter told me, 'The guys at the gym tell me I'm mad – they say King will rob me like he robbed all the others. But I say to them, before you can be robbed you have to have money. In boxing King has the money. Better to be robbed by a big man than a little one. That way you get to keep some of the money.'

Eventually, I typed out a list of questions which were faxed to Tyson and the following day King triumphantly read out the answers. He said that Tyson was still enraged by the coverage of the second fight. He was not ready to sit down with a journalist, but here were his reactions to the main questions. Perhaps they had been fed to and filtered through the damage control department, but they did have a certain force and certainly my sports editor at the *Express* was pleased enough to receive them.

Said Tyson, 'As long as I live I will regret what happened that night. But I cannot change anything. I can only start again and hope that I get another chance. I tasted blood that night when I bit the ears of Evander Holyfield. Yes, I went over the edge. I felt I had been pushed back into the streets. I've spent so much of my life admiring the great fighters and striving to be one of them, so think about it. Do I want to be remembered for something so bizarre? Do I want all my years of battling to be washed away by something like that? It's the last thing I want and something I will fight against as long as I can. Why did I do it? You have to understand I grew up in the streets. I didn't have any protection. A lot of my friends died or went to prison. Our role models were drug dealers and pimps. They were the ones with the diamonds and the cars. That's not an excuse but I have to explain there were no rules. You just had to survive, hurt someone who wanted to hurt you.

'I have the greatest respect for Evander Holyfield and after the first fight I held out my hand and paid my respects. It would hurt me terribly, more than anything, if the only thing people remembered about our fights was that I bit his ear. As I said right away, I snapped. In boxing I learned to follow rules which, coming from the streets, is not your instinct. But I felt in this fight the rules were not being observed. Holyfield was butting me and he was getting away with it. I was fighting for my life, for my children, and I got so frustrated because I felt Holyfield was using his head illegally. I told the referee I wasn't getting any help. So I went back to the streets. I cannot defend it, but it happened, it was bizarre, it was a freak.

'I cannot complain about the Nevada Athletic Commission. I have always respected those people. They gave me respect. They treated me well. I just want to tell them how badly I'm hurting. I desperately want to fight again. I'm a student of boxing. I've spent so many hours watching film of the great fighters. I feel a lot of emotion when I look at those old films. When Roberto Duran lost to Sugar Ray Leonard in that bizarre fashion it was the worst day of my life, or so I thought. I was only a kid, but it hurt. He was a warrior. I love all the great fighters, Jack Johnson, Jack Dempsey, Joe Louis, Stanley Ketchel, Henry Armstrong, you name them. When I was a kid Muhammad Ali came to Brooklyn. I was in awe just looking at him. I've been to the graves of great fighters and I've identified with someone like Sonny Liston, who felt he was an outsider, who *was* an outsider. What happened against Holyfield in that last fight is a big problem for me. I know a lot of people hate me, like to see me down, and they have made judgements. But I do know a lot of people want to see me fight and that gives me encouragement. My biggest incentive to fight Holyfield again is that I may be judged again as a fighter, win or lose. People do different things in life. All I do is fight. I must fight again. And I must fight Evander Holyfield.'

King made it clear, when I finally sat down with him, that his need was just as pressing. Yes, there were problems with Tyson, problems with the Feds, but Holyfield–Tyson would carry all kinds of redemption. It would celebrate King's inevitable defeat of the FBI in the Federal courthouse in New York. It would underpin the finances of Don King Productions by another $10 million or so. Patriotically, I mentioned the claims of Lennox Lewis, the reigning WBC champion, but they were brushed aside. 'Lewis–Holyfield or Lewis–Tyson can happen anytime, and they would be big fights, but Tyson–Holyfield is different. It is now. It is a fight of the streets, of the blood.

'Tyson–Holyfield III would be the biggest fight in history and it

51

would not even matter if Lewis in the meantime came along and beat Holyfield. Yes, Holyfield–Tyson III is a fight of the blood. It would have people going crazy if it happened in the Roman Colosseum. Mike Tyson is contrite, no doubt. But someone has to speak for him, explain where he is coming from and what happened to him that night.

'Something came up in him that was so strong the rules of boxing no longer applied. Mike is a generous man. He went to a party in New York City and Winnie Mandela was there. He heard she was in trouble so he gave her $50,000. He knows nothing about politics. He just reacts instinctively. But in the ring he has had to learn to control those instincts and for so long he did that. When it went wrong against Holyfield he was confused and angry. And when fighters snap you don't always know which way they are going. What happened is not unique. Andrew Golota bit an opponent and was then disqualified in two fights against Riddick Bowe. His reward was to fight Lennox Lewis for the world title. Mike has to live with something I know about. You can make mistakes, you can atone for them, but they don't let you forget. When I went to New York to go straight after some statutory illegality [or manslaughter and numbers running] the authorities would not accept that I had done my time. You have to remember this is a deeply racist society. There are two sets of rules. The FBI have this place bugged. They spend millions trying to put something on me and they call me a mobster. They try to put me in prison as they did Al Capone. But in my case I pay my taxes – and my lawyers. Capone only paid his lawyers. The FBI have combed through everything and all they have is one charge of fraud, which is not true. They say I defrauded Lloyd's of London. But they ask Lloyd's what I am to them and Lloyd's say, "Don King is good business."'

Unstoppable, a King interview invariably becomes a monologue. It hits a series of crescendos, skitters through original syntax and outright malapropisms, but has a narrative power rarely touched outside the most passionate theatre, both farcical and dramatic. Clearly he was on the edge here in Florida. The Feds had got under his skin and if he had conjured for me a series of highly quotable answers to the Tyson questionnaire it had obviously not been his easiest task of the week. On half a dozen occasions he had tried to contact Tyson in my presence but his prized commodity was plainly on the loose, slipping away from his influence and even examining harshly the roles of his old companions Rory Holloway and John Horne, co-managers who with King were shortly to feel the fighter's intense wrath.

At that point it would have been hard to imagine King in his triumphant role at Madison Square as Lennox Lewis and Evander Holyfield prepared to do battle. The word from the Federal prosecutors was that they had King at last. Tyson would soon touch bottom again with violent road rage which would send him back to prison. He was on his way to buy a new gleaming motor bike, the fad of the moment, when he was involved in a minor collision. He jumped from his car muttering oaths and struck two middle-aged motorists.

For more than 25 years King had been keeping the balls in the air, juggling with careers and law suits and always keeping his eye on the main chance, but you could cut the tension in the air at his command post in January 1998.

He told me how he could earn Tyson at least another $50 million when his licence was restored. He recalled a late-night scene in a Las Vegas bar the previous November, when Holyfield had rallied against Michael Moorer to retain his WBA world title belt but also left Showtime TV with losses of $11 million. Said King, 'There was no Tyson and the excitement was down. A few of the players [high-rolling gamblers] lined up a series of drinks at the thinly populated bar. They were saying, "This is for old so-and-so" and a whole lot of characters who hadn't made it to the fight. Why? They told me, "Man, you don't pay to go to church." They said they needed the buzz of Tyson. Holyfield was a great fighter, a true warrior, sure, but Tyson was wild, Tyson was dangerous, Tyson gave that buzz in full measure.'

Now King was talking about the buzz of Lewis and Holyfield, fighters who in the past he had accused of being unable to 'draw flies to a garbage dump'. Now he was selling them on the impeccable, unchallengeable basis that they were the best two heavyweights around. He had christened the fight, 'King's Crowning Glory'. It wasn't that but it did have a certain glory. The glory of Lewis's steadfast march to a moment of truth, uncompromised and unencumbered by the machinations of King, and the glory of Holyfield's defiance of the years and a whole series of bigger, younger opponents.

Unlike Tyson, neither Lewis nor Holyfield had required more from King than simply the chance to fight. Holyfield had contrived his chance with an oddly untypical performance against ill-considered Czyz. Lewis had made his opportunity by the sheer doggedness of his ambition. When King had given the floor to the fighters at the climax of the hype, they had both spoken briefly and with dignity.

Lewis made a small joke, saying he respected Holyfield's warrior qualities and how he wished to make clear he had called him a hypocrite – a reference to the charge, which had inflamed Holyfield, that his opponent spoke religion but lived otherwise in siring a series of children outside of his marriages – and not a 'hypoquit'. Holyfield refused the bait on this occasion and pointed out that he had risen above the challenges of James Buster Douglas, Riddick Bowe, Michael Moorer and, finally, Tyson, and that Lewis, too, would be mastered. There was no talk of graveyards or coffins, no sneers about the quality of an opponent. Just the statements of intent of real fighters going into a real fight. Suddenly, the fluted, fractured oratory of Don King was redundant. The fact was that a decent proportion of the world was, as Ali would say, already slapping on the cologne.

But then with King there are always questions, always concerns. When Douglas hammered Tyson in Tokyo, separating him from the undisputed heavyweight championship of the world, King came within an inch of restoring the belts on the grounds that Douglas had enjoyed a 'long count'. When Tyson came out of prison, he was magically restored to the head of the WBC's ranking list at Lewis's cost. King skilfully plotted that Tyson comeback, earning him nearly $100 million with the graveyard raids on the bodies of Pete McNeely, a bar-room scuffler from Boston, the powder-puff hitting Buster Mathis Junior and the panic-stricken Bruce Seldon and Frank Bruno. King, it seemed, had the capacity to do anything he chose in boxing. Hence that irrational surge of fear when Lennox Lewis found his way to the Madison Square Garden ring suddenly barred. Some eyes turned to King with apprehension. But he stood there in the ring, his jewellery glittering, his arms extended proprietorially along the ropes, so benign he might have been at his annual chore of handing out Christmas turkeys in the ghetto. This, he was saying, was his gift to boxing. It wasn't of course. It was a fight which simply had to happen.

A Warrior's Pain

Something happened to Evander Holyfield between a bright January morning in Miami in 1999 and the night he stepped into the ring with Lennox Lewis at Madison Square Garden six weeks later. Whatever it was, it was more affecting than the mere tick of the clock. Gone was something fine, almost imperceptible at first, but as the fight wore on, as the seed of controversy sprouted like the plant in the Little Shop of Horrors, the need to remind yourself that this was a fighter of the ages, a man for whom adversity always lit flames of extraordinary defiance, became progressively stronger.

Holyfield would later blame it on cramps in his legs and his stomach but boxing was generally unimpressed with excuses from such an unlikely quarter. Before fighting Lewis, Holyfield's performance levels may have dipped from time to time, but always he fought with a conviction that even on his worst nights he would find a way to win. In Atlanta in 1991 he had been ambushed by the ill-considered Bert Cooper and was obliged to fight his way through a storm of punishment which at one point threatened his unbeaten record. Against the ancient George Foreman and Larry Holmes he was required to rely more on sweat than inspiration. The common factor in such victories was a self-belief so fierce it always seemed guaranteed to consume rather than negotiate crisis.

I saw him twice on the build-up to the fight before he arrived in New York, once on that morning when Don King wheeled him into a big breakfast-room filled with American sportswriters covering the Super Bowl and then later in the gym in Houston known as the House of Pain. He worked before dawn broke over some of the less salubrious streets of the city.

He was rampant in his confidence in Miami. His ambition was so intense you fancied it might warm up the coffee he reached for with an arm of such sculpted muscle it might have come from an old piece of Greek marble. He tossed aside the arguments of ageism and sizeism with outright contempt. Yes, Lewis was three inches taller, a good two stone heavier, his reach advantage was more than seven inches and he was three years younger. But such measurements were meaningless, said Holyfield. They ignored by far the most important parts of the equation, the equalising impact of Holyfield's heart and his will.

'People have always talked about size all my career but I see it as a joke,' Holyfield declared. 'In a fight like this the only thing worth measuring is mental strength and I believe I'm the bigger man in this respect. I admire some of Lennox's qualities. He's a straight character, he conducts himself well and I've always liked the way he presents himself for a fight. He's a good fighter and that's why I'm going in with him. There is so much to prove. But I've done a lot more than him, you only have to look at our records to see that. I've been in places so bad he couldn't even dream about them, and I've come through. What gives me so much confidence is that I can look at Lennox Lewis, and then at my own life, and I can say that I've looked into the face of danger so many more times and I know this will carry me through.

'Nothing can stand in my way because I believe it is my destiny to win this fight, to reclaim the undisputed heavyweight title of the world. I see it as my right – and this makes me believe that with the help of God I can achieve anything I want in the ring. All my life I've been told I'm too small and now I'm being told Lennox Lewis is too big for me, that I cannot handle big fighters. Well, they will see soon enough. It's not how big you are but how strong you are in your mind and your body. I'll be too strong for Lennox in both areas.

'It is right that people are excited about this fight because we are the two best heavyweights left standing. It is a fight that had to happen. How will it end? There are two possibilities. One is that I beat him in a fight which boils up in the first round and finishes around the third. The other is that I beat him in a bad fight. And if it is a bad fight I'll get him around the seventh. But however it goes, I'll get him.

'Lennox's style is good for me. Like all men with a big right hand, he keeps his neck stiff to throw it. I can get inside when he's loading up. He has power but Tyson still has power – and I proved against him you need more than that. To beat me you've got to fight, really fight, inside. People wonder if I've lost some of my appetite because I'm in my mid-thirties – not at all. I always look at a fight the way I'm looking at this one. I just ask myself, "Can I beat the man? Have I got more equipment?" As long as I do that and can say honestly I know I can beat him, I go on. When I get rid of Lewis, I'll fight Henry Akinwande, maybe in South Africa, and then I'll stand beside Nelson Mandela – a hero of mine. He's another guy who has beaten the odds.'

Holyfield was implacable in his confidence that morning. Away from his entourage, and his now estranged wife Janice, the religious card was brandished less extravagantly. He talked a little of his boyhood in Alabama and Georgia. He was looking forward to the Super Bowl later that day, confident that his hometown Atlanta Falcons would get the better of John Elway's Denver Broncos, but he was no great fan of the gridiron. It was a game dictated by coaches, by players who became merely the pawns in some great strategy worked out in a darkened video room by middle-aged white men with clipboards and a liking for military haircuts and the lingo of war.

'I chose boxing as a kid,' Holyfield recalled, 'mainly because my mother said I had to be respectful of authority and that if I played football I would have to listen to everything the coach said and obey him. But I didn't like that because it all depended if the coach liked you. You weren't in control of your own progress. It wasn't a question of how good you were but whether you were respectful enough.

'I concluded that maybe you had to be a con-artist to succeed. It is so different in fighting. In fighting you make your own career and if you are good enough you win. That's the only question mark – and only you can provide the answers. You don't have to win any favours. You don't have to convince anyone how good you are. It's all down there in the ring. The better man wins.'

You suggested that maybe the sheer size of Lewis, coupled with his natural ability, might just cause a flicker of doubt, a hint of intimidation. Holyfield remained unimpressed. 'Tyson tried to intimidate me but it didn't work. He stared at me hard in the ring before the first fight but it had no effect. I was just thinking how I was going to beat him. I said to Tyson, "You cannot scare me – no one on earth can scare me. The only person I'm scared of is God." People think when I pray to God I'm asking someone to come out of the sky to help me. It doesn't work like that. God is deep inside you. That's the only way he can work for you.'

The fight was still six weeks away, there was so much terrain of the psyche still to cover, but Holyfield was filled with certainties. 'Sometimes in boxing,' he said, 'a fight is thrown up which is the ticket – and no other ticket means anything. Holyfield–Lewis has been the ticket for some time. Maybe it should have happened some time ago but Riddick Bowe messed that up when he threw away the WBC belt. Lewis can't shirk all the blame. Maybe he could have fought when he first won the WBC title and then when he won it back. But that doesn't matter now. The fight is on. I'm ready – like I'm always ready.'

It seemed that for Holyfield the older he got the sweeter became the simplicities of the ring. Within the ropes everything was so 'controllable'. You fought well, you dug deep down and you won. If you didn't, you lost. It was so simple, so clean. Beyond the ropes there were all kinds of intangibles. Your mother died. Your brother was murdered on a roadside. Your marriage, bathed in the white light of evangelical religion, celebrated modestly in a fast-food joint, could end almost before it began – and with crushing financial penalties. Trust was elusive and when it broke down it was gone forever. So you demanded a DNA test of your wife to prove the paternity of one of your children. You were zealous in your religion, but you also kept producing offspring out of wedlock, and you became angry when this was pointed out. Maybe it was after Lewis noted this inconsistency of Holyfield, and mentioned the word hypocrisy when talking to some American writers up in his training camp in the Poconos hills on the border of New Jersey and Pennsylvania, that the change came in Holyfield. He was, no question, a different man in the House of Pain five weeks later.

The direct gaze, the declarative statements had gone. The dawn was still several hours away when he arrived at the gym at the wrong end of Clay Street. A hobo, wrapped in a tattered copy of the *Houston Post*, slept in a doorway. The American Noodle Company across the street was still in darkness. Eerily, Holyfield crooned along with some gospel muzak as his trainer, Don Turner, bandaged his hands. His helpers massaged his body. He performed stretching exercises as though in a trance. When he finally sparred with two big men loosely impersonating Lewis, he looked businesslike enough but the homage of his followers seemed heavier, more cloying than ever before. The Amens were thunderous when he mouthed the words of the tape between rounds . . . 'In Your presence that's when I'm strong. Oh Lord, My God, that's where I belong, touching your grace.'

One of the crowd, a small black man who looked somewhat like a refugee from the set of *Guys and Dolls* dressed in a white suit, a black shirt and tie decorated with images of baseball greats and a white fedora, sniffed at the idea that Holyfield's final definition as a fighter would come in Madison Square Garden. 'If any man has already defined himself it is Evander Holyfield,' said the black Stubby Kaye. 'What more could he have done to explain himself as a fighter, as a man? Maybe only carve his face on Mount Rushmore.' But if there was serenity around him in the gym, it seemed less apparent in the heart and the mind of Holyfield.

He snapped when I began to shape what was planned as a gentle opening question. I said only, 'If you beat Lennox Lewis,' but he cut in, 'No, brother, it is not if I beat Lennox Lewis it is when I beat him and I've just told you that will be the third round. I see it so clearly. Before any fight you go through different stages. You first pick out the fight in your mind. It's the one you want and the promoters say, "Oh there ain't so much money in this fight" but you say, "Well, I want to fight this guy." In the case of Lennox Lewis there was both a real fight . . . and real money. I wanted it and the promoters and the TV people just had to get it on. Lennox says he wanted it but I'm not so sure. He had his contract with HBO and I was tied up with Showtime, so the way it works in boxing he could keep saying I was ducking him, knowing the odds were that the fight wouldn't happen. But I went through that. I said, "Give me the fight. I want it, boxing wants it, the people want it." And now it is threatening to break all records because it is a real fight, a real big fight. It's getting closer now and I'm feeling better all the time.'

But was he? His manager Jim Thomas was already deeply worried about his mental state. Later he would say, 'The closer the fight got to New York I realised Evander had made a mistake – one he had never made before. He had let Lennox Lewis get under his skin. Lewis's claim that Evander was a hypocrite did the damage. It provoked Evander into predicting a third-round knock-out. He had always stayed away from that. He always said it was a counter-productive thing, a no-win situation. You flagged the achievement of something which would bring its own credit, and if you didn't do it the pressure was on you and your opponent felt that much better.' If it was a profound mistake, it was also irreversible. The furies of Holyfield's will, having been launched, permitted no compromise.

Again he reviewed passionately the profile of his career. He included both the highs and the lows of a campaign which had relentlessly challenged the view that he would always be genetically challenged when taking on the big men for the greatest prize in boxing. He went back again to arguably the very peak of his career, the losing fight against a talented Riddick Bowe who would never be better prepared than that night in Las Vegas when he became the first undisputed champion since the young, cyclonic Tyson and the last before this fight due in New York in ten days' time. Before that fight the remarkable trainer Eddie Futch had talked triumphantly of his winning crusade to drive away the indolence which alone threatened the prospects of Bowe. Futch told of how he had finally accepted the assignment. He had gone to meet the young fighter in Reno, where he was in training. Futch knew Bowe's quality but had also heard stories of his indiscipline. He told Bowe that he had to fly home to Vegas later that day, but he wanted him to step up his work – and if he got the right response he would accept the job. Futch suggested that Bowe ran in the hills outside the city before dawn the following morning.

Futch didn't fly home that night. Though in his eighties, Futch was vigorous enough, a fact underlined by his recent marriage to a beautiful young Swedish woman and his comfortably administered knock-out of a particularly arrogant racist in a Las Vegas parking lot. He booked an alarm call for the early hours and drove up to the hills before sun-up. There he saw Bowe toiling up a hill, the morning frost forming on his track-suit as he sent up great billows of steam. That was good enough for Futch – and too good for Holyfield, despite an unforgettably courageous performance.

Holyfield now remembered his mood as he left Vegas after losing the points decision. 'I was shattered and embarrassed. I couldn't believe I had lost. It was very painful. I went back to Georgia and tried to nurse my wounds. It took a long time. But when I looked at the fight again I took pride. I thanked God I hadn't been knocked out, and I could see I had gone right to the limit of what I could do. So there could be no shame.

'That is what fighting is all about in the end. It's going somewhere unknown. Going to a place you never knew before. That's what Lennox Lewis faces in New York. He's got to go to a new place – a foreign place. But I'm at home.' Yet three years earlier Madison Square Garden had not been overwhelmingly hospitable to either fighter. On the same night Lewis had fought his war of attrition with Mercer, Holyfield had teetered on the edge of credibility against Czyz. Looking back now, Holyfield saw that as the greatest crisis of his fighting life. Yes, he agreed, he was way ahead on points but he looked terrible, a shell of the man who had waged such war with Bowe. 'I panicked. I knew I was ahead but I also knew I looked bad and I could hardly deal with it. I had lost to Riddick Bowe in the third fight and suddenly I felt embarrassed in the ring. I had felt a hell of a lot of pressure in the ring over the years, I had often wondered whether I had any gas in the tank in the course of a particular fight, but I'd never felt embarrassed. Man, that was something unknown, and of course it made me think the worst thing of all. It made me wonder if this was the end of the road, this nothing fight against a guy I was beating easy. I had told people I would be carrying the flame in the Olympics in my home town of Atlanta and now here I was struggling to beat Bobby Czyz. I just thank the Lord I didn't do what was on my mind. I didn't walk away.' Had he done so, one of the most extraordinary passages of boxing history would have been aborted. He would never have handled so brilliantly Tyson at that point where long accumulated rage slips into madness. Holyfield said, 'Yes, I believe it was the Czyz fight which got me the shot with Tyson. I believe it made me a big-name opponent who the Tyson people thought had turned soft. Maybe deep down Mike Tyson didn't believe that – I suspect he didn't because of the way he came into the ring with me – but his people were convinced, they said he would kill, and for a while he just went along with that. Also, he needed the money.'

You had to wonder if Holyfield had indeed lured Tyson into an elaborate trap. Holyfield thought for a moment and then a small smile flickered across his warrior's countenance. 'No,' he said, 'even if that plan was partly in my mind, my ego just got in the way. I couldn't go in the ring to look bad – that would go against everything I've stood for ever since I came out of the "projects", when I didn't even have enough to eat properly.'

He ate now, as he prayed and bought new horses and improved his properties and fathered children with women other than his wives, with something which could be only described as zeal. As he trained he drank from long, calorie- and vitamin-laden flasks. He would eat mounds of pasta, trays of eggs, the best steaks and he would still not come within two stones of Lewis when they weighed in at the Garden. His masseuse Sharon Stewart said,

'We'd love Evander to come in at around 220lb [15st 10lb] but he will be at least five pounds less. His metabolism is unbelievable. He eats only to stop his body invading his muscles, his power.' But the weight, which would be so vital as ballast against the sheer strength of Lewis, was elusive. 'People are making a lot of this, but I pay it no mind. Weight is weight, talent is talent. What is inside is most important. Lewis will see I overcome all disadvantages. What you do is adapt, find a way to win.'

Flying up to New York for the drive into the Poconos to see Lewis, it seemed to me the mystery of Evander Holyfield had never run deeper. Idly, I scanned a list of fight predictions which only confirmed the extraordinary spread of opinion about the coming fight. The former champion Holmes was particularly hard on Lewis. 'Everyone knows he is a scared fighter,' sneered Holmes. 'Holyfield has more heart, more know-how – he's just so much more of a fighter.'

British promoter Frank Warren, who could never forgive Lewis much, perhaps least of all that he wasn't his property, declared confidently, 'Holyfield will stop him, likely late on.' But Mickey Duff, long the prevailing intelligence of British boxing and a man never scared to put his money where his mouth is, was even more emphatic in the other direction. 'Lennox Lewis is the best British heavyweight ever – and the most capable since Muhammad Ali. If he doesn't make any silly mistakes, if he uses his jabs, fights Holyfield at a distance, as he can, he must win by a decison.' Duff had backed his opinion with a bet of £10,000.

You could simply take your pick on the predictions. 'Lewis, definitely,' said Britain's former world cruiserweight champion Glenn McCrory, who had sparred more than 100 rounds with Tyson and had been crushed by Lewis after taking a fight which had appealed more to his business instincts than his always thoughtful appraisal of the game he had distinguished with guts and no little ability. 'Holyfield is the challenge to bring the best out of Lennox. He needs to get up for a fight. He has so much talent, his tendency has been to cruise along. But you can't do that against Holyfield. Nobody needs to tell Lennox this.'

Former world bantamweight champion, the Las Vegas-based Ulsterman Wayne McCullough declared, 'It's close but if you force me to pick a winner I have to go with Holyfield.' Ray Mercer, who pushed Lewis so hard at the Garden, said, 'I'm going for Lewis, narrowly on points.' Angelo Dundee, mentor of Ali and Sugar Ray Leonard, knew the answer, saying, 'Holyfield will win because he's got ten tons of heart.' But it was the call of Teddy Atlas that was most intriguing. Indeed it carried me back from that plane seat to an afternoon in Las Vegas on the eve of Holyfield–Tyson I.

Atlas was in town with his fighter Michael Moorer, who was performing on the undercard against Francois Botha. Atlas had long fascinated me. If he hadn't been born the son of a doctor in Staten Island, the tough little community which is a short ferry ride across Manhattan's harbour, the author of the classic fight novel *Fat City* would have been required to invent him. I first met Atlas while covering Tyson's first slide beyond the boundaries of American society.

A decent but unremarkable pro fighter, he had been the iron prodigy's first trainer under the management of the maker of champions, Cus D'Amato, in the sleepy little upstate New York town of Catskill. Tyson came to D'Amato raw and jumpy from his days in reform school, where gang rapes were commonplace, and Atlas saw early that the need for discipline, kindly but firm, was absolutely essential to the boy's future. Atlas was well equipped to apply the necessary restraints. He was a tearaway of serious proportions in his youth, and carried a long scar – administered by an iron bar in a street rumble – to prove the point. After that incident he had gone to his father's surgery with a bloody head, but the doctor pointedly dealt with all his other patients, mostly sniffling pensioners, before sewing up his son.

It was not the style of the elderly fight man D'Amato. Atlas saw early that the old man, who had groomed Floyd Patterson for his world heavyweight title and had also handled the fine light-heavyweight champion Jose Torres, had no stomach for the hard task of controlling Tyson. D'Amato could see plainly that Tyson had all the raw talent to deliver him his last world title. He wouldn't put at risk this crowning prospect by disenchanting Tyson. So when it was reported to Atlas that Tyson had been bothering a local girl he took a gun to the young fighter and said that if there was any repetition he would use it. Atlas reckoned only such a dramatic gesture would impress a kid hardened by the scabrous streets of his native Brownsville, Brooklyn. D'Amato was unimpressed and fired Atlas, but not before the trainer had delivered an impassioned speech about the certainty of Tyson's end if he went unchecked. 'I told the old man,' Atlas recalled, 'that he alone could influence the kid. He could tell him how much he was putting at risk. I said that if Tyson had to choose between living in a nice house in the country, with a fight career and big money in the pipeline, and going back to those streets he wouldn't be indecisive for too long. He might run off to the streets but he would surely come back with his tail between his legs soon enough.'

Atlas's distaste for the course of Tyson's life, his collection of friends, his status as a pawn of Don King, had grown down the years and that week in Las Vegas for the Holyfield fight his scorn had become open. He had attended the final press conference at which Tyson's former friend and co-manager Rory Holloway had revolted the gathering in a big banqueting suite with his warning that Holyfield risked death if he stood too doggedly in the path of his man. Atlas's blood was already running high. He had been confronted by one of those characters on the fringes of boxing who inject themselves into the affairs of the men who shape the game. This one had taken to calling Atlas's answering machine when one of his fighters had lost in order to leave a gloating message. Atlas briskly slugged his tormentor, then recoiled at the sentiments of the Tyson entourage. 'When I walked out of that room,' he said later, 'I had an overwhelming need of soap and water. I felt dirty. I just wanted to wash those people away.'

By the time of that press conference I had built in my mind a clear case for tipping Holyfield. He had done it before, when he upset the odds and beat Bowe in the second fight when the 'Fan Man' had come gliding in from the desert night, and despite the discouraging evidence of the Czyz fight I concluded that Tyson, the classic bully, had also shown clear evidence of eroding powers in the series of fights against hapless opponents on his release from the Indiana Youth Centre, where he had done his time for rape. Tyson was ripe for exposure, I believed, and I would have been surer in my conviction if I had known then the word being put about by his former wife, the actress Robin Givens. She reported how Tyson had always been in awe of Holyfield, how he had become tongue-tied in his presence, and that it was a legacy of their time together in the Olympic team, when Holyfield had offered the lisping, awkward boy a little relief from the baiting of team-mates led by Tyrell Biggs. Biggs would later pay dearly for his insults when Tyson held him up in their fight in Atlantic City not out of compassion but from the need to prolong his punishment. Later Tyson expressed his pleasure at the night's work. Gleefully, he reported that Biggs had 'screamed like a girl'. But for Holyfield the legacy of those amateur days was sharply different. It was one of respect for a man who stood on his own. Even without the Givens testimony, I had talked myself into going for Holyfield – until I sat down with Atlas in the coffee shop of the Desert Inn.

Slowly, relentlessly he demolished my argument. Yes, he said, Holyfield had infinitely more character than Tyson. Yes, he was a much more inventive fighter, but did I not understand that my theories and enthusiasms were based on a fighter who no longer existed. 'That Holyfield is gone,' said Atlas. 'He's 34 years old, and that might not seem so old, but look at the mileage on the clock. Look at the fights he's been in – look at the punishment he took in the Bowe fights, and remember how he just couldn't raise enough power to put him away in the third fight. Remember how shot he looked in that Czyz fight. He grew old in that fight. He became a shell. It is right to honour the character of Holyfield, and right to remember that it is the most important thing in boxing. But he has to be supported by good legs. Holyfield cannot support his character any longer. It's sad but you have to say it's over.'

The result, you may have guessed, was a travesty of a fight preview, a trailing of possibilities delivered from a firm seat on the fence from which I was finally dislodged in the third round, when Holyfield had absorbed the first furies of Tyson and then began to back him up with sweet combinations which signalled an end that would come five rounds later when the referee decided the resurrected Holyfield had delivered enough punishment. Such, I reflected on the drive in to my Manhattan hotel, was the enduring aura of Evander Holyfield.

Soon enough I would have to make another fevered prediction. I would have to commit for or against the man who had earned, as much as any fighter in history, his nickname the Real Deal. Only one thing was certain. This time I didn't have to seek out Teddy Atlas. His company, and his knowlege, remained among the most enjoyable in boxing but his view was already on the record. And all it did was deepen the mystery.

Touch of Class

In the first exchanges Lennox Lewis oozed authority. He looked like a man who knew his moment had arrived. Suddenly, Evander Holyfield was de-mythologised. He was another fighter trying to win a foothold on hazardous ground. When he rushed Lewis, as he knew he must to get inside the big reach, he did so tentatively against the force of a long, stiff jab and a freely thrown right.

Lewis romped through the first round. Secure behind his defence, confident in the release of his punches, he was setting a business agenda which would soon enough require Holyfield to rummage in his briefcase. The suspicion had to be that the ruffling of this Lewis might require Holyfield to fish out a hand grenade – or a left hook of unprecedented surprise and violence, perhaps accompanied by a practised thrust of his gleaming skull.

From Lewis it was an opening statement to quell the angst which had risen in the chests of his most fervent supporters. I cannot say my own concerns were placated. An opening round is often a fisherman's first fly skittering across the water, an initial testing of possibilities. But sometimes a pattern is set, a calling card put down. The message on Lewis's card was printed boldly enough for even the most sceptical, a fact, it would be wryly noted, that was underlined on the cards of the judges. Even Eugenia Williams, her view at this point presumably unhindered, scored the first round for Lewis.

As the bell sounded and Lewis turned for his corner like a guardsman standing down, some words he had uttered in the Poconos, philosophical musings which perhaps at the time might have been dismissed as a little airy, fell into place. 'When I think of the fight,' Lewis had told me, 'I can freeze a moment, a little window of time when it will all be decided. It will take Evander and me into the vacant ground you find in every fight.

'On this vacant ground two things are there. There's the courage to win – and something else. It was something else for a great fighter like Michael Spinks when he faced Mike Tyson. He was down on the canvas and he had blood on his face and he must have thought, "The millions are in the bank and do I really need this?" That was the end of Michael Spinks. Maybe Holyfield is a different kind of man. Definitely, he has survived these moments, these little dangerous windows of time, but I believe they keep coming to every fighter, whatever he has achieved. Holyfield has achieved a lot but there is always going to be a day when a fighter loses if he stays around too long.

'Muhammad Ali said it and I know he is right now. He said the longer you go, the harder it is to prepare yourself to fight. I'm sure Holyfield has never trained harder, or under so much pressure, than for this fight. He did well in his three fights with Riddick Bowe, but Bowe threw away his big advantages by mixing it. That was exactly how Holyfield wanted it.

'In fighting, like anything else, you just don't throw away your edge. I'll exploit my advantages as a boxer-puncher. Holyfield has three problems. He has to get past my jab, which I've been working on more than ever before and I know it is a great weapon when I use it properly. Then he has to face my right hand, which is harder than anything he has experienced. His last problem is my uppercut. I believe I will have the chance to tear him apart with my uppercut.

'I don't dismiss Holyfield. Yes, he is a great fighter. He's always been a warrior. But he's a small warrior and the one big heavyweight he's beaten, Bowe, threw it away mainly because he didn't prepare correctly and fought the wrong fight. Holyfield has never faced anyone like me and when people say, "Yes, but you haven't fought anyone like Holyfield", that's true enough. But the real point is that everything depends on how you handle yourself, how much you believe in your ability when you reach that vacant ground I was talking about.

'That's the time when the ring becomes a little unsteady under your feet and the crowd is screaming for blood. But to be honest, deep down I see this as another fight. I know I'm facing someone who will probably convince himself that he can beat me, but let's look at the evidence of his recent fights. Evander looked bad against Vaughn Bean – and who is he? – and before that he beat Tyson twice. But Tyson is a washed-up fighter, as we saw when he faced Francois Botha, and the only reason Holyfield got the Tyson fight was that he looked so bad against Bobby Czyz, who isn't even a real heavyweight. The same night in the same ring I got a lot of criticism when I fought Ray Mercer, but I was glad I went through that war.

'You need a few fights like that, when you have to dig down. I know my trainer Emanuel Steward was pleased, even if he didn't like my whole performance. He said afterwards, "I liked the way you stayed in there and fought it out. You can build on that."'

There was so much upon which to build this night in New York. So many times he had been investigated both in and out of the ring. So many questions had to be answered and sometimes he had wearied of the process. Questions about his origins, his loyalties, his sexual preferences. Invariably, he was candid, and not least on the matter of his return to the land of his birth, and the first 11 years of his life – Fitzsimmons, the expatriate Cornish blacksmith, had spent just nine in Britain – to launch his professional career after winning Olympic gold in Canada's colours.

He was a dual citizen of Britain and Canada; he had his attachments in both countries, his mother Violet in Kitchener, Ontario, his half-brother Dennis in North London, and the choice fell to him. He noted the extravagant support the British public had given to Frank Bruno, and he measured his talent against that national hero. He also recognised the bigger British market and the nation's yearning to have a heavyweight champion of the world. The idea had been put to him originally by Lawrence Lustig, a photographer for the *Daily Star* who saw Lewis in Las Vegas while covering the British world welterweight champion Lloyd Honeyghan's fight against Marlon Starling. Lustig sensed Lewis's frustration with a round of talks with American suitors and, with a sharp journalistic instinct which would change the course of British boxing history, recalled the Olympic champion's East End origins.

Tenaciously, Lustig arranged for Lewis and his American lawyer John Hornower to make a midnight call to the London office of Frank Maloney, a publican and jobbing South London boxing man who instantly saw the point of re-uniting Lewis with his British roots. Lewis elected to fight for Britain and was a little bemused when it became clear that it wasn't enough to recognise the flag, to make slightly uncomfortable journeys back to his old roots in the East End and to fight opponents like Steve Garber and Calvin Jones in places like Hull and Gateshead and knock them out inside a round. Perhaps, he reflected, he might have to hire a scriptwriter, as Bruno had, and have him shape endearing phrases for moments of maximum exposure, or maybe he could take elocution lessons from Harry Redknapp, the Cockney manager of the football team of his childhood, West Ham United. Or perhaps he would just fight.

I first saw him fight professionally in the Wembley Arena in March 1991. He arrived there as European champion with a record of 14–0, 13 of the wins inside the distance with only the veteran Ossie Ocasio taking him the distance, albeit painfully. His press notices were not overwhelming. He had power, certainly, and the cachet of the Olympic title, but the charge, one that in some quarters had still to be withdrawn even as he stepped into the ring with Holyfield eight and a half years later, was that there was too much of the amateur in his big, perfectly formed bones. Gary Mason, though, was said to be a first significant test of Lewis's undoubted natural ability. He was reigning British champion and ranked, for reasons which became rapidly obscured by Lewis, number four in the world. Lewis stopped Mason by a technical knock-out in the seventh round after a merciless attack on his opponent's right eye, which had been operated on for a detached retina the previous year.

Lewis's trainer John Davenport, a dour and unhelpfully anglophobe American who in the opinion of many critics had failed to develop seriously the fighter's natural ability and would soon give way to another American, the quickly discredited Pepe Correa, came up with a strategy expressly designed to work on Mason's weakness. In training camp Lewis's sparring partners had had targets taped on to their headguards above their right eyes. It is an unpleasant image, but the idea was eminently practical in a business which will never qualify as a charitable endeavour and Lewis applied it with near-perfect precision. Davenport, as his successors Correa and Emanuel Steward would also be required to do from time to time, urged Lewis into more intense effort, saying later, 'At the end of the fifth and sixth rounds I was

75

scolding Lennox. I said, "Look, we have come too far, worked too hard. Why are you carrying this man? We've got him drunk as a skunk. We've got him ready to go. Let's get out of here. So we finished it and I felt really good."'

So did I. About Lewis, that is. I had been away from Britain from 1979 to early in 1987, working for the *Vancouver Sun*, and when I returned much had changed on the sporting landscape of Britain and, it seemed, little for the better. Midfield football players of even a smattering of craft had virtually disappeared – the Scottish dynamo Gordon Strachan and the briefly blossoming Paul Gascoigne being notable exceptions – and English cricket was dwindling desperately in the fading footsteps of Ian Botham. Barry McGuigan, the brilliant Irish world featherweight champion, was also on the wane, which meant the pursuit of excellence in most corners of British sport had become forlorn. The first football match I covered on my return was Manchester United against Everton at Old Trafford. The afternoon was grey and windy, the game was goalless – and witless. Alex Ferguson had still to get a firm hold of United and Tommy Docherty, sitting in the press box, nodded agreement when I complained about the quality of the play. 'Aye,' he said, 'it's a bit like watching a shuttlecock in the Bay of Biscay.'

But nothing reflected more this general decline of British sport, it seemed to me, than the elevation of Frank Bruno to the status of national hero. An amusing character, no doubt, but as a serious contender for the heights of the game his claims seemed starkly untenable. It was a point I thought might have been established beyond doubt in 1986, when I covered for Canada the equally ill-fated nuptials of the Duke and Duchess of York. At that time Bruno was fighting Tim Witherspoon for a version of the world heavyweight title at Wembley. The *Daily Mail* trumpeted that Bruno would destroy Witherspoon with his 'atomic punch'. But though Witherspoon was a bloated parody of the young fighter who some thought was cheated when he lost a points decision to the formidable champion Larry Holmes, he eventually savaged Bruno with the cleanness of his technique and the timing of his punches. It was a triumph of residual class over absurd pretension.

So, yes, I was thrilled by Lewis when he ripped through Mason's illusion that he was an authentic challenger for a world title, that, like Bruno, he could glean from such slender talent at least one huge paynight. I wrote from ringside, 'Lennox Lewis will never be Frank Bruno. He will never invade our hearts. But nor will he insult our intelligence. We should learn to love him anyway for one great shining possibility. The new British champion with the soft Canadian accent might just step into a world title ring with more purpose than the collection of a huge blood-smeared cheque. Lewis has more potential than any British heavyweight since the war.' Quoting oneself in a prophetic mode is dangerous practice, I know. There is always a chance that someone will unearth other predictions, like, for grisly examples, my suspicion that the clever Spinks would absorb the demonic fury of Tyson in Atlantic City, or an indifferent reaction, as a cub reporter on a local paper, when a much-hyped pop group named the Beatles came to town.

But then, naturally enough, I'm happy to stand on that first assessment of Lennox Lewis. It was not, as I see it now, any great triumph of insight. It was an announcement by Lewis of superior class, of that special excitement created by performers in any walk of life who suggest that they have the means not just to prosper but to climb clean to the mountain top. That conviction about Lewis was put under most pressure when he lost his WBC world title to Oliver McCall in the same ring three years later, but if his recovery from that disaster has had its tentative moments, if his whole career has been shot through with a hint of ambivalence towards his chosen theatre of action, there has always been a glint of quality, a strand of evidence that one day all the doubts will shrivel to nothing in the fierce heat of talent and strength perfectly realised.

The Mason fight was something of a watershed. It marked Lewis's first victory over world-ranked opposition, it drew a line under the extra dimensions of this British heavyweight contender – and also, ironically enough for his embattled sponsor, Roger Levitt, it marked the point when financial control of his career passed to his current promoter Panos Eliades.

It is hard to imagine two men so distant in their approach to life as Levitt, the fallen lion of insurance sales and quick profit, and Lewis, the fighter whose patience and resolution relentlessly countered the schemings and the string-pulling and the compromises of professional boxing. When Levitt's empire crumbled – he would eventually be sentenced to community service – Lewis hired him as a business manager, but the new relationship lasted just a year. Lewis's biographer Joe Steeples nicely summed up the style of Levitt when he wrote, 'The trouble with Roger Levitt, generally speaking, is that he is generally speaking. The smooth-talking supersalesman is so loquacious that members of his Levitt Group, behind his back, used to call him Roger Rabbit.' Maloney, now Lewis's diminutive, resilient and notably honest manager, also went to the heart of the Levitt phenomenon when he said, 'The thing with Levitt is that he never really said anything. He just talked.'

Soon enough, Levitt would talk his way out of the affections of Lewis, whose initial reaction was one of loyalty, natural enough in that Levitt for all his excesses of nature had bankrolled the first phase of the fighter's career, to the tune, Levitt later reckoned, of £1.25 million. Levitt managed to estrange almost the entire boxing community, bewildering South African-born, American-based promoter Cedrick Kushner in a business meeting which Kushner later described as 'a complete waste of time, from A to Z'. He caused exasperation in America with a much hyped but eventually abandoned fight between Larry Holmes and George Foreman.

Levitt, who owned a luxuriant moustache and a stream of Cuban cigars, probably reached his nadir on the fight scene when he went into King's office during a promotion in Nashville, Tennessee, which had on its undercard the world welterweight champion Felix Trinidad and the British fighter, Kevin Lueshing. Levitt, who claimed to be Lueshing's business manager, demanded of King's man Bobby Goodman that all monies due to Lueshing should be handed to him directly rather than to the fighter's promoter Frank Warren. Goodman thought it prudent to call Warren, who rushed down from his hotel room to confront Levitt. They had a brief verbal exchange which Warren quickly deemed to be futile. He then delivered a short, crisp right hand to Levitt's head. The punch was promptly celebrated on *The Sun's* front page, the paper's boxing writer Colin Hart reporting that Warren had achieved the ambition of all those investors who had trusted Levitt with their life savings.

Eliades, a highly successful liquidator, also talks somewhat but to rather more effect. What Levitt's successor lacks in knowledge of the nuances and the customs of boxing is compensated for by a fierce belief in his product – and a willingness to take on someone like Don King. Some might say that a less confrontational style, a willingness to take boxing as it is rather than as it should be, would have prevented the loss of some vital possibilities, particularly a fight with Tyson which was aborted when Lewis accepted $3 million-worth of step-aside money to enable the former champion to fight the quaking Seldon – a relatively insignificant amount when set against the scale of ring earnings which now approach $100 million. It might be argued that Lewis, so proud of his record of facing every challenge in the ring, should have intervened in the haggling between Eliades and King and insisted on a fight which most of the *cognoscenti* would have expected him to win quite comfortably. The impact of such a victory would certainly have enriched a career profile which too often had been starved of the oxygen provided by a truly 'big' fight.

Yet if Lewis's basic goals have always been clear enough, he has never neglected to give them a practical slant. After negotiating a superb deal with the Levitt group, which gave him an unprecedented financial security, including £750,000-worth of life insurance, the use of a house in Kent and a Mercedes, Lewis told Steeples, 'All boxers are used. I realised that I would be used during my professional career because so many people have to take their cut of the money a boxer earns. But I only wanted to be used to a certain extent. I wanted to make sure that I retained a clearly defined percentage of whatever I earned and that I had control over my own destiny. There are too many boxers who go through their whole careers being told what to do and who to box, and they end up badly off.

'There are so many fighters who are left like Marlon Brando in *On the Waterfront*, thinking about what might have been. I was determined it wouldn't happen to me. I've studied what happened to some of the great heavyweights like Ali and Joe Louis. What dragged some of the greatest men in boxing down were drugs, drink, bad managers, bad financial advisers, hangers-on, bad fights, bad health and bad women. I was determined that none of these things was going to happen to me. I wanted to leave boxing with my finances secure, my brains intact and no gold-digging female homing in on me because of what I'd earned, not because of what I'm like.'

Such was the basic 'business plan' of Lewis, who while long on solid principle and unforced pride, is sometimes a little too passive both in and out of the ring. He fights, he relaxes in his new home in Miami or in Jamaica, performs those publicity tasks that are deemed absolutely necessary and largely lets the details of his career fall into place where they may.

Some suggest this speaks of a lack of passion, a clinical involvement in a sport which has always tugged at the very entrails of the greatest performers. But as a fatherless boy, watching his beloved mother eke out a survival existence and being forced to send him back to England and an elder relative for a while when her move to Canada initially failed to provide even bare subsistence for the both of them, he absorbed some brutal lessons. He learned the value of independence. The result is a style which instinctively leads to a cool evaluation of possibilities, good and bad. Lennox Lewis's wine glass is neither half full nor half empty. Its last drop requires attentive tasting and, quite regularly, is spat out.

Eliades is rather more pro-active and sometimes the policy has backfired – not least embarrassingly when, a few days after announcing to the London *Evening Standard* that he was one boxing citizen above suspicion and also arguing that the constant threat of indictment hanging over Don King's head should have excluded him from any role in negotiations for Holyfield–Lewis II, he was arrested on a charge of defrauding the government.

Ron Borges, the American writer who had charged Lewis with cowardice, wrote gleefully, 'Sometimes what goes around, comes around. And now it has come around and slapped Lennox Lewis's promoter in the mouth – and embarrassed Home Box Office television executives. In the final months of negotiation among King and representatives of Lewis, Time-Warner, HBO's parent company, insisted that King sign a clause which would allow him to be removed as promoter of the re-match if he received a federal indictment again for boxing malfeasance, as it was widely rumoured he would. King steadfastly refused, citing his constitutional right to the presumption of innocence and claiming that before the ink was dry a government lawyer would present him with an indictment, whether it had merit or not, just to put him out of business.

'HBO countered that it did not want to abrogate King's rights but was concerned about guaranteeing huge purses for a fight for which pay-per-view sales might be severely affected if King was indicted on racketeering or fight-fixing charges. In the end King refused to sign and HBO refused to guarantee Holyfield's $15 million purse. So King guaranteed Holyfield's purse – and had not been indicted going into the fight. Meanwhile, HBO guaranteed Lewis's $15 million only to see his promoter arrested in his pyjamas in the middle of the night in the home of a woman other than his wife by officers from Scotland Yard.'

King's reaction was predictably serene. He said, 'The good thing about all this is, even if they indict me tomorrow, Panos done beat me to it. He's made getting indicted palatable at HBO.' The television company pointed out, through gritted teeth, that in America Lewis's promoter of record is the Duva family's Main Events organisation. It is in this context of deal upon deal and deal within deal that Lewis's resolve to do the fighting, and to collect the money, makes such eminent sense. He had said much earlier in his career, when Riddick Bowe was on the run from him and Tyson's career was collapsing, 'I don't suppose boxing will ever change fundamentally, but it's like a lot of things in life – you have to take the best of it. I hate so much of the business, the politics, the need to make the hype. But you have to put up with it if you want to go in the ring, if you want to get to the thing which you have marked down for yourself – the right to call yourself the best in the world.'

The point and the glory of Lewis when he came into the ring in New York was that he had ridden the most unpromising of circumstances from the start of his life in East London, when his mother Violet found herself alone with two children and a desperately hard living to make, first in a plastics factory in Plaistow, then in a hospital in East Ham, without any warping of the spirit. If there is anger in Lennox Lewis, and when you examine the details of his life it seems inconceivable that there is not, it remains under remarkable control.

One of his principal defences is the careful selection of his people. Davenport and Correa were banished after careful examination of what they brought to his cause, and any lingering need to keep faith, out of gratitude and loyalty, with the self-destructive Levitt was abandoned when his behaviour became just too irksome.

Eliades's style can be gauche indeed when set against the rough practices and coded language of boxing. He once gave me an extremely bad moment or two at a press conference announcing a Lewis fight in America, quoting a piece I had pitched on a particularly high moral plain and which reached the conclusion that Lennox Lewis represented 'truth and decency' in a desperately compromised game. Several careworn American colleagues could not suppress their titters, then and at the cocktail hour. But in the face of the mouth of the cannon – or, to put it another way, in the face of Don King's mouth – Eliades, everybody had to agree on the potentially momentous night in Madison Square Garden, had done brilliant work. He had brought Lewis to the promised land of a fight for the undisputed heavyweight title of the world, and without the strings that King had always attached to such an epic opportunity.

If Lewis won this fight, he would have no obligations. Eliades could make his deals with Seth Abraham and Lou DiBella, the HBO chiefs, without hindrance from King. Eliades jubilantly told the boxing correspondent of *The Times*, Sri Senn, the erudite former Oxford boxing blue and one of the few British fight specialists to express consistent if not unreserved belief in Lewis's world-class potential, 'HBO tell me I will be the most powerful man in boxing if Lennox beats Holyfield. Seth Abraham said, "You better leave your insolvency practice to your top people because in boxing for the next two years you're going to be the man."

Lennox has put at risk his $80 million contract with HBO. They would have the right to tear it up if he lost to Holyfield, so he is taking an enormous gamble all because he wants to bring that undisputed title back to Britain. It's a case of who dares wins. Ninety-nine per cent of fighters would pick up the $80 million first but that's not Lennox's way. The step is consistent with everything he's done.'

Eliades sometimes sounds like a man who idly dropped a quarter into a slot machine at Caesar's Palace and landed the jackpot. But having done so, was not likely to allow the profit to go unexploited. 'I did not want to be involved in boxing. I thought it was a bit of a sport for gangsters. Then I was convinced that with a couple of hundred thousand pounds I could make Lennox world heavyweight champion – and earn a lot of money.

'I did not tell my wife of my intentions to put in $200,000 because she said, "Don't invest in that type of sport. I don't want you to get involved in shady deals. Don't you dare get involved." It was all done behind her back. I invested just before the Gary Mason fight without realising Mason was the favourite. Had Lennox lost I would have lost my money. When I sat down to watch the fight I said to myself, "What the hell have you done?" It was not until the Razor Ruddock fight a year and a half later she found out. At that time I stood to lose £1.8 million. When she saw me jumping for joy she knew I was a little more than a bystander.

'I work four hours liquidation, 14 hours boxing a day. Financially, my business is consistent every year for the next 20 years. I can earn $1.5 million every year as long as I live. Boxing is not consistent. I can make more money than in my other job in one hit. Lennox and I could earn $250 million with the right fights . . . with a Holyfield re-match and a Tyson fight.' However, the idea of ultimately supplanting King, of sending tentacles out into every corner of the boxing world, to sweaty little time-worn gyms from Nicaragua to Sydney, has little appeal for Eliades as he ignites a large Cuban cigar in his office in Bloomsbury Square.

'I can't believe I'll be bigger than King,' he says. 'King is King even if he is complaining at the moment that he will be working for the "Greek" for the next ten years. He has even brought Helen of Troy and the Trojan Horse into it. He says, "Beware of the trickeration of Greeks bearing gifts."' Eliades chuckles happily at the idea of being cast as a devious force, as a master of 'trickeration', by Don King. It is, no doubt, a little like being hailed for niftiness by the Artful Dodger.

Eliades is right. He will never be Don King. He will never sniff out the hunger and the need of a vulnerable fighter or manager with the bloodhound acumen of King. He will never invade or flatter or bemuse a potential business victim or potential ally as beguilingly as the man from Ohio. He will never dream his manic Barnum dreams as relentlessly as someone who sees no contradiction in checking his office for FBI bugs on a daily basis and then declaring himself the embodiment of the American dream of freedom under the law and security in 'due process'.

But it is an intriguing, diverting idea for a man whose fortune was made sifting through the detritus of broken businesses and scrambled dreams. Certainly it was another reason for Panos Eliades to strain forward in his seat, his face rapt, wide-eyed, as Lennox Lewis pressed forward in Madison Square Garden.

The Sun – and the Shadow

Lennox Lewis also won the second round with an easy mastery and as Panos Eliades's pulse quickened at the thought of his expanded empire, and the great winning gamble, another spectator, a short, middle-aged woman sitting nearby at ringside, thought not of the possibilities of the future but of one long miracle of the past.

As the tumult of the ring spread up to the rafters of this most famous of sporting venues, as Lewis jabbed and punched and shoved his smaller opponent around the ring as a prefect might quell a malcontent in a school corridor, she thought of all the pain and the hardship of her life, all the disappointments and the terrors of uncertainty, of not being able to see her way through to make a decent life for herself and those she loved.

All her life, from the warmth and bright light of her native island, through grey and gritty East London to the vast whiteness of Canada, came spinning back to her. She thought of her worst and best days, and how they had carried her to this clamorous night, potentially one of ultimate celebration.

She mused at the odds she would have made against the possibility of such a night when she counted her small change and wondered how she would get through another day. She thought of the irony now that all of God's tender mercies – and the greatest material gifts of this life, of which she could never have dreamed on the night shift at East Ham General when she worried whether she could pay the rent and the light and for the most basic of food – should come to her via so brutal a place as the boxing ring.

Most of all, she thought of the slender line of chance which had carried her to this momentous night, when the man who had been the centre of her life for so long, the repository of so much of her love and her hopes and her pride, was so close to the fulfilment of all his strivings.

She had formed an alliance with the big man dominating the ring which ran deeper than any contract pored over by a division of Wall Street lawyers. It was an alliance of blood formed against the classic vicissitudes of the Caribbean diaspora, the dichotomy between carnival and tough existence, warm blood and a cold climate, and always the shifting patterns of work and relationships and, ultimately, the need to survive, somehow, against heavy odds.

Lewis's mother Violet had been buffeted many times on her journey from the Jamaican seaside hamlet of Boston Bay, where her father Cedric and her mother Margaret fought a losing battle to provide for 12 children from the meagre income which came from selling primitive 'slush puppies' – a sticky blending of maple syrup and crushed ice – to the local children and taking in washing. Violet always seemed to lose out in the shuffle for subsistence. She moved in with various relatives in nearby Port Antonio, a harbour town at the mouth of the Rio Grande where the extravagant Hollywood film star Errol Flynn hurtled hedonistically towards his early end and American plutocrats fished for marlin and sampled all of the local delicacies. Violet watched the dissolution from a distance. She worked on a vegetable stand. From there she formed the impression that the carousing Flynn was 'very loud'.

At the age of 18 she followed her aunt Gee on the classic West Indian odyssey to the gold-paved streets of London. Much later she would recall, 'I'd heard so much about England. We had been brought up to regard it as the mother country. So I was just happy to be there. Never mind about the fog and the queues. The one thing about the place I really didn't like, though, was the queues. Nobody ever queues in Jamaica. The impression I got when I was a youngster was that money grew on trees in England. The first pay packet I got was £4.12s. I felt I was the richest person in the world. Since it was my first wages, I had a spree and spent it all on myself. It seemed a huge amount of money for someone just over from Jamaica.

'I used to write home to a friend and tell her things were so lovely over here you could pick money from the trees. So silly. A silly girl enjoying every minute of a new life.'

But real gold was elusive, of course, and she had to work long hours to maintain herself and then her first son from a failed relationship, Dennis, and when she became pregnant with her second son — named Lennox by the delivering doctor at Queen Mary's Hospital, Stratford in the East End — she faced an utterly pivotal moment in her life. Against heavy advice, she had decided to continue with the pregnancy despite the bleak economics of her life and the fierce disappointment of her discovery that the father of the child, a Dagenham car worker named Carlton Brooks, a Jamaican who she admits was the love of her life, was already married with a family of his own. When he said, 'I'm sorry, Violet, I cannot marry you,' it was as if a big iron door slammed in her face. For a little time she could only harvest despair and futility from the English trees.

Violet speculated on how many young women of her islands

had faced the dilemma but many years later she would say, 'As soon as I had Lennox in my arms I knew I had made the right decision. As I cuddled him to me I knew I would never regret it because he was so precious. I suppose that is why Lennox and me are so close, because he was all I had to cling to. I did care for his father – and I suppose that's one reason why I poured all my love on Lennox. I don't know if it was wrong of me to do that, to show him so much love. In spite of all the heartache and hardship he put me through I'm grateful to Carlton because he gave me a lovely son who is my pride and joy. He is the loser because he has missed out on the love of a marvellous boy, and I'm the winner because I've got my Lennox.'

In the way of these things, Carlton Brooks re-surfaced in the life of his son. Not at some moment of extreme crisis, of course; not when mother and son had to be separated because of the harsh circumstances of their lives, when she could provide scarcely enough food for her gangling son as she went hungry, when the boy went off to a special school in the English countryside and played sport with an often overbrimming enthusiasm because it seemed he was obliged to compensate for his pain, which was re-doubled when his mother went to Canada to try to make a new life, and then, after calling him to her, was obliged to send him back again to England for another period of desolation. No, Carlton Brooks didn't come back into his son's life at a critical point. He came when the partnership between mother and son had grown unassailably strong at all the broken places.

He returned to Lennox Lewis's life when the English newspapers were filled with the world-beating prospects of the son he had abandoned, when Lewis faced his biggest fight, against Donovan Razor Ruddock at Earl's Court on Halloween night in 1992. Carlton thought it would be nice to go to the fight. He cared for his son and he had thought of him often, but you know how these things are, and now he wanted to be part of his life. Lennox Lewis was polite but icy. He had a mother but he knew nothing of a father, nor did he want to know anything now. Too long had passed, too much had happened and it had gone beyond repair.

The strength of the relationship between mother and son, the fact that it was so central to their lives, was clear enough at ringside after Lewis had ransacked Ruddock with the most ferocious performance of his career. It was an assault that stunned even the most experienced onlookers. George Foreman, moving towards the money-making apex of his extraordinary comeback 18 years after he had been so diminished in his African drama with Ali, was at ringside for HBO television. He was wide-eyed. When I asked him if he fancied getting into the ring with Lewis, he mugged in amazement and said, 'Are you crazy, that man's dangerous – that man could rip your head off.' It was good hype for Foreman's employers, but there was no questioning the impact of Lewis's destructive work. Bill Cayton, the austere manager who had been rejected by Tyson and now handled Ruddock as well as the up-and-coming movie-star fighter Tommy Morrison, left the arena with the expression you normally see at the roadside on the face of a victim of a car crash. Violet Lewis fought her way through the frenzied crowd, past the officials and the television crews and buried her head in her son's chest. He embraced her in a way that excluded the rest of the world.

Usually, Violet watched the fights in a fever of apprehension, concerned for the health of both her son and his opponent. After Lewis pounded Andrew Golota to a dramatic first-round defeat some years later, she waited anxiously until the Polish-American fighter returned from hospital and then, drawing on her nursing experience, took his hand and looked closely to confirm the hospital conclusion that he was without serious damage. But in Earl's Court that Halloween night she screamed and bellowed for the first time at ringside. She said, 'When Razor went down I was jumping up and down. But I always believed Lennox would win.

He told me and I believed him, as I have always believed him. He is a son you could always trust. Naughty, yes, untrustworthy, never. A lot of people thought there would be a problem with this fight – but they didn't have enough trust in him.'

Lennox Lewis said, 'I've seen video of my mother watching me fight, and if I ever doubted she was with me every punch that was the end of it. She gets so into it, it's frightening. People may say it is unusual for a fighter to be a mother's boy, but I'm proud to say I am. She has always been there. She gave me everything, and I'm just happy I can do a few things for her now. She will never have to worry about money ever again. This is the least I can do. In boxing you learn quickly that really you are on your own. You have friends and people who work with you and whom you come to trust, but in the end you have to go into the ring on your own and you have to do it for yourself. That concentrates your mind on what is most important in your life – and when things have been at their worst, after I lost to Oliver McCall for example, I have always known that she was the one person who would always be there.'

Such recognition of a mother's power over a son is perhaps not so common around a boxing ring but then it is true that Joe Louis, arguably the greatest heavyweight champion of them all, had a healthy fear of his mother Lily, especially after smashing his rented violin over the head of a sneering friend while neglecting his music lessons for the gym.

Lewis has never attempted to disguise his emotional reliance on his mother, even in the most provocative of circumstances. Under the needling of inquiries about his sexual preferences, he will say that his love of his mother does not preclude close relationships with females and his friends laugh at suggestions he might be gay. They talk of a longstanding affair with a former cheerleader of his youth in Ontario, Marcia Miller, and many more fleeting friendships, some of them spectacular in their intensity – especially after the months of celibacy he imposes on himself in training camp. 'Man, it's like being is prison. But it's good. It makes you feel mean, you know.' There is a persistent rumour of his liking for a certain Toronto exotic dancer, but Lewis insists on his privacy and the speculation is that this particular lady might not flourish if she is ever taken home to meet mother.

Climbers are often asked why they scale mountains. The stock reply is, 'Because they are there.' It is the same with reporters probing the personal life of Lennox Lewis. They might say that is because they presume it is, like the mountains, there, somewhere beyond their sure knowledge, no doubt, but at a time when well-paid football stars dress up in white suits and sell their wedding celebrations to glossy magazines the need to illuminate some of Lewis's bastion of seclusion is insistent. Such, anyway, was the pressure on Colin Hart of *The Sun* when he made his trek to the Poconos on the build-up to this night in Madison Square Garden. Hart is Fleet Street's most experienced specialist boxing writer. He has been part of the foliage of the big fights since the early seventies, when he made a spectacular splash with his prediction that Ali would indeed invade the imagination of the world and beat the ogre Foreman in Zaire. Out of choice, Hart would no doubt write exclusively of the intrigues and the tactics of the sport he defends vigorously against attacks from outside, assaults which he believes are often built on a combination of naïvety and hypocrisy, but as a former newshound and a long-time servant of *The Sun* he has the surest instinct for his market.

Thus Hart filed the following report to his newspaper a few weeks before the big fight. 'Lennox Lewis sat in his mountain retreat and spoke openly on how the world sees one of its toughest men. People want the macho Lewis image shining through outside of the ring as well as in. But when you are the gentle type awkward questions can crop up.

'Lewis, at 33, is still a bachelor and rarely seen with a girl on his arm when making public appearances. In fact the WBC heavyweight champion has become known as a mummy's boy. His mother Violet is an important part of his entourage and cooks all his meals. His secluded training camp is a tranquil resort that caters for honeymoon couples. At the entrance to the grounds there is a heart-shaped hoarding which says, "Welcome to the land of love."

'It might seem an unusual setting for a fight camp – and for Lewis in particular. Rumours. We met in his comfortable wooden chalet on the edge of a frozen lake, to discuss his future should he unify the heavyweight division by seeing off Holyfield. Yet as there were only two of us in the room I decided to take my life in my hands and ask him the question that has been bothering so many back home. I hadn't the bottle to put it to him straight – "Are you gay?" So I said, "Do you know the rumours that have circulated about you for years?" Lennox grinned and replied instantly, "You mean the ones about me being gay? I must say I find it comical. But let us put the silly rumours to rest once and for all. I'm certainly not gay. I love and adore women. I date girls and do not date boys. I had a very serious relationship with a woman that lasted eight years. Unfortunately we split up, but I'm glad to say we're still friends. At the moment I date several girls, though no one serious."'

So far no offence, indeed in a sense, no story, but Hart was of course right about the rumours and he could not have hoped for more unequivocal answers. It was with that sense that Hart filed his story. What he couldn't have imagined was that beside his piece there would be a prominently displayed panel seeking further clarification on the love life of a man who in a little time would be attempting to become Britain's first undisputed heavyweight champion of the century.

Clarification from where? From the streets, that's where.

THE SUN — AND THE SHADOW

Anyone, girl or, presumably, boy, who had experienced even the briefest romantic collision with Lennox Lewis was invited to spill all the details in the pages of *The Sun*. Such an invitation, we can only suppose, was seen as a brilliant labour-saving device. No need to tramp the byways of London's night, no need to check out the rent-boy agencies or the gay bars. If you have anything on Lennox, *The Sun* seemed to be saying, even if it is the merest smear of compromise, let us know and we will spread it all over our pages.

Lewis's camp was appalled. Angry phone calls and faxes were fired off to *The Sun* in London — and soon enough a grovelling apology was received. Of course. It was, after all, another day, another search for truth wherever it might be found and in whatever dubious company. Who really cared? Lewis was more philosophical than most of his camp. Courtney Shand, Lewis's normally easy-going fitness coach from Canada, was caught on a promotional video tape calling Hart 'a bastard'. Maloney, the knowing South Londoner, pointed out that the writer would have had nothing to do with the insidious call to the streets for a dishing of dirt. Lewis simply rolled his eyes and shrugged. It was as though practice had taught him to absorb the cuts and the slights so that they could be allowed to fly over his head like artless punches, irritating only in their requirement to be charted and thus, with minimum footwork, avoided.

In fact the gay 'hare' had been set running from time to time over the years and this time it had put its ears over the stubble even before Hart plucked up his nerve to ask a question as uninvited as Basil Fawlty's musings to German tourists on the subject of the Second World War. An American writer, one of a pack hoping to prise a line out of Lewis on a telephone conference call arranged by the promoters, moved on to the subject with even more circumspection than the man from *The Sun* — and without the excuse of being face to face with a glowingly fit, 6ft 5in, 17-stone plus heavyweight developing that prickly edge which inevitably comes after long weeks on the monastic coalface of a fight camp.

The Observer's Kevin Mitchell reported, 'In a vintage week for sexual innuendo, an American reporter wanted to know if Lewis had a "significant other", a query delivered over the phone (which, if you are going to ask such a pointed question of a 33-year-old, unmarried, hugely rich, 17-stone boxer is probably the way to do it).'

Lewis said, 'Pardon me, what does this have to do with boxing?' and when the American offered various justifications for the question and asked, 'Well are you . . .', Lewis said softly, but firmly, 'No.' This naturally didn't stop the posh *Observer* making a little hay out of the thin homophobic harvest – few things do in that part of the Street longer on syllables than a willingness to own up to its readiness to both hunt with the hounds and run with the hares. They offered a clever headline, 'Cruising for a bruising', and several conclusions which explained both the American reporter's and their own need to spice up the apparently barren scenario of the two best heavyweights in the world finally stepping into the same ring at precisely the same time.

'What's the best way to stir up interest in "our boy" before his fight with Evander Holyfield?' asked a sub headline. The answer: 'Ask him if he's gay. By phone . . .' Disappointed by the result of the initiative, the only conclusion for the paper was that, 'Lewis is reliable, intelligent, unblemished. This makes for a fine citizen and a son every mother would love. In boxing it moves tickets like stale bread.' Yet on this occasion, that was demonstrably not true. How, indeed, could it be that the Garden's 21,000 capacity had been sold out for several months, and that a dozen British journalists routinely awarded ringside seats for the big fights between Americans were obliged to spend a few anxious days wondering whether they would need to hire opera glasses? Not solely because of the warrior charisma of Evander Holyfield.

Though six months earlier Don King had done a remarkable job in selling Holyfield's fight with the obscure Vaughn Bean, the fight was in Atlanta, where hometown boy Holyfield is at least as popular as the high-flying baseball Braves. More relevantly, Holyfield's last big fight – against Michael Moorer – had left Showtime TV with a sickening loss of $11 million.

No one could say Lewis had pulled off a late *tour de force* in the publicity department. No, he had not suddenly charmed a nation whose boxing writers had been rubbishing him for the five solid years since he defended his WBC title in Las Vegas and left with both the belt and a barrow-load of Don King's money. But the Garden was sold out. There was no limit to the dismissals of Lennox Lewis as a fighting man. There were question marks not just against his sexuality – he had after all yet to be convicted of statutory rape of a member of the opposite sex and, unlike Holyfield, he didn't have as many paternity suits as the average resident of London's West End – but against his stamina, his professionalism and, most disgusting of all, his basic courage. So why were the ticket scalpers preparing for a coup? Why were they selling not stale bread but the hottest boxing ticket New York had known since Ali and Frazier made war 28 years earlier?

It was because Lewis, while behaving with dedication and inherent dignity, breaking no laws and donating £1 million and considerable unrecorded time to a remedial training college in Hackney, indeed doing nothing more heinous than pursing his privacy in the warm clime and relaxing rhythm of his mother's island, spending some time in the Ontario of his youth and buying a home in Florida to go along with the one in Hadley Wood, and yes, dating girls of dazzling beauty and normal appetites, had presented himself as the only valid challenger to Evander Holyfield as the undisputed champion of the world. This, so extraordinarily, so bewilderingly to the psychology of great swathes of the media, especially in America, was apparently deemed more important to the public than whether Lennox Lewis secretly yearned to enter the ring to the sound of 'YMCA' by the Village People.

It was an agreeable state of affairs for boxing and for Lennox Lewis and he made this clear enough on the cold, snowy day in the Poconos when he was preparing to break camp and head for Manhattan. He shrugged dismissively at mention of the gay controversy and brightened considerably when told that he appeared to have penetrated the skin of Holyfield with his charge of hypocrisy. We talked after a session of sparring in which Lennox had worked easily and powerfully in the hothouse gym outside of which there were flurries of snow over the neighbouring lake and such stillness you could have heard a deer snap a twig deep in the woods.

Lewis had worked too seriously for his top sparring partner Jeremy Williams, a low-slung, quick heavyweight out of Los Angeles who carried a record of 34–2, 15st 7lbs and at least a few other characteristics of Evander Holyfield, most relevantly a rushing style hinged to the principal weapon of a left hook. Lewis pounded him pitilessly for four rounds and trainer Steward wanted him to come out from his corner one last time. Williams would have none of it. Once he threw chairs and trashed a room when he was told he would not be part of the American Olympic team, and now there was another small point of rebellion. 'No way I'm coming out,' spat Williams. 'He's hit me enough for one day.' Lewis shrugged again, wiped away huge beads of sweat and stretched out on the canvas, from where he announced, 'We've watched a lot of Holyfield videos and we've reached certain conclusions. One is that I do not go for his chin. I go for high on his right temple. That's where he seems most vulnerable.

'So the perfect scenario is that I catch him there early and just put him away. People talk about my Caribbean blood and say I'm just too laid-back. Well, I can't deny my blood, but you know something about it . . . on the surface it may seem I don't care enough, that I'm not as committed as Holyfield, but people who think that are making a terrible mistake. My blood comes to the boil very quickly. Under the calm there is a fire, and it burns up in a moment. So if you think you see a big difference between me and Holyfield, don't be mistaken. I don't sing hymns all the time and I don't come over as hyperactive. But I do care. So much, in fact, that I can't see beyond the fight. The normal things in life are just in abeyance. They do not exist for me now – and they won't for another week or so. In some ways it is the most terrible time. You do not live it, you exist through it.

'I'm not overwhelmed by any of this. I'm just anticipating it, looking forward to the moment when all this work – the hardest of my life – is done with, when Holyfield is down and I can start living my dream.'

What he couldn't express quite so clearly was the feeling that comes at such moments of triumph, even deliverance. 'I can't really put it into words,' he said. 'At that moment I cannot speak. It is just something that takes over. It is so basic. It just happens. People keep telling me Holyfield fights inside and I don't. But then Muhammad Ali didn't fight inside. Does that mean he wasn't a great fighter, that he couldn't deal with any challenge that was put in front of him. I don't think so.

'I have the clearest idea of what needs to be done. Bert Cooper, who had no great reputation, did it to Holyfield in Atlanta in 1991. I saw it happen, I was fighting on the same bill. Cooper caught him high and Holyfield was in terrible trouble. He took a real beating, but he got very lucky. The referee helped him out. But in the Garden he will be beyond anyone's help.'

You could see a certain serenity here. The television cameras were not whirring and if his pronouncements were war-like it did seem he was more interested in convincing a sceptical listener

99

than himself. You would see the composure again in his last work-out in the garden as he struck in an easy rhythm against the hand-pads and told a great pack of journalists and television crews, 'Yes, I feel great – and a little impatient.'

Back in the Poconos Lewis offered the final advice: 'What people should do when they come to analyse this fight is examine the reasons why Holyfield is so famous for his heart. They are to do with the fact that so many times he has to put his courage on the line. Look at my career and apart from the night McCall caught me you see none of that. You don't see instances of me having to lay my heart on the line, you don't see me in such an extreme position because I don't let it happen. I have too many tools. I control things because I have the means. But tell me, how can people say I don't have heart? My heart is fine. All my life has been building to this moment in time. So of course I'm going to grab it.' Lewis was breaking camp and so was his abused workmate. Jeremy Williams threw his gear into a dishevelled heap, piled it into a grip and left with the classic valediction of the sparring partner for his paymaster. 'Yes, he is ready. He's mean. He hits hard. If you don't believe me, look at my face.'

As the second round wound down, Holyfield's face was set along grim lines and already he had pink blotches where Lewis had scored freely with a jab – a jab which never looked longer or firmer or more integral to the fight plan of its owner.

In the corner Emanuel Steward felt no urgency, no pressure at this point. It was going pretty much as he hoped. Lewis was establishing command. He was building to something and the pressure was mounting on Holyfield with every fresh exchange. Steward, like every trainer, has the vision of a perfect performance. Down the years he had come close to it often enough; Tommy Hearns had fought a dream of a fight before Sugar Ray Leonard injected nightmare in the 14th round and Holyfield, when briefly under his guidance, had delighted him with his comeback victory over Riddick Bowe in 1993. But maybe now, Steward fleetingly speculated, he was seeing the shaping of a masterpiece, an inexorable demonstration of superiority in all of the basics of fighting – class, power and, most vital of all, will.

Panos Eliades, in his necessarily less technical way, was also pleased. The gamble looked good. But for Violet nothing had changed since the first moment she watched her boy step into the ring. She could only pray that God would keep him safe.

6

Evander's Anvil

Now, as the bell sounds for the third round, we can see the scale of Evander Holyfield's boldness. But you have to ask: is it really boldness? Could it be something more disturbing; is it that madness the destructive gods cook up in your brain before you fall?

Certainly this is the round which permits him only one serious option. For some reason which he hasn't begun to explain logically these last few weeks – but then how do you coherently articulate a flipping of your brain? – it is three minutes in which he is committed to knocking out Lennox Lewis. Three minutes which could conjure untrammelled glory, a vindication that even the great sorcerer seer Muhammad Ali might admire. Or, on the other hand, Evander Holyfield's credibility as a fighting man could simply fall apart before our eyes.

If Holyfield was faced now with doing no more than merely achieving a degree of dominance over Lewis, even just turning back the tide flowing so clearly in his opponent's favour, the evidence of the first two rounds would not be encouraging. Unless he has been playing a game of possum more complete, more deceiving than anything anyone around this old battleground can begin to recall, his realistic goal is mere parity in the volume of punches and the body language of confidence. Yet this is the least of the challenge he set himself when Lewis casually pointed out the difference between the piety he expressed and the life he led.

At first Holyfield had dismissed the charge of hypocrisy quite contemptuously. There was no ugliness, he said, in the old question about the compromises a man sometimes imposed on his deepest beliefs. It was true he had nine children by five different women, with five of them coming outside of marriage. Yes, he had fathered two illegitimate children since marrying Janice, the treasurer of the religious rally he attended, white-suited, bible-carrying, before his first fight with Tyson, but hadn't anyone heard of the concept of original sin? Tom Archdeacon of the *Dayton News* certainly had. When Holyfield said that he really paid the views of Lewis 'no mind', no more than he did his physical bulk because he was just like any other man deep down, he had to take his trousers off from time to time, Archdeacon shot back, 'Yes, but not as often as you.'

Yes, Holyfield was happy to do business with Don King, the patron saint of amorality for whom godliness would always run a poor third to profit and survival. 'I made mistakes, Don King made mistakes, but in life you have to see the error of your ways and march on,' said Holyfield. 'I'm born again and I strive to do right.' The King connection was just business. 'He is the best promoter in boxing. We know that now. He proposes and I listen. I have a very smart lawyer.'

A smart lawyer, a forgiving wife, backslapping sparring partners, an adoring media, a private line to the heavens, why wouldn't Holyfield ride through Manhattan as much on his personal cloud as in the black stretched limo which in recent days had whisked him away from his workplace in the neighbourhood of Wall Street and Skid Row, of quick wealth and slow despair?

But you had to suspect this sublime confidence which provoked Lewis's cornerman Steward to say, 'Holyfield's trainer Don Turner seems to have him really believing that he is some kind of chosen one. He's saying that Lennox is a nobody, a big, clumsy kid. He talks as though I should be putting Pampers on him instead of saying he's a great fighter. He is making a big mistake in not showing Lennox more respect. Anyway, maybe it's in our favour. Maybe he really doesn't understand what he faces. Maybe he really thinks he can make his own rules – in and out of the ring.' It is clear enough to everyone now and, not least the fighter himself as he springs from his stool, that Holyfield has talked his way into a corner.

Holyfield has to snap in punches that will penetrate the big reach and the stifling strength of Lewis. The trouble, everyone knows, is that Holyfield lacks the power of one single punch which can topple the big man. He cannot look at Lewis, as Muhammad Ali once did at the towering basketball player Wilt Chamberlain, who briefly, ludicrously, considered the possibility of stepping into the ring with the great man, and say, reasonably, 'Timber . . .'

No, a single, dismembering chopping stroke is beyond Holyfield. The only time he managed such a blow against a big man was when he separated James Buster Douglas from the undisputed world title under a moonlit Nevadan sky in 1990 and then the suspicion was that a tap of a feather duster might well have had a similar effect. The short right went in and Douglas, who had thrown high and wide, jiggled rather like a bowl of blancmange and went down with a sigh. He then stared reflectively at the moon from his prone position. He had come to the weigh-in a bloated parody of a reigning champion. His preparations had been neglected so scandalously, Holyfield's trainer Lou Duva sneered, 'He must be the only fighter who puts weight on in the sweat room. He calls room service when he is in the sauna.'

The Mirage owner Steve Wynn was aghast. He had invested $24 million in this fight, having earlier been disappointed by the failure of Sugar Ray Leonard–Roberto Duran III to create even an echo of their first wars, and he couldn't quite believe that this wanton Douglas, who at the start of the year had been hailed as the Lion of Tokyo, the conqueror of Iron Mike Tyson, was guaranteed such a huge paycheque.

For Holyfield it was boxing's ultimate soft option. Now, he has to go into the dangerous flight path of Lewis's big right hand and deliver clusters of punches; he has to throw lightning blows in a blurring sequence, a jab, a right to the head, hook, maybe he must double up on the hook, and toss in an uppercut or two. He must simply dance on the bones of the big man. He must knock him out. But to where does he look for inspiration? Back, perhaps, to the time he started to make Tyson retreat in the third round of their first fight, when he shrugged off Tyson's punches and countered with solid, telling blows, none of them decisively destructive in themselves but each one carrying the ineradicable message that that was his fight, his terrain. Holyfield's problem is that it is three years ago now since he last confounded the imagination of boxing and Lewis isn't Tyson. He is a much younger, stronger fighter and has hunger and serious hopes where Tyson had only a pack of demons hampering skills already eroded by neglect and general dissipation. In the first two rounds here he has looked about as vulnerable as a newly commissioned ship of the line nosing into a yachting marina.

My round-by-round notes are muted little songs of reassurance but anyone who cares for Lewis – and it has taken this early skirmishing to remind me how much I do – would have settled for them at the sound of the first bell.

Round one: Lewis jab immediately in use. Peppering Holyfield. Good right hand to Holyfield's head – and a flurry of jabs. Holyfield bemused? Holyfield counters with left hook to the jaw and then heaves Lewis on to the canvas as Lewis attempts to weigh down on Holyfield with all that extra weight (31lb). Referee (Arthur Mercante Junior) speaks to both fighters. Lewis resumes control. Lewis round, 10–9.

Round two: Holyfield stiff, almost inert at stalls in the low-key action. Can make little impression on Lewis's jab. Passive mid-round from both fighters, but Lewis's jab is working sweet enough and sets up one excellent uppercut. Holyfield looks deeply reflective at end of round. Locked into his prediction of a third-round knock-out now. Lewis round, 20–18. So it's knock-out time, when Holyfield has to put flesh on the bones of his stunning projection of Lewis's downfall.

If this hasn't happened in three minutes there will be a formidable argument that the fight is already over; that Holyfield, always facing an uphill battle, has the additional handicap of a massive loss of face. In some fighters this wouldn't be so much of a problem. Ali could throw his prophetic doggerel into the pre-fight hype and if the predicted round was passed without a decision he could shrug his shoulders, pull a comic face and companion dance routine and say something like, 'Okay sucker, now it's for real.'

As Hugh McIlvanney once wrote, 'Ali only needs to look into the bathroom mirror each morning to re-invent himself.' In the ring he made the task seem as routine as throwing a jab, and on the build-up to his astonishing fight in 1971 with Frazier he had never been so mesmerising. He told more than 700 journalists who had come to New York from all corners of the world, 'Fifteen referees! I want 15 referees to be at this fight because there ain't no one man who can keep up with the pace I'm gonna set except me. There's not a man alive who can whup me. I'm too fast. I'm

107

too smart. I'm too pretty. I should be a postage stamp. That's the only way I'll ever get licked. When I go in the ring here they'll be waiting everywhere; England, France, Italy. Egypt and Israel will declare a 45-minute truce. Saudi Arabia, Iraq, Iran; even Red China and Formosa. Not since time began has there been a night like this. People will be singing and dancing in the streets, and when it's over Muhammad Ali will take his rightful place as champion of the world.

'Joe Frazier will be nothing but a target for me. I'll be dancing and moving and Frazier won't be able to find me. Joe Frazier will be reaching and straining with those hooks and they'll get longer and longer and he'll get more frustrated. Things are going to happen so fast Joe won't be able to keep up with them. Pop, pop, pop! Plus I'm talking to him. Come on, Joe, come on, Joe, you're no champ. Come on, you lost three rounds already. Like my poem says:

> Joe's gonna come out smokin'
> But I ain't gonna be jokin'
> I'll be pickin' and pokin'
> Pouring water on his smokin'
> This might shock and amaze ya
> But I'm gonna destroy Joe Frazier

Excruciating poetry, perhaps, but what a statement of intent, what an earnest resolve behind those lines of jokey hype. One pitched no less than for the invasion of the imagination of both the fearsome Frazier and the entire world. Not for nothing does Bryant Gumbel, a household television name in America and one of the first black men to smash beyond the stereotypes of the nation's racial perceptions, still talk of the meaning of Ali in those days of his breathtaking prime.

The Gumbel of today could have walked to ringside 28 years

ago with backslappers and autograph hunters at his side every step of the way, but then he was just another ambitious, smart young black man fighting to make his way and he told Thomas Hauser, author of *Muhammad Ali, His Life and Times*, 'It was a tumultuous night [when Ali fought Frazier]. I was living in a third-floor walk up on 46th Street between Eighth and Ninth Avenues in New York. The only way I could find out about the fight was to listen to the radio and after every round they gave a quick capsule. I nearly died that night because this was the night when it all came together and if Ali lost it was as though everything I believed in was wrong.

'It's very difficult to imagine being young and black in the sixties and not gravitating towards Ali. He was a guy who was supremely talented, enormously confident and seemed to think less of what the establishment thought of him than about the image he saw when he looked in the mirror. The fact that he won all the time made it all the better. You know, for all our passions of those years, we didn't have a lot of victories. So the fact that Ali won was gravy. It's hard to believe all those years have passed since then. And when Ali lost I was devastated. It was awful. I felt everything I stood for had been beaten down and tramped.'

But of course Ali would nurse his broken jaw and go on to beat Frazier in their second and third fights, going, as he said later, 'close to death' in carrying the Thrilla in Manila. Three years after that first fight Ali would re-invent himself so spectacularly George Foreman was left beaten and bemused in a jungle clearing in Africa and Ali, beyond any prospect of contradiction or reproach, could declare, 'I done fucked the world's mind.' Ali could change his coat with the ease of a chameleon, but any role he played was subservient to the point of his being, the imperative of being competitive, of thinking on his feet and fighting effectively in any conditions against any odds. Nine years after the first Frazier fight, as he prepared, against the counsel of all those who revered him, to fight the clinical Larry Holmes he told me in a log cabin in his training camp in Deer Lake, Pennsylvania, 'The world thinks I'm going to take a beating, but there's going to be a little doubt, because deep down the world knows it can never really know quite what I'm going to do.' As it happened, quite dreadfully, the world was right in its suspicions and grown men cried in the backlot at Caesar's Palace in Las Vegas when Holmes pounded him to defeat. They mourned the greatest sportsman of the century, the man, who like no one else in the history of the ring, could change himself, take on new life, under the heaviest pressure.

Holyfield, by comparison, will always be stuck with himself. He is and will always be part warrior, part evangelist and, in the ring at least, somebody who would sooner place his head on the axeman's block than quit on the idea that he should burrow down and find a way to win. On several epic occasions his has been a wonderfully satisfying presence, but never one that permitted any easy adaptation. No fighter, possibly no man, ever needed to believe himself more emphatically than Evander Holyfield.

So why did he do it? Why did he declare, with increasing volubility as the pre-fight weeks wore on, that he would knock out Lewis in the third round? He had never done it before, not even in those days when he was building up to a fight with Mike Tyson. Then, he needed to create for himself an aura that would begin to match the dissembling one of the man he stalked all the way to Tokyo, only to see it split apart in an orgy of geisha girls and punches from a Douglas who had for a sufficient number of weeks grasped the essential contradiction of having cheeseburgers brought to the sweat-room. But in this fight against Lewis, when Holyfield should have had only one imperative, the classic one of finding a way to win, and however it came, ugly or beautifully, quick or slow, the manner of victory had never mattered less.

Holyfield's old pro cornerman Turner had, despite Steward's

charge that he had helped detach his fighter from reality, been appalled to hear Holyfield picking his round and he was still frowning deeply when his fighter continued to make the claim, as if it was some religious incantation, right up to going into the ring. Turner shook his head and said, 'Don't ask me why Evander is doing this. He doesn't need to say a damn thing other than that he is going to fight his fight. Man, there's enough pressure in there without putting a heap more on yourself. Evander is going to win, there ain't no way he can't find a way but saying you're going to win in a certain round, man, that's making problems for yourself. You can hit some guys with a baseball bat and they might not go down. Then what do you do if you picked the round? Maybe you get it right in the end but that's a whole lot of stress and trouble you just don't need.'

The pressure is showing as Holyfield jumps out of his corner and takes the fight to Lewis. Clearly, he has jerked himself into life. Perhaps he is remembering the intensity of the speech he made in that little dungeon of a gym down near Skid Row a few days earlier. Could he forget it? Only if he casts off proclamations as easily as a one-night stand.

There, in a roped-off, low-ceilinged room where the air tasted as though it had been sieved from a bucket of sulphur, Holyfield pounded on the body and the head of big James Gaines from Knoxville, Tennessee. It was another explosive expression, hazardously late, you had to think, of his belief that life is all about praising the Lord and loading up the ammunition. The punishment was mercifully brief, however, just three rounds of it, and Gaines retreated into shadows teeming with television cameramen and sound recordists with the relief of a man just sprung from purgatory. It was the end of long weeks of programmed hitting and gospel-punching and hymn-singing and swooning and now Holyfield leaned over the ropes and told the sweltering pack of media, 'I feel so fine. It's going to be a great fight, a short night. Write it down now, or write it down later. It's all the same to me. Lennox Lewis is going down in three rounds. I keep saying it, but I'm not putting Lennox Lewis down. I give him respect. I'm just letting you know what's going to happen.'

No crusader approached the walls of Jerusalem with more zeal. As Holyfield towelled away the sweat and headed for the showers, Gary Bell, another Holyfield target in the gym, attracted a knot of inquisitors. As sparring partners go, Bell tends to be a superior witness. I've yet to hear one say, though, that the man who was paying his modest paycheque was heading for destruction, making his own fate by indolence in the gym and waywardness in the night. Usually the testament is of another kind, and one recalls the time a group of sparring partners stood forlornly outside the Golden Gloves gym in Las Vegas, where for some days they had been taking a desperate pounding from a Mike Tyson at the peak of his savagery. Several carried the scars brought by Tyson's fury and one of them, with the blackest of humour enhanced memorably by a crooked smile, simply opened his mouth when I enquired about his health. It was a smile largely minus teeth. One of his workmates reported bleakly, 'It's been hard, man, so hard. This morning I tried to lighten things up when Mike came into the gym. I said, "Morning, Mike, howya doin', champ?" He just stared at me for a few seconds and said, "I'm going to knock your fucking head off."'

But Bell is a fighter of decent record and sharp expression, his front teeth were in place and he was happy to talk. On this occasion his evidence carried more than normal weight. He had previously worked with Lewis, notably before his victories over Ray Mercer and Tommy Morrison, and now he said, 'Evander's edge is his speed – and it's a big one. He's been working real hard to beat Lewis's jab by straightening his right hand. The basis of his work, its real strength, has been his hand speed. Evander is quicker, more versatile than Lewis, and I'm sure that will tell in the end. Hey, I'm not knocking Lennox. He has a lot of strengths, he is a good boxer and he has power. But this is a fight which is going to be settled by instincts. Evander has the better instincts.'

In the warren-like gym at the bottom of Manhattan, the force of Holyfield's presence was strong. He is a man who could turn a phone booth into a prayer hall and the strength of his evangelism was near overwhelming in the old building decorated with classic fight posters and fading pictures of Jack Dempsey and Joe Louis. An hour or so later, his impact was somewhat diluted when Lewis worked lightly in a big, airy room at Madison Square Garden. Lewis was unmoved when he was told that Holyfield was stoking up belief that he would win with a third-round knock-out. 'I really don't think he has done himself much good with his knock-out prediction. He says he's going to take me out in three rounds. It doesn't make sense. I'm his toughest fight and he is talking about knocking me out in three. He should have done that to Vaughn Bean in his last fight. But he didn't and Bean is a nothing fighter. Really, Evander looked quite bad.'

When Lewis's dismissal was reported to Holyfield his reaction was predictably serene. He shook his head and said, 'There is just no comparison between the Bean fight and this one. It was enough for Vaughn Bean to be in the ring with me. He knew he couldn't beat me so he just wanted to show the world he had a right to be in the same ring. He was very cautious. He didn't want to take any chances. Lennox will be different. He has to try to beat me. It is the climax of his career, his biggest fight. He has to do so much more than he has ever done before. He's never been in this class. He has to stretch himself to the limits and that's when a man makes mistakes, when he's out on the edge, when he has to take a chance.'

No one could argue in that sweatbox of a room in Lower Manhattan but now in the ring, as he and Lewis work towards the first significant crescendo of their fight for all the spoils, the certainties of Evander Holyfield are peeling away.

But are they? Holyfield comes out for the third with the demeanour of a fighting bull and if it is a performance, a jaunty whistle while walking past his own graveyard, it is a good one. Indeed, long before the round is over we know we're having at least a glimpse of the authentic Holyfield. Lewis maintains his jab but Holyfield now sweeps away the pressure building around him.

How profoundly and for how long he has achieved this we cannot yet know but this, for the moment, is the classic Holyfield, barrelling in, suspending the tyrannies of time and size and weight and pushing back the big man with a waspish assault. Holyfield had to make a show and he is doing it now. A jab lands on Lewis's jaw with unsettling force and it is followed in a flash by a short hook. The crowd gasps, roars and rises to its feet. The Real Deal has returned, burning again, smoking with all the old furies. There is animation again in the sculpted, muscular body of the man who for so long has rejoiced in the title of People's Champion. Lewis is back on his heels and Holyfield is surging forward. He connects with a crisp, perfectly timed right – then follows it with a harder one. Lewis is retreating and Steward is screaming and suddenly the eyes of Panos Eliades gleam with a little less expectancy. Violet's face, inevitably, is contorted with concern. But if Lewis is troubled, if Holyfield has seized the middle of the ring and is driving him towards the ropes he has yet to trigger the worst fears of his people. These tend to come with shocking swiftness when an opponent breaks the plain of his concentration and his confidence.

Frank Bruno, of all people, did it in the small hours of a cold, damp Cardiff night when he fought the best four rounds of his life, achieving a stunning momentum as he backed up Lewis, who at one point seemed in danger of tripping over his own feet. Shannon Briggs, the personable young heavyweight, who scarcely believably comes from the same Brownsville streets as Mike

Tyson, did it in Atlantic City early in 1998 when he caught Lewis and seemed to open a floodgate of confusion. On both occasions Lewis rose mightily from the depths of his disarray.

Against Bruno he cleared his head between the fourth and fifth rounds, controlled the fifth with a re-discovered jab, and in the sixth Bruno, sensing that the ground he had won so dramatically in the early rounds was beginning to fall away beneath his feet, delved down into his reserves for the attempt to get himself back on to a winning course. His reward, as he moved Lewis towards the ropes, was to receive a perfectly thrown left hook flush in the face. For a man said not to have a true finishing instinct, Lewis was remarkable. He brought a closure from hell, hammering Bruno about the head relentlessly. It was as if Bruno's entire nervous system had shut down when the hook landed. He stood against the ropes a forlorn and unprotected target. The referee had no choice but to stop the fight. It seemed like the end of the carefully confected Bruno story then, a fact reflected by the bitterness of Bruno's wife and manager Laura when Lewis's man Frank Maloney offered his sympathy and said, 'That's boxing.' Laura Bruno spat in his face.

Bruno, who believed he was so close to the greatest victory of his career, would later, remarkably if briefly, hold the WBC world heavyweight title after beating an Oliver McCall fresh from drug rehabilitation. The extraordinary resurrection of Bruno was only made possible by the negligence of Lewis when McCall landed his shattering right hand at Wembley, a punch which at the time was reckoned to have cost the victim as much as £30 million.

When Lewis was wobbled by Briggs there were fleeting fears of a similar disaster, but again he found enough equilibrium to buy the time in which first to survive, then crank up the power. Briggs went the way of Bruno in the fifth round, overwhelmed by a superior force, no doubt, but not before revealing the point of vulnerability Holyfield is now required to invade with authority and passion and the harsh knowledge that he alone had created this violent necessity to topple the big man at a specific time.

Holyfield is clearly heartened by his ability at least to break the pattern of the fight, but the seconds are slipping from him as he throws another flurry of jabs and hooks and right hands to the head and the body. If Lewis has been shaken away from his easy authority he is showing no signs of buckling.

When the bell sounds, Lewis turns for his corner with the impression of a man not so much hugely relieved but rather as though he has negotiated a street crossing which, while not blazing with hazard, certainly demanded his full attention.

By comparison, Holyfield is down. His shoulders slump as he returns to his corner, where Turner, no stranger to life on the edge, has to massage back the will of a fighter for whom self-belief has never been so casually put at risk.

Later, Holyfield will reveal the extent of the desolation he carried on this brief journey back to his stool. He will say, 'Right then, I could have walked back to my corner and through the ropes and right out of the arena. I didn't feel right and I knew I had done wrong picking the round. It gave him an advantage, no question, when I failed to knock him out at the point. But sometimes you feel something so strongly you have to say it. But then I got in the ring and I didn't feel right. Something was missing. Yes, I could easily have quit, but I didn't because that's not my thing. Quitting is for other guys.'

So he fights on, straining, stretching for contact with Lewis's head or body but never with the conviction that has until now been as much part of him as the gunfighter's gait and the shining, dangerous skull. On the balance of pressure the fourth round is close, but it is Lewis who finds his target the easier, who seems to have reserves of power as yet unused. Steward yells, routinely, jab, jab, jab and Turner counters with cries of stick and move, but there is an impasse now and it is unbroken even when Holyfield produces a left hook, right-cross combination that lands with some solidity but leaves Lewis's legs still as upright as pines in the lightest breeze.

It is time now for one of these two fighters to lay claim to the most lucrative prize in all of sport. Holyfield, driven by his own unravelling agenda, has made his big move and Lewis is still occupying the centre of the ring, still jabbing at will, still encouraging his admirers to believe he is gathering himself for the climactic surge of his fighting life.

Maybe the fifth round will tell us a little more. Maybe it will tell us everything.

Failure in the Fifth

Perhaps this fifth round isn't telling us everything about the fight – or about Lennox Lewis. But the boxing world will take some convincing that Lennox Lewis isn't defining himself, once and for all, both as a fighter and a man.

Muhammad Ali will always be known for his ninth round against George Foreman, Marvin Hagler and Sugar Ray Leonard for their third and 14th rounds against Tommy Hearns. They made action which separated them from their contemporaries, gave supreme points of focus for their applications to join the élite. Now, can Lennox Lewis do the same?

The questions are so intriguing and will become so big over the course of the next few months, because from a perspective that no one can say is outlandish, there is a *prima facie* case that Lewis is turning his back on a dramatic onset of all-round superiority, a sea change of power so profound that in most eyes his task has become utterly formal. Indeed, if Lewis grows any bigger, and Holyfield shrinks still further, the temptation will be to believe we have joined Gulliver on his travels.

Lewis has come on enormously in this round and Mickey Duff, sitting at ringside and warmed by the prospect of landing his big bet, will score it 10–8 for him. But Lewis has yet to bear down truly on Holyfield as he ducks his head, that always dangerous head, and bobs and weaves against the ropes in a desperate effort to avoid the big one, the equaliser, the punch that weighs more heavily than any judge and jury. The case against Lewis is one of unfolding neglect.

Against a tide of contrary opinion, he will always insist it is just not so; and those who apply to him the mantra of the old pros that when you put a man on his way, when you unlock his defence, you are obliged to finish the job with maximum force, will be reminded there are two points from which truly to judge the action – and all of a fighter's options. One is from outside the ring. The other is from inside, where you can see and smell and sense things beyond the range of any witness, however informed.

He will say what we are seeing is not an opportunity lost but a potential disaster avoided. His trainer Emanuel Steward will never agree. Steward is spending almost the entire round yelling for closure. I have to admit, inside, so am I. In Steward's case the instincts of a lifetime are speaking to him with overwhelming force. He is ready to go home, the work done, the mission complete. For me, it is no doubt more that I want it to be so and so I am excited by the sudden surge of Lewis's apparent command. His bad days, the doubts and the fears, are surely on the point of a great, climactic expulsion from the career of a good fighter, a good man.

Suddenly, it seems to me that it is over. Lewis's mission isn't impossible after all. All the duplicities and the evasions that have threatened to condemn his career to limbo are shrivelled up now. They are consumed by the decisive force of a beautifully economic right hand that lands on the side of Holyfield's head and sends him spinning, stunned and disorientated, into the ropes. Lewis has opened the round with authority, his jab piston-like again, and the right hand the announcement of superior force. Or so it seems.

Holyfield has cried his defiance to the gods, made the push for victory his raw, wild prophecy had insisted upon. But Lewis dwarfs him now. He pins Holyfield against the ropes, bombards him with heavy blows. But if they are heavy they are also speculative and Steward is seeing this with mounting horror. The hard centre of Steward's philosophy is to take a man out of the ring just as soon as you sniff his blood. It is a logic implicitly acknowledged on the streets of his native Detroit and when the trainer screams now for its implementation he voices disbelief as well as exasperation. Steward can see Lewis has Holyfield now. You can see it, surely, from any number of rows back in Madison Square Garden.

But where is the *coup de grâce*? Where are the sledgehammer blows that shut down Bruno's system in one savage sequence? Where is the invasion of Andrew Golota? Where is the destruction of Razor Ruddock and those long, shattering right hands which set so much of boxing running scared?

It is, we will know soon enough, all locked up in Lennox Lewis. The truth is – and Lewis will admit it to me when this action has cooled – there are three men in the ring apart from referee Arthur Mercante Junior. There is Lewis. There is Holyfield. And there is the ghost of a fighter named Oliver McCall. A ghost of a fighter, a ghost of a man, a broken former world heavyweight champion whose adult life had veered crazily between police cells and rehab centres and mental institutions but who on the night of 25 September 1994 took up more or less permanent residence in Lewis's psyche.

Then, at Wembley Arena, Oliver McCall threw the punch of his life. It scrambled the senses of Lewis and deprived him of his

WBC world heavyweight title with a shocking abruptness. More than that, it took something away which had been Lewis's constant companion when he stepped through the ropes in an unbeaten career which had brought him Olympic gold and made him Britain's first twentieth-century holder of a share of boxing's greatest prize.

Lewis admitted, 'You could say that Oliver McCall is part of my growing pains in life, and yes, you could also say he's a bit of a ghost for me. What happened at Wembley that night shocked me so much it has definitely made me more cautious. Going into that first fight with McCall I just didn't believe I could be beaten. I had all the title belts in my sights back then, and I felt that nothing could stop me becoming the undisputed champion of the world. It was my destiny, what I was born for.

'Then I made a terrible mistake – and I paid a huge price. The punch came from nowhere as far as I was concerned and I would be lying if I said it didn't affect the way I look at fighting now. Before I had only half the picture. I knew about my own ability – my particular strengths. But what happened that night at Wembley told me there was more to it – and I'll never forget that lesson.

'After the defeat by McCall I escaped into the hills in Jamaica above my mother's home in Port Antonio. It was so painful for a long time, but gradually I came to terms with what had happened. Friends tried to help me, said that everything would come right, but I told them I had to work it all out for myself. I didn't think any less of myself as a fighter. I still believed I could prove myself the best in the world. But I had to change a lot of things. I had to change my trainer, maybe the way I prepared for a fight, but most of all I had to change something in myself.

'I still thought of myself as a warrior. But now I would be a smart warrior. I would make sure I didn't give anyone else the chance I gave Oliver McCall.'

As Holyfield cowers against the ropes now, as Lewis towers

FAILURE IN THE FIFTH

above him, but warily, like a hound who has cornered a particularly cunning badger, the nightmare of McCall inevitably billows back into focus. Lewis was so different back then. He was never arrogant in any overt way. But he had always won. He was Violet's darling boy. He was a cheerleader's dream, and when pressure had been applied to him on the campus of his Canadian high school by random bullies, jeering at his strange, East End accent, needled by both his aloofness and his ability to hold a basketball so easily it might have been a baby pumpkin and his unwillingness to sue for peace on any terms but his own, he stood and fought and invariably won. Olympic gold was the imprimatur of all his facility in life and in sport. Oliver McCall smashed all of this, perhaps not permanently, but for a little while his effect would be cataclysmic.

Lewis threw a lazy right and McCall stepped inside him and sent a perfect counter to Lewis's jaw. Lewis went down, and when he got to his feet his legs wobbled and his eyes were glazed. When referee Lupe Garcia looked into his eyes he decided the fight was over. Lewis argued that he could have gone on, that he could have smothered the aggression of McCall and fought his way out of trouble, but when he claimed that he had been 'totally robbed' the phrase sounded alien and unconvincing to everyone, perhaps even himself, on the lips of a man who had for so long been above the scrabbling self-justifications of jobbing fighters whistling in the dark reaches of their professional doom.

He left via the bowels of Wembley Arena, surrounded by a stunned entourage who were still trying to absorb the fact that a programme of fights, including possibly, finally, one against Riddick Bowe, had been wrecked by the most expensive punch in boxing history, one reckoned to have cost the recipient roughly $30 million. Lewis was struggling harder than anyone with the reality of his fall. Before disappearing down a stairway leading to the basement carpark, and possibly oblivion, he told me, 'It's too soon to know how I really feel. This has got to sink in. I've got to look at myself and my situation. Right now I still think of myself as a champion. If I no longer think like that when I wake up, who knows what will happen . . . ?' His brother Dennis had no clearer vision of the future, saying, 'Right now I'd say it's 50–50 whether Lennox carries on. He has a lot of pride and he may not want to leave the memory of his career here, but then he knows what he faces, he knows the politics of boxing very well.'

That the tentacles of those politics would hinder him for years to come, if indeed he did decide to bite on the bullet fired so devastatingly by McCall, was made clear enough by one backward glance at the ring. There, Don King embraced the man who had so improbably returned him to the heart of influence in the heavyweight division.

Tyson, King's ultimate means of influence and fortune, might still be languishing in his Indiana prison cell, but the promoter had some leverage again in boxing's most lucrative neighbourhood. Lewis, who had scorned all of King's gifts and had caused him to take a heavy loss on the Tucker fight 15 months earlier, was on the outside now.

In the mean small hours in the empty arena it was hard to see any easy route back to the high ground. One imperative was to sign a new trainer. Pepe Correa had to go. It was one of the few easy decisions Lewis could make as he was driven away from Wembley. Correa's most discernible contribution to the fight preparations had been to throw a woman's suspender belt at McCall in a press conference. Certainly there was no evidence of progress since the victories over Bruno in Cardiff and Phil Jackson in Atlantic City, fights which had ended in eruptions of destructive power from Lewis, but not before he had shown dismayingly lazy reliance on the power of his big right hand, at the expense of one of his most valuable assets, a long, hard jab around which real dominance might be built.

Correa had been suicidally complacent before the McCall fight. He sneered at McCall's background, said he was a glorified sparring partner wrecked by self-indulgence. He had been similarly dismissive of Tony Tucker before Lewis's first defence of the WBC title awarded to him when Bowe ceremonially threw the belt into a rubbish bin. Tucker, like McCall, had been caught up in the desperate dislocations of drug abuse, but he was a fighter of distinct talent who had once embarrassed Tyson over 12 frustrating rounds – despite a damaged hand and such mismanagement by his father it appeared that around 120 per cent of his contract had been sold off to a dizzying number of investors.

Correa said Tucker was a shell of a fighter and a man but if it was something to know, it wasn't to say and though Lewis put Tucker down twice – the first occasion the former IBF champion had gone to the canvas – Lewis had failed to capture the American market. The damage was compounded a hundred times by the failure against McCall. Correa had simply told Lewis to get McCall out of the ring as quickly as possible. It was simply a matter of loading up and delivering the big right hand. In the other corner, Emanuel Steward had been at work on behalf of McCall. Relentlessly, he had hammered home the one possibility of McCall's victory, a quick, explosive exploitation of Lewis's flapping jab and telegraphed right hand. McCall had to beat Lewis to the punch once and his fortune could be made.

Steward had long agonised over the neglect of Lewis's development as a fighter. He had led the pack to sign him after the Seoul Olympics. Steward acknowledged that Lewis's first trainer, Davenport, was a man of thorough methods who knew something of the fight game, but he dismisssed his dour personality and his – bizarrely expressed in the circumstances – contempt for all things European and, especially, British. Davenport had a military background, which might have been good for training a unit of infantryman but worked less effectively when applied to a complex, highly individualistic, chess-playing young fighter who might just be prepared to run through a brick wall, but only after being given an extremely plausible reason to do so.

As far as Steward was concerned, Correa was without redemption. He regarded him as 'a braggart', who spuriously claimed credit for playing a vital role in the career of Sugar Ray Leonard. That disdain crackled on the underside of Steward's reaction to his own training achievement on behalf of McCall, one that most would hail as another masterpiece by the man who founded the Kronk production line of champions in Detroit.

Said Steward, 'When I look at Lennox Lewis I see a terrible waste. This is a man with all the tools, with ability which would make any trainer worth his salt drool. But for some time it has been clear to me he hasn't been progressing. If he had been improving, we wouldn't have had such a clear target in this fight, we wouldn't have able to keep on saying to Oliver McCall, look, this is his big weakness, work on this, take advantage of it just once, and you can be champion of the world. You just cannot compare the natural ability of these two fighters. I've always said that Lennox Lewis had more talent than any fighter I've seen since Muhammad Ali. You cannot say any more than that. Lennox Lewis can come back and be champion of the world, I've no doubt about that. But he would have to change a lot of things. He would have to open himself up to new training methods. He would have to hurt in the gym, hurt in his training – and he would have to take a few blows to his ego. Whether he's willing to do this at this stage of his career, when he is 29 years old, well, that's the biggest question.

'Would I train him? Yes, I would, I would be delighted to – but only if he met those conditions.'

Lewis did satisfy Steward with a new resolve. He went off into the mountains of Jamaica wounded and shocked. He ran back the spool of his life, analysed how much he had achieved – and how much he had lost, and when all his accounting was done it was clear to him that he had to go back into the ring. He had to grow strong at the place McCall had broken. But was he healed at that vital place? How much baggage would he carry the next time he climbed through the ropes? Could he put away the ghost of McCall? We wouldn't know that for nearly three years, not until the fighters faced each other again across a few feet of canvas in Las Vegas. But we might get a clue in Sacramento, California, on the night of 13 May 1995 when Lewis faced Lionel Butler.

Bob Marley's *Redemption Song* might have been the musical score for Lewis's training camp in the San Bernardino mountains. This was the most critical time in the delicate relationship between fighter and trainer. Some in boxing were sceptical when the relationship was first mooted. They wondered about the basic chemistry. Steward is emotional and intense, Lewis takes himself off to a chessboard. If Steward applied his hand more forcibly on the work of a fighter it could only be by transplant. Lewis had always thought of himself as his own man with his own habits and it was said that one of the few merits of Correa, in Lewis's eyes, was that he could be guaranteed not to challenge the whims of his fighter.

But the work went well. Steward talked, sometimes yelled. Lewis listened. The first thrust of the trainer was to shorten the fighter's punches, increase his tempo. Lewis could control fights from outside with a renovated jab, but he also had to sharpen his work inside. He had to lift himself to a new competitive level. Lewis was impressed with Steward's knowledge. The trainer had it confirmed, extravagantly at times, that he was working with a fighter of brilliant, and still largely unexplored, possibilities.

For a while the politics also went well. Frank Maloney came back from the World Boxing Council's annual convention in Thailand satisfied that Lewis–Butler would be an eliminator for the title smashed and grabbed by McCall. But then nothing is quite how it seems when Don King has a hand to play. While Tyson did his jail time, some of the more ambitious spirits in boxing, and notably Butch Lewis, who handled the career of Michael Spinks and took the sartorial initiative of wearing dinner jacket and bow tie minus a shirt at the big fights, believed they had a chance of prising the man-child former champion away from King. The American media said that King was on the outs with Tyson, that the fighter had been listening to stories of the promoter's betrayals, and that when he came out of prison it would be with a new spirit of independence forged under the chains of imprisonment. Tyson was a new man; he had filled his prison cell with the work of great writers, had the images of Mao and Arthur Ashe tattooed on his skin, and for a while the fact that his sudden eruption of self-education had not quite carried him to a pass in the high-school graduation test, which would have given him an earlier release, was lost from the re-assessment of the fallen megastar.

No, everything had changed for King and Tyson. The fighter would go back through his financial affairs as they had been affected by King. He would do the first serious accountancy of his profligate charge through the late eighties and the early nineties, and the consequence would be an inevitable separation of King from his meal ticket at the Waldorf Astoria. For the moment, though, it turned out to be so much wishful thinking by that large section of sceptical humanity the promoter dismisses as doomsayers and naysayers and traducers of the 'American Way'. Whatever Tyson thought of King, and there was clear evidence that he had wearied of his effusive, mock evangelical style, he knew who could best generate the quick, necessary money from the comeback trail. The immutable fact was that when Tyson emerged from jail in the garb of his new Moslem faith on a frosty morning in March he stepped into the limo of Don King.

Lennox Lewis in Times Square to promote his fight against Ray Mercer. On his right are Emanuel Steward and Floyd Patterson

Ray Mercer ambushed Lewis with the fight of his life, but Lewis survived – just

Lewis demanded
$15 million – a
nice slice of the
big apple

For a while, Lewis
had to stand behind
Frank Bruno – and
the puppet master
Don King

King had to ride a storm of anger over the Lewis–Holyfield 'draw'

Lewis v. Akinwande: referee Mills Lane disqualifies Henry Akinwande for not
fighting

Oliver McCall breaks down as Lewis regains his WBC title

Lewis takes the WBC belt after Oliver McCall is disqualified

In Atlantic City before fighting Mike Dixon

With Emanuel Steward
– the partnership
which won it all

Lewis KOs Andrew
Golota – a statement of
brutal intent

Lewis – the warrior who likes to play chess

Training in Phoenix, Arizona

Lewis v. Holyfield I: Lewis lands a right cross to the head of Evander Holyfield in their controversial fight at Madison Square Garden, 13 March 1999

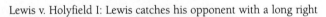

Lewis v. Holyfield I: Lewis catches his opponent with a long right

Lewis reads about the decision after his first fight against Holyfield

Lewis hit back at the American press – in the ring

The end of the mission: Lewis is the undisputed
heavyweight champion of the world

The rest were nit-picking, King laughed, and he had some evidence of this when he was accused by several leading American boxing writers of a killing gaffe in his catering arrangements for a homecoming party at Tyson's Ohio mansion. The fact was that any irritation caused the fighter by the arrival of trays of American, infidel food, was smoothed away quickly enough by arrangements for a $30 million paynight against the hapless bar-room brawler from Boston, Pete McNeely. Never, we would see soon enough, had so much money been enticed from the public for so little.

King's days with Tyson would prove to be numbered, and destined for courtroom battles, but not before he had orchestrated a return to the ring which would be described by one embittered promotional rival as 'the gouging of a canteloupe until every pip squeaked'. The operation started in classic King style as Tyson was whisked from prison before dawn and within minutes was being ushered into the local Nation of Islam mosque. There Tyson, in the role of a humble penitent, prayed, flat on his face with his hands stretched towards Mecca, shook hands with and served breakfast to Muhammad Ali.

It was, even by the surreal standards of Don King, an extraordinary *tour de force* of publicity, a fact one mirthlessly noted at several points, not least when being required by a cold-eyed Indiana State trooper to abandon a hire car and march across frost-whitened fields in order to answer the call to the faithful. The tone had been set by Wally Matthews, columnist of the *New York Post*. When the King cavalcade swung out of the prison grounds and turned left rather than right on to the highway for the airport, Matthews, rather like Lawrence of Arabia urging his followers to Akaba, yelled above the hubbub, 'To the Mosque!' Nor was Jeff Powell of the *Daily Mail* enchanted when asked to add his Gucci shoes to a great pile at the entrance to the holy place. But the real victim, again, was Lennox Lewis.

Despite having his fight with Butler officially approved as a final eliminator for his old title by the WBC in Thailand, Lewis was shocked to see that the moment Tyson walked away from three years of imprisonment he was installed as the WBC's number-one contender. His dismay, which would eventually provoke court action and the awarding to him of $3 million-worth of step-aside money as Tyson's 'comeback' reached new levels of farce against a terrified Bruce Seldon, was not lessened by the fact that Tyson's last two fights before going inside had been laboured performances against Ruddock, the man who had been destroyed by Lewis in two rounds at Earl's Court.

But it was not as though he was unfamiliar with such caprices and he said what he had to say when Butler came into town. Butler was a man of wild reputation, mountainous debt, dangerous habits and a punch powerful enough to encourage King to believe that Lewis, having been so severely derailed by McCall, might now be pushed over the cliff edge. Said Lewis, 'Whatever action my people take against the WBC is not so important to my situation now. I have one priority here. I have to prove that what happened against Oliver McCall was a fluke. I have to show the progress I have made with Emanuel Steward over the last few weeks. I have to pick up on what I was doing before McCall, I have to show that I can get right to the top whatever Don King and his friends come up with.' Most of all he had to prove that what McCall did to him had left no lasting damage.

Butler was in many ways an imperfect divining rod for Lewis's future. He had genuine power, no doubt, but you could see when he came into the ring at the Arco arena, a half-filled stadium in Sacramento's rustic suburbs more familiar with high-school basketball than collisions pivotal in the lives of heavyweight fighters, that his training had probably not matched the intensity of Lewis's. He wore a big leather coat into the ring and it was stretched against his bulk. His style was extremely basic. It consisted of a few shuffling steps and the throwing of big, looping punches. Throughout boxing he was known as a dangerous, unpredictable customer capable of detonating all kinds of unpleasant surprises – in and out of the ring. In the days before this fight there had been a bizarre accumulation of rumours about the chaos of his life. Police had been called to his motel room – a mean, sad place which defined the boxing class system acutely enough as it mouldered just across the freeway from Lewis's more generous quarters at the sprawling Radisson Hotel – because of disturbances between Butler and his wife, and there was a report of guns in the room and also of a package of dubious white substance left in a taxi vacated by the boxer at an unlikely hour.

But if Butler's life was a mess – and how deeply so we would only know after the fight when a series of court-imposed 'liens' on his purse by various creditors and former managers meant that he had, barring some unlikely act of compassion by the promoters, effectively fought for nothing – it was scarcely more chaotic than that of Oliver McCall. Like McCall, he also had a punch – indeed, some said he had the hardest punch in boxing.

This in itself would have been a good enough reason for caution by Lewis but of course any hint of indecision, any blurring of authority in the face of Butler's wild aggression, would be taken for far more than the reaction of the moment. It could be seen as the consequence of McCall's devastation, and of course it was.

Along with his leather coat, Butler brought with him an outrageous swagger and a somewhat sinister half-smile. The smile disappeared soon enough, as did his threat to wreck Lewis's career, but while it lingered Lewis was obliged to call up some of the lessons of the gruelling seminar he had attended at the top of Big Bear Mountain. He had to jack up the level of his jabbing after Butler landed a big overhead in the first round and in the second and third rounds, before his opponent's energy visibly drained, he felt the impact of several powerful hooks. What his critics would feast upon though was a transparent mood of caution, an excessive concern about the potential of an opponent demonstrably both seriously unfit and out of his class.

This point of criticism, inevitably, survived Lewis's powerful finish in the fifth round, when he put Butler down with a quick right hand and then returned him to the canvas with two more big rights, the second delivered a little recklessly as the beaten man slid down the ropes. Though much of the fight aftermath was taken up with politics, King loudly declaring the legitimacy of Tyson's annexation of the role of number-one contender, WBC boss José Sulaiman protesting that everyone would be treated fairly and Lewis producing huge sarcasm with the comment, 'I've every confidence the WBC's word is golden', a harsh spotlight again fell on a man who was still seen to be at a crossroads of his fighting life.

Lewis said he was happy, but he was also defensive. He said, 'When you come back from a defeat – and especially when it was the first of your career – you naturally have some doubts in your head but throughout the fight I felt strong and confident and I know I can make a lot more progress under Emanuel Steward. He has already unlocked the door on quite a few problems and this situation between us will only get better. Whatever the politics, and I do expect them to go on for some time, I know we'll reach a point together where I just cannot be ignored when anyone talks about who is the real champion of the world.

'We worked on my balance before this fight, shortening my punches, getting inside more positively. I knew I had to be patient against a fighter like Butler. He has fast hands and a heavy punch. I had to remove that threat without taking any silly chances early on and in the end I was happy with the way I got the job done. It was an unusual situation for me, coming in off a defeat and that can play on your mind if you let it. I wasn't going to leave myself open to any kind of sucker punch.' Steward also said he was pleased, at least to a point. 'This was a good start. I'd given Lennox eight of ten for tonight's effort. Next time out you'll see a whole lot of improvement.'

It wasn't such an easy situation to sum up back at the Radisson in the small hours, and not helped by the fact that my hotel neighbour, a lady who was perhaps not all that she should have been, noisily entertained several male guests at regular intervals before the dawn and by the sound of it, concurrently rather than consecutively. My problem was two-fold. The writing desk was attached to a thin wall by a connecting door, which meant that cold analysis of Lewis's future was somewhat hindered by the warm revelries of the present. But one could only follow the lead of a colleague who was a victim of a spoof phone call from his office in London, allegedly from the editor. He declared, 'It is an honour to be a journalist and I'll do all I can to pull off the assignment', after he had been ordered to seduce a woman of easy morals then in the public eye – and to have a photographer on hand to burst into the room at the moment of success.

I was obliged to labour less spectacularly, and as the sun came up over the Napa valley I was concluding, 'There is no doubt there is much work to be done in the re-making of Lennox Lewis but this was a hazardous place, in and out of the ring, to make a start and it could all have ended almost before it began. But it did not, which means that for a little while at least the politics can wait. This was not about politics but redemption. It happened.'

It had happened to a degree, at least, but no one could be surprised that the graph of Lewis's renovation would move up and down, crazily at times. He looked less than awesome barely two months later when finishing in four rounds a short, fat Australian named Justin Fortune in Dublin, but one huge excuse was easy to find on this occasion. Lewis could claim extreme embarrassment caused by a grotesque mismatch. In October, three months later, there was a touch of majesty about him in Atlantic City, where he disposed of Tommy Morrison in the sixth at the end of arguably the most complete performance of his career. Morrison, despite good looks and a left hook of no little merit, had never been far from pathos and he touched bathos when he was ambushed by Michael Bent, who would later lose to Herbie Hide, in Tulsa, Oklahoma, an upset that deprived Lewis of the $7 million he was due to receive for fighting Morrison in Las Vegas.

Maybe the memory of that disappointment helped to give Lewis an edge, perhaps it was simply the progress he and Steward were making in the gym, but, for whatever reason, he simply dismantled Morrison, strafing him with a long, impeccable jab and landing effortlessly with both hands to the head and the body. It was the end of Morrison's fading dream as both 'white hope' and a putative Hollywood star in the tradition of his distant relation John Wayne (aka Marion Morrison). Soon after, Morrison tested positive for HIV, a tragic prelude to a series of collisions with the Oklahoma police.

After the highlight of the Morrison performance, Lewis stepped back, at least in the minds of many critics, when he survived that desperately close decison against Mercer in Madison Square Garden. The effort was judged to be pedestrian, but Steward liked the visceral content of Lewis's refusal to give way in a street fight. 'Lennox will perform a lot better than that,' said the trainer, 'but he won't often be required to produce so much character in the ring. It's the kind of performance I can live with. He showed me he had guts, that he wasn't going to run away when the going got tough.' But the question that still had to be resolved, and was still being asked in this fifth round against Holyfield, was as insistent as ever. Had he really recovered from the McCall episode? Were the scars, and the inhibitions, it imposed in danger of becoming permanent?

We assumed we would know better when Lewis returned to the ring in the company of McCall on 7 January 1997 – two and a half years after the night of catastrophe. But we would not. We would have only fresh evidence of the depths to which boxing can descend. The first fight was a shock. The second was a nightmarish convulsion which involved Lewis mostly as a spectator, an innocent one who did what he had to do but, yet again, found himself caught in the very entrails of a game which seemed to be losing everything – its head, its soul, even its point.

McCall behaved eccentrically in the days before the fight, at one point throwing a handful of dollars from his car window to a bemused bagwoman on Las Vegas Boulevard, and in his room at the Las Vegas Hilton he rambled from one subject to another, leapt up to make phone calls of suddenly overwhelming importance, then quietly resumed a monologue of sometimes haunting strangeness. He was fresh from drug rehabilitation, was accompanied by a psychologist and facing various indictments across the country after the fight. Later, Lewis's American promoter Dino Duva claimed that he argued with the authorities about McCall's mental fitness to fight. But Don King deflected the concerns, maintained McCall's right to fight for the vacant WBC title he once held, and when the time came McCall was in the ring, his eyes wide, a manic expression on his face and voluble claims that he would beat Lewis again on his lips.

What followed, to everyone's horror, and not least Lewis's, was a public nervous breakdown. When I filed my report to the *Express* I felt like a voyeur of something very personal and almost unutterably sad. I started thus: 'Lennox Lewis is the WBC world heavyweight champion again but as he stepped into the desert night and his red stretch limousine he knew better than anyone that this wasn't his resurrection. It was the final professional crack-up of Oliver McCall, broken by drugs and the chaos of his desperate life. Lewis was awarded a technical knock-out win in the fifth round but his punches had been accessories after the fact. Defeat had come in the tortured mind of McCall, who wept,

135

walked distractedly around the ring and refused to return to his corner. Lewis collected his title from a pugilistic madhouse.

'It was the night boxing, for reasons which scarcely bear scrutiny in a civilised society, offered Lewis up a recovering junkie with inevitably severe mental problems. It wasn't the triumphant rise of Lennox Lewis. That may come later. It was the pitiful descent of McCall.'

Given that if McCall had behaved in the street as he did in the ring that night, he would have been taken gently away from the public gaze and into custody for his own protection, it seemed scarcely believable to me that the burden of criticism on Lewis was that he didn't wade into McCall, heap on top of his other miseries the pain of a severe and sustained beating. As it was, Lewis mostly kept his distance, jabbing and watching McCall as a supervising police officer might eye a potential suicide teetering on the edge of a top-floor balcony.

In the wake of the fight the extent of McCall's problems became even clearer. His veteran trainer George Benson shook his head and said, 'I always feared this would happen. McCall is recovering from drug addiction. His behaviour hasn't been normal. He has been talking incoherently today and for some time. He was in no condition to fight, that was clear, and I did what I could but it wasn't enough. I saw the evidence. I spent too much time around addicts to miss it. Televison may say it didn't get value for money but it did get a mega-million lesson about drugs. It should show it to all the kids of America.'

The promoter Duva was savage in his criticism of King and Sulaiman, the WBC chief. He said, 'Oliver McCall has been a crack addict for a long time and he has only been off the stuff for six or eight weeks. The ring is no place for a recovering addict. We pleaded that he should be withdrawn and Lennox fight the next ranked opponent but Don King said McCall would be fine. They pushed him into the ring and we saw how fine he was. We feel great sympathy for him and hope he can put his life together again.'

Before doing that, McCall had to untangle problems with authorities in three states. He had to report to the police in Nashville,Tennessee, to clear up his rampaging behaviour the previous December, when he threw a Christmas tree across a hotel lobby and had to be restrained by eight police officers. In his home state of Virginia he had to settle matters with police seeking to charge him with possession of crack cocaine. In Chicago he was wanted for parole violation.

That he had gone beyond his limits, that the accumulation of drugs and angst had created a total failure to deal with the requirements of life in and out of the ring, was not even an argument now but this did not prevent King calling a morning press conference in which he railed both against criticism of him and suggestions that McCall had been utterly unfit to enter the ring. I wasn't immune from the indignation of the McCall camp, having been quoted in the *Las Vegas Revue Journal* that the fighter appeared to have become as 'mad as a hatter'. But as King and McCall spoke, the tide of evidence was mounting against the moral basis of this desperate affair. Several nights before the fight, McCall woke up his wife Aletha so that they could exchange bible readings. They agreed that boxing just wasn't 'godly'. It involved too much hurting, too much humiliation.

Lewis had a different kind of pain. It was to do with his fear that wherever he went within boxing there would be some cloud or other over his head. Occasionally, he enjoyed clean, uncomplicated victories, like the destruction of Ruddock, the smooth negotiation of Morrison, but mostly it seemed the best he could hope for was a fair hearing in some rancorous debate. Now his moment of redemption, his return to the company of champions, had been grossly flawed. He was philosophical, indeed saddened deeply by the spectacle of McCall's disintegration, but how could he be criticised, he wondered, for his circumspect approach? McCall appeared to him to have gone mad. Do you talk to madmen, let alone fight them, in the normal way? Wasn't it true that one of the reasons the formidable Sonny Liston was so untypically anxious before the first Muhammad Ali fight was that he was convinced that his opponent had gone clear off his head?

As Lewis walked out to his red limo, he said to me, 'This was a terrible night for everyone – Oliver McCall most of all, but also boxing and in a much smaller way, me. Losing to McCall was the worst thing that ever happened to me as a fighter. I wanted to wipe away the stain of it tonight. I wanted to show how much better a fighter I was than McCall, how that first fight was such a freak event. But now I'm told I wasn't aggressive enough, that I should have put him away. Well, I'll tell you something, it's not so easy being aggressive towards a man who is breaking up before your eyes, who's walking away from you and shaking his head and weeping when he should be fighting you.'

A few months later, over lunch in north London, where he keeps a large house – he also has a home in Miami and his mother's house in Ontario – he gave his last words on one of boxing's most desperate nights. 'I felt sorry for him, of course, but there were other factors, and they took me back to the first fight,' said Lewis. 'When McCall started playing up, when he started weeping, I was cautious mainly because of what had happened before. I didn't really know whether or not he was playing tricks – but I knew I would beat him. What I think happened was that although his life was in a mess and he was going through drug rehabilitation, he had been talked into believing he could beat me again. But when I hit him in the second round with a really big uppercut it was as though his belief just drained away. It wasn't how I imagined winning back my title and there was absolutely no sweetness in it . . . no, I felt cheated, but then I thought the important thing was that I had my title back and as I long as I had it I would have strength.'

That strength, so imposingly marshalled at the start of this fifth round in the Garden, was now on the brink of perfectly timed expression. In the following months Lewis would be relentlessly required to explain the course of this brief, ultimately vital window of time. As always, he would bring much logic – the logic of the chessboard rather than the ring, his critics would say – to his carefully considered answers.

It is, however, more than likely that if Mike Tyson or, more relevantly, Evander Holyfield had been placed in Lewis's position, Oliver McCall's conversations with himself would have been interrupted not by referee Mills Lane but by a disabling punch on the jaw. Lewis, though, isn't Tyson, and we have to wonder if this isn't the root of the problem as the bell sounds for the end of the round with Holyfield still on his feet.

8

The Scent of Scandal

The fifth round was big and potentially decisive for Lennox Lewis. We all knew that as surely as we did the time of our commuter train or the way the sky looks before a storm. But Lewis will always deny it was laden with special significance, not, certainly, as the third round had loomed so large in the fevered psyche of Evander Holyfield.

Emanuel Steward might have sucked in his breath and slapped the apron of the ring in his disappointment when the bell signalled Holyfield's survival, but he knows his man still controls the fight; indeed he is winning it almost as he pleases. The pattern of the first, second and fourth rounds is resumed. Lewis's jab lands with production-line regularity and there is a tattoo of right crosses, uppercuts and hooks which, while not on a floodtide, are frequent enough to remind Holyfield who is in charge. Of course, Holyfield being Holyfield, he seeks to break up his tormentor's rhythm. In the sixth round Lewis idles for a moment, drops his guard and Holyfield leaps in with a left hook, his signature punch.

Encouraged, he produces a flurry of punches. But Lewis smiles – and re-activates the jab. In the seventh, Lewis is quickening the pace a little and is landing with a series of right hands. Holyfield's left eye is closing.

Maybe it has become too easy for Lewis. Maybe he has too much time. Too much time to think of ambush, of running out of gas, of the dangers of seizing the moment too eagerly, too rashly. I have him winning the seventh, eighth and ninth rounds comfortably enough, although no doubt he is waging war less aggressively now. Steward will say, with disgust, that his man is reverting to the chessboard, too much thinking and not enough bruising and battering and sheer atavistic bludgeoning home of a point already elaborately made. 'I hate that chess shit,' says Steward. 'People think it's a joke with me. But it's not. I'd like to take that chess set and burn the damn thing.'

Holyfield is straining to get back into the fight but the running of the gauntlet of Lewis's jab is showing on his face. The entire left side of it is swollen. At the end of each round Holyfield walks back to his corner with leaden steps. Back in the House of Pain he swooned like a zealot. Now he plods like a field labourer at the end of his shift. None of it is happening as he said it would on that blue-skied, optimistic Florida morning. Then, the picture was so simple. Lewis would be ponderous and Holyfield would sweep to the point of attack, ducking inside the jab and the big, telegraphed right hands, launching stinging hooks which would spin Lewis into a new line of attack from a man too quick, too alert, too much of an all-round fighter. Instead, Holyfield is being force-fed a diet of Lewis's jab. It is draining both his strength and his belief.

But it is the corner of Lewis which is reflecting crisis at the end of the ninth. Steward is tearing into Lewis, slamming his right hand down for emphasis. Lewis has to work harder, he has to move Holyfield around with greater authority, he has to charge beyond his opponent's fading resistance. He has to think of Holyfield not as some mythical figure, the last obstacle on the long road to final glory, but as just another fighter to be moved out of his life. He has to think of him as he did Ruddock when he rose up at Earl's Court and told boxing that he was indeed someone both fierce and special. Or as he saw the big Golota, who had been built up as something big and wild by the American writers but who was simply consumed by that first raging assault.

Lewis looks impassively ahead as Steward pours out his belief in the need for a new urgency, offering a few token nods. Manager Frank Maloney wonders about the volley fired at the fighter by the trainer and as the tenth round unfolds – one of only four I give to Holyfield – he shouts to Steward, 'Manny, what's the problem? The television has Lennox winning easy.' Steward snaps back, 'It doesn't matter what the television judges say. Television judges don't matter. It's what these guys at ringside say that counts.'

The trainer is yet to know of the weird arithmetic being compiled by judges Eugenia Williams and Larry O'Connell, but he understands the culture of boxing like few men ever have or ever will. He senses trouble before it arrives, like some goatherd on the mountainside eyeing the sky for signs of bad weather. He knows the subliminal forces, of reputation, of crowd noise, of what might be the most popular decision in the minds of those who make the fights and who decide who gets to travel to them on full expenses in cities they might not otherwise ever see, that can influence a judge; he knows that any two people can see a fighter throw the same punch and interpret it quite differently. Nothing in sport is perhaps as subjective as the scoring of a fight. On the face of it, it is straightforward enough. Points are scored by the landing of punches, clean punches, not slaps or aggressive body language, by fire not smoke, but anyone who has been around boxing for any time knows how badly things can go wrong.

Months later Steward would still talk with agitation about the fears that began to grow around the ninth round. Once he did so in the company of Don King, demonstrating his theories with the huge promoter used as the nearest available recipient of the two kinds of punches, the ones that should score and the fake ones that shouldn't. Both kinds he threw lightly enough not to discomfort King physically.

If you shared the growing frenzy of Steward back in the fifth round, his snapping impatience at his fighter's apparent lack of understanding of how vital it was to settle matters with his own hands, it was not so much because of a particular lack of confidence in Lewis's continued ability to dominate the course of the fight. It was because of the number of times you had stood at ringside cursing the whims, if not the corruption, of ringside officials.

You remembered the bleak fury of the fine champion Larry Holmes up in his suite at the Riviera hotel in Las Vegas after he had lost a points decision to Michael Spinks in their second fight, and how, as he poured out his bile, you looked at your notebook and totted up the points again and saw that, yes, you agreed with his grievance – by a margin of at least four rounds. Holmes had committed one of his periodic acts of folly before the fight. He had bad-mouthed King and the judges of Las Vegas, calling them cheats. Some said he lost to Spinks the moment he uttered that phrase, but Holmes filled that sweltering, jammed suite with his fury.

You also recalled the time Pernell 'Sweat Pea' Whitaker counter-attacked Don King's fighter Julio Cesar Chavez so beautifully in San Antonio that long before the end the Mexican was charging forward with the futility of a maddened bull twisted this way and that by the grace and the timing of a master torero. How Whitaker slid and rolled and, with the finest balance, came back with such clean combinations Chavez was backed up all the way to the ropes. And how even the Mexicans who filled the hall shuffled away shamefacedly when the fight

144

was called a draw. The Mexicans adored Chavez, even this one who had become a parody of the old implacable warrior with the red bandana and the proud furies of a Zapatista warlord. But they also knew boxing and even they recoiled at the injustice of what they had seen.

In the post-fight press conference Whitaker was inconsolable, and his pain was heightened by the refusal of Chavez to accept the possibility that there had been even a hint of injustice. Chavez said that he believed he had won. Whitaker said, 'You spend your life working towards certain goals, you train hard, you hurt and you create in your brain the way to win a fight – and then you execute it as well as you hoped you would. You feel proud because you have done what you said you would. You know you have won, clean as you like, and then somebody comes along and steals it from you. Man, it's very hard to take.'

Steward knew which result would most accommodate Don King and at least one of the sanctioning bodies, the IBF, on whose behalf Ms Williams was doing her work and who were already deeply enmeshed in a major probe by the Federal Bureau of Investigation. But he would never charge wrong-doing. He would always think of judges as unmanageable hazards, factors beyond the control of fight men. They can jump any way, even beyond the boundaries of the simplest logic.

He will later explain why he launched into Lewis so strongly at the end of the ninth, saying, 'It wasn't that I thought Lennox was losing the fight. Quite the opposite. He was completely in charge, completely the better fighter. But I never trust judges. I don't say any one of them is corrupt. But I know how they can score fights, I know how easily they can get it wrong, and that is why I've always told my fighters not to forget that they will always be the best judge and jury at a fight.

'Lennox was on top but I worried that the judges might not be seeing this as clearly as me – or Lennox. So I said he had to make it completely obvious. Maybe when Holyfield threw one of his little punches, and Lennox blocked it easily and threw a counter that scored, this just wasn't being picked up by the judges. Sometimes, when you think of all the factors surrounding a fight, the prejudice of the crowd, the background of the fighters, you get an instinct that things might be not quite right. For some reason I had a feeling things were not right. I wanted Lennox to put away Holyfield – and my fears. I thought, "If it's anything short of a knock out, Lennox could lose out."'

If it was so, it was maybe the final crushing extension of the fate Lewis had confronted when we had that lunch back in London. 'When it all started, when I first started to fight as an amateur in Canada and realised I was good, that I had a lot of gifts, it was all so straightforward,' Lewis had said. 'I would win the Olympics, which I did, then I would win the world title, which I did – well, at least a part of it. I would make a lot of money. I would look after my mother, who had done so much for me when I was a kid, when I didn't have a father to look out for me, only her, and then I would retire. I would be around 30. But now I'm a few years older than that and I know it has got so much more complicated.

'I want to be recognised as the undisputed heavyweight champion of the world. People may have laughed in the past when I've said that was my mission, but they were wrong to say that. I could have gone on earning millions of dollars every six months, having a nice big piece of the pie, but I've never wanted to settle for that. It is why I chased Riddick Bowe so hard and why, when he has disappeared, I asked, "Whatever happened to the stuffed chicken?" It's why I've always wanted Mike Tyson and why I'm putting so much pressure on to get Holyfield into the ring.

'I want to know if Holyfield is there and if he is listening, because if he is, he won't like what I'm saying. I'm appealing to his pride, his manhood. He says God is on his side and that he is proud of his career. It is right that he should be – but only to a point. He has to fight me if he wants to keep that pride. I have the WBC belt, the most prestigious one, the one worn by Muhammad Ali, but it's not enough. I want to fight Holyfield and Tyson, I want to finish the business and I know at some time I will get the opportunity because I just don't see how Holyfield can run away without fighting me. The people aren't stupid. He's fought Bowe three times, Tyson twice and I've been around all that time. Why not me? He signed a letter that said he would fight me, but there's a lot of dust on that now.

'Sometimes I wonder about the value to me of putting in an overwhelming performance, like I did against Ruddock and Golota. Did the fact that I just blew Golota away affect Holyfield's thinking, make him back off when he got the contract put in front of him? Did the way I beat Ruddock put me on ice for so long?

'In the end, though, I have to agree with my trainer Emanuel Steward. You cannot hold anything back, you have to fight the best way you can . . .'

Now, those words might have been uttered on another planet. Lewis had had Holyfield against the ropes, bundled up like an old sack but it was almost as if he had been chasing too hard for too long so that when his quarry was finally tracked down, cornered and awaiting dispatch, he couldn't quite catch the reality of it. His sense of impending triumph was mixed in, maybe, with too many bad memories, too many times when, quite beyond his control, the moments of satisfaction had been whisked away.

But, still, he controls the fight around which his life has revolved for so long. The tenth round is more even than the others, and I mark it to Holyfield by a fraction, because of the desperate energy he has brought to the fanning of the embers of his talent, the dogged refusal to go back to Atlanta without some last sign of pride and resistance. He throws a hook of merit, he lands with a decent right, and if these blows are again neutralised, maybe even surpassed by the relentless scoring of Lewis, I score conservatively and give it to Holyfield, perhaps because I feel that such a gesture is affordable so close to a moment of triumph for the man I have believed in for so long.

The 11th is Lewis's, which on my card restores him to a three-round lead. He is home, I tell myself, barring some superhuman eruption from the tired Holyfield, and my ringside neighbours Hugh McIlvanney and Sri Sen agree. Sen is quite clear about the outcome. 'He's boxed Holyfield's ears off,' he says. 'Och, it's Lewis,' agrees McIlvanney, who had agonised over his prediction, finally deciding it was impossible to go against Holyfield's ferociously executed instincts inside and the powers of resurrection which had confounded Bowe and Tyson and suggested to some that his birthplace should go down as Bethlehem rather than Altmore, Albama. On the eve of the fight McIlvanney had written, as memorably as had become his habit over more than 30 years of covering all the big fights, 'Unless our man's power proves irresistible, the result could be decided by comparative depths of desire. Holyfield's competitive nature is a bottomless well. So long as there is a flicker of consciousness left in him, he is at war. I find I just cannot oppose such purity of will.'

But, as befitting a man of such experience, McIlvanney gave plenty of consideration to the possibility that whatever the scale of that extravagantly proven purity of Holyfield's will, he might easily be left at risk by both the physical advantages of Lewis and those separations of desire and execution created by the sheer march of time. He wrote, 'There are so many imponderables, such a variety of obstacles to confident analysis, that any prediction could be swamped by devastating embarrassment. The most worrying question about Holyfield's prospects concerns his age and the many debilitating ring wars he has endured. At 36, he is three years older than Lewis but the relevance of that discrepancy may be increased by the younger man's easier journey to the top. When a fighter of exceptional calibre reaches Holyfield's age the roof can fall in on his career at any moment. The capacities that made him great can desert him suddenly and without warning, so that he can appear to age a decade in a round or two . . . it may be that the sense of continuing deadliness associated with Holyfield has been exaggerated by the terminal decline of his most celebrated recent victim, Tyson.'

McIlvanney's words are echoing through the final round. Lewis's dominance of the fight is more pronounced now than at any point other than the fifth. Holyfield is dragging himself around the ring, making gestures rather than throwing punches and all the serious work is coming from Lewis. He stuns Holyfield with a long, hard right. Holyfield seeks the respite of a clinch. Lewis pushes him away with a hint of contempt and when, a few seconds later, the bell sounds for the last time he raises his arms in triumph and briefly embraces Holyfield, who turns for his corner without even a hint of challenging his opponent's confident assertion that the spoils are his.

As the final scorecards are collected, as Lewis savours these moments of impending triumph, as Holyfield inhabits pain and weariness he has never quite encountered before, a computer is spewing out the fight statistics.

Rarely have such details been collated into such a one-sided story or so challenged Benjamin Disraeli's dismissive reference to lies, damned lies and statistics. Certainly they speak of the fight I have just seen. They say that Lewis threw 613 punches, Holyfield 385, and that Lewis connected with 348, Holyfield 130. They also offer, redundantly you think, the itemising of a slaughter that lacked only one killing stroke: power punches thrown, Lewis 249, Holyfield 214; power punches connected, Lewis 161, Holyfield 78; jabs thrown, Lewis 364, Holyfield 171; jabs connected, Lewis 187, Holyfield, 52.

In the wait for the scoring, a formality you believe to rank with that of the returning officer announcing an old Labour victory in some Salford or Gorbals soviet, you accept the congratulations of an American colleague, and if you point out that you didn't actually throw a punch, that of all fighters Lennox Lewis surely got here on his own, and against a sometimes revolting tide of prejudice and sneers in America, you inevitably feel a flush of national pride. That, and a surge of relief that indeed there had been a point to all these trips on the coat-tails of Lennox Lewis.

You remember the time you were standing in the lobby of the Mirage Casino Hotel in Las Vegas when Lewis came up on your blindside and applied a withering bear hug before announcing that he was on the trail of Evander Holyfield and he would get him in the end. That was seven years ago and Lewis had still to be sickened by the lurching deceits of boxing, its endless capacity to duck and dive and shape events not out of any rough sense of justice but from a relentless need to feed the hopes and the illusions of brave young men and battered old ones into a vast, cynical maw of profit. Looking back over those few years, he seemed so young and guileless then and he didn't take too much offence that not too many gave him much of a chance of breaking through. He rode the jibes about his essential lack of 'Britishness' and the sniggers when he reported how his brother Dennis had taken him to watch West Ham United at Upton Park. He absorbed the charge that deep down he would always be an amateur, a man of talent for whom the hard edge of a true champion would be as elusive as the touch of genius which turns an able draughtsman into an true artist.

He had rarely been treated with more than token enthusiasm by the media and he could not look forward to any immediate improvement, especially that weekend in Vegas when Lewis had been frustrated over ten rounds by a journeyman named Levi Billups. He was no kind of scalp to boast of but the fact was that Billups was a notorious spoiler, one of those opponents who should be avoided by up-and-coming fighters as veteran actors steer a careful path around animals and kids. Lewis insisted he would march on. The cries of *Bruuuno-Bruuuno-Bruuuno* might drone on for some years, celebrating victories which had credence only in the making of bogus dreams, bogus fights and would finally deliver brief ownership of the WBC title after a collision with the King-owned Oliver McCall, who came to the Wembley arena fresh from another rehab centre, but we should always keep an eye on Lewis. He would get there in the end. He said that through gritted teeth when the Union flags unfurled at Wembley Arena and Bruno took over the title he once held in a fight so lacking in distinction patriotic celebration had to be dredged up as you might recover some spurious family heir-loom, the orginal of which had been hocked some generations earlier.

Now, surely, Lewis has done it. His coronation is just a few long seconds away. He can put away the anger and the angst. He can forget the night he overwhelmed inside a round Andrew Golota, the man who effectively ended the career of Riddick Bowe, only to be told that the big Polish-American had had a curious spasm in his dressing-room before the fight, one that would remain thoroughly unspecified. He can forget, too, the surreal afternoon in Lake Tahoe when Henry Akinwande, another King property, spent five rounds clinching and clutching and refusing to fight until an exasperated referee Mills Lane sent him back to his corner, and Lewis went off for the second time in a year to face charges that he failed to impress against a man who wouldn't fight.

Akinwande! He was supposed to help pull boxing back from the brink of self-destruction that strange afternoon in the little showroom in Tahoe. It was the year of Tyson's ear-biting and McCall's nervous breakdown. It was the year when boxing was seen to be going mad.

John Morris, the chief of the British Boxing Board of Control who was the official supervisor for the WBC, spelled out the task for Lewis and Akinwande in the days before the fight. He said, 'This is a fight which can make a new start for heavyweight boxing, show that its spirit and its image does not have to be dragged into the gutter. This is the first fight since Tyson bit the ears of Holyfield, and Lennox Lewis and Henry Akinwande are not just fighting for themselves but for the real meaning of their sport. I know them well and I know that they are good fighters – and good men.'

Akinwande had certainly shown a degree of resolution since breaking free of a dominating father in Lagos, Nigeria, and investing everything in boxing, for a while working as a street cleaner for the City of Westminster to keep himself fed while going to the gym and waiting for his chance. Now, despite an awkward, deeply unpleasing style, he had made enough money to own a fine home in Florida and if he could beat Lewis, well, he was set for life. Unfortunately he didn't fight against Lewis. He froze with fear, despite the encouragement of a flash knock-down which referee Lane unaccountably failed to register. The referee's preoccupation, though, had been to nurse Akinwande into a fighting mode. Repeatedly, he demanded more action, then, his patience spent, he waved Akinwande back to his corner and ended the fight.

Lane's trademarked injunction to fighters before the first bell is, invariably, 'Let's get it on', but on this occasion his task was hopeless. Earlier in the year he had been overwhelmed by the outrage of Tyson, bitterly saying in the acrid aftermath of that controversy, 'It is maybe time for boxing to be moved from the sports pages to the business sections. What matters in the game today except money?' Now this spry little US circuit judge, a former marine, was knee-deep again in boxing's scummiest tide.

Like Lewis he had come to do a job, to help lift boxing from the edge of the abyss to which it had been carried by first Tyson, then McCall, now Akinwande. In all the anger in Lake Tahoe it didn't go unremarked that all three fighters were the promotional property of Don King.

Lewis's American promoter Dino Duva, not for the first time, angrily asserted that this was another boxing disaster caught in what he saw as a sinister web woven by King and the men he manipulated so effortlessly. Duva said, 'Boxing is sick and it will continue to be so while it plays the alphabet-soup game, when the various sanctioning bodies cook up fights like this, when fighters in the condition of McCall and with the background of Akinwande are pushed into title fights. The WBC broke its own rules to make Akinwande the number-one contender. It insisted on Lewis fighting McCall when we knew he was an opponent who wasn't fit to be in the ring. It has got to stop.'

But Lewis had to wonder where it would end when he finally disentangled himself from the desperate embrace of Henry Akinwande. He shook his head and said, 'The truth is I get more practice in training than in fights. I attacked him from the start, but when I moved to jab, to do anything, he was draped all over me. It would have been quite simple to have knocked him out if he had agreed to fight.

'I could feel his fear as soon as he came into the ring and it just got worse. But if you want to blame anyone, blame the people who run the sport, who put up these Don King mandatory contenders who shouldn't really be in the ring with someone like me. I want to fight Evander Holyfield and Michael Moorer – the best fighters around, champions like me – but my last two fights have been against opponents who have been incapable of making a fight of it. I want boxing fans to see there is one true champion of the world. I believe that is going to be me, but the important thing is that real fights happen. Boxing had another lesson to

153

learn tonight . . . it is that boxing must have the best fighters in the ring at the same time. It can't go on as it is now. The smell is just too rotten.'

He was not to know that the aroma would grow even more atrocious soon enough. Within months of running up the white flag so pathetically, Henry Akinwande, not Lennox Lewis, would be matched against Evander Holyfield in a world heavyweight title scheduled for the spring of 1998.

The fight was sanctioned by the International Boxing Federation and the World Boxing Association for the titles held by Holyfield. It was as though Tahoe had not happened, that all traces of that afternoon, when we walked out on to the sunlit shore of the pine-fringed lake feeling that even a place underpinned by the addictive force of gambling had been defiled by a visit from the fight game, had been removed from not only the conscience but the very records of boxing. When Lewis heard of the proposal he speculated on what they would call this grotesque matching of Holyfield and Akinwande – the Final Insult, the Last Outrage, the Thrill at the Till. We could take our pick and still be left with understatement. As it happened fight fans responded to the prospect of Holyfield–Akinwande as if they had been invited to some ceremonial incubation of bubonic plague. Anyone not totally familiar with the workings of boxing might have reasonably asked: how could it happen?

Inevitably the story was to do with money. The WBC and IBF worked through the top of the rankings, inviting such as Frans Botha, Zeljko Mavrovic, Golota and Corey Sanders to fight an eliminator for the right to meet Holyfield, but all of them declined. They didn't want to immerse themselves in the risky business of fighting for the right to win the big title shot which would leave them on easy street for the rest of their lives. They preferred that it came to them not as a right fashioned in the ring but by way of clever negotiation by their manager or promoter, and in the cases of Botha and Mavrovic their decisions would be justified. Soon enough Botha would fight Tyson and Mavrovic would meet Lewis. Right there we had the kernel of boxing's problem. The object of the exercise for so many fighters – and nobody exemplified this more completely than Bruno – was to win the 'shot' not the prize. Bruno never won a fight that truly mattered, the outcome which his backers were not certain of before the first bell, if we exclude the one with McCall, which I think we have to on the basis that McCall would have been rather better off under sedation than starter's orders. Twice Bruno fought Tyson, the first time when the champion was veering off on the path of self-destruction which would lead to defeat by Douglas in Tokyo – his next fight after Bruno. Bruno was immobilised by fear in his second fight, and ultimately outclassed by a bloated, drug-raddled Tim Witherspoon. But, like Akinwande, Bruno was a property, a pawn, and four times he fought for boxing's biggest prize. Akinwande's fight with Holyfield never happened. Shortly before he was due in the ring, he tested positive for hepatitis C.

Now, though, we could consign all that to the past. For the moment we could celebrate a real fight for the undisputed heavy-weight championship of the world. Before the first bell Don Majeski, veteran fight man, had turned to his friend sitting beside him in Madison Square Garden and said, 'You know, boxing needed Holyfield to fight Lewis more than anything but I still can't believe it is really happening. I can't believe that within the next hour we're going to have an undisputed heavyweight championship of the world.'

Now Majeski would know the identity of that man. Lennox Lewis held his head high, savouring the moment, and Holyfield, grimacing in pain, waited with resignation as Jimmy Lennon lifted up the microphone.

Rages of Indecision

For a little while almost everyone was just stunned – Lewis, most visibly, big George Foreman sitting on the first row, his moon face framed by a broadcaster's headpiece and his eyes opened wide, Lewis's people, Holyfield, drained and so diminished, and even Don King's expression suggested a rare moment of reflection.

It was a draw, it was a stench, it was boxing's latest dive into irrationality and corruption. But what kind of corruption? The bald corruption of money exchanged, of the fix going in, of a formal conspiracy to deny one man a modicum of justice? Some would say so in the first rush of disbelief and anger, and the Governor of New York State and the Mayor of New York City would immediately launch official probes. The FBI, already deep in their investigation into corruption by the International Boxing Federation, had a new and juicy bone upon which to pick. Others were more philosophical; they talked not of a fix but of a 'culture of preferment', of judges who scored fights from perspectives which, if not warped by specific motives, were informed by an instinct for the most desirable result; desirable, that is, to the men who make the fights and distribute the profits and the perks. There were other factors to feed into the stew of controversy. Was simple incompetence at work in the case of the American judge, Eugenia Williams? Did Britain's Larry O'Connell, who was already under a cloud in America for his eccentric scoring of the Oscar De La Hoya fight in Las Vegas a few weeks earlier, strain too officiously to show himself unbiased?

All these questions would be asked relentlessly for weeks running into months. But for the moment anything like cold analysis was impossible. Frank Maloney stood close to Lewis as Lennon announced the scoring. He was shocked when Lennon said that we had a split decision. How could someone score it for Holyfield? Lewis frowned. Lennon first gave the scoring of South Africa's Stanley Christodoulou, and there was no problem here. Christodoulou had it for Lewis by 116–113, or three clear rounds. The problem was Eugenia Williams, who scored 115–113 in Holyfield's favour and, quite shockingly, had awarded him the fifth – the one upon which Lewis would be critically impaled for not converting a huge advantage into a knock-out, and which Mickey Duff said should have gone to him by a two-point margin. There were muted oaths in the Lewis corner but Maloney recalls thinking, 'Oh well, it's going to be okay because the last score is Larry O'Connell's. He's British, he's experienced.' But O'Connell, and he would admit later it was also to his own amazement, had made it a draw. Like all the judges he had handed in scoring slips at the end of each round. When his score was announced O'Connell gasped. The crowd was silent for a little while, absorbing the scores, the impossibility of Lewis not being at this moment crowned undisputed heavyweight champion of the world. Then the boos came in solid waves.

Maloney reports, 'I've known Lennox Lewis for ten years and I've never seen him so emotional. He shouted, "What's happening, what's going on? Somebody tell me what's happening." We had to tell him he hadn't won it.' Tears of rage appeared briefly in Lewis's eyes. When he got back to the dressing-room he slumped on to a bench and stared at a wall. 'I feel so empty,' he said.

Walking down from ringside to the big area of the basement cleared for the press conference was to have one's own sense of outrage confirmed at almost every step. I walked past the HBO broadcasting booth, where frontman Jim Lamplay was telling his audience of more than a million £50 subscribers, 'What we have here is a fraud. Boxing's cesspool has opened up to give an unconscionable odour. You have seen the fight. Lennox Lewis won the fight and two judges converted it into a draw. Lennox won it in every way imaginable. The draw means there is no undisputed heavyweight champion of the world – but there should be.'

Budd Schulburg, the novelist, raised his arms and asked me, 'What's happened to the British? Why didn't they riot? This was sickening. This was disgraceful.' Richie Giachetti handed me the slip of paper with his scoring so hugely in Lewis's favour. Henry Akinwande who, having been cleared on the hepatitis scare, was back, amazingly enough, as a leading contender to fight for one of the belts and stood to gain most from a Lewis defeat, said, 'I gave it to Lennox by three rounds. I'd be happy to stand aside for a re-match. It's the least he deserves.'

Larry Merchant, HBO television's ringside interviewer and analyst, was perhaps the most eloquent and impassioned witness. A sophisticated, witty former columnist of the *New York Post*, Merchant had long cleverly and decently walked the line between the need to sell the fight product of his company and objective comment. A few years earlier HBO had proved their regard for him when Mike Tyson insisted that he would only re-sign for them if they fired Merchant. HBO boss Seth Abraham refused to make the deal. Merchant was banned from Zaire in the hiatus between

Foreman suffering a hand injury and the eventual fight between him and Ali in 1974. He had been less than complimentary about the régime of Mobutu. Now, Merchant was blazing.

He said, 'It is almost beyond a stench. Lennox Lewis suffered so many slings and arrows in America. He has a really wonderful career and despite being the best fighter in the heavyweight division he has been shamelessly avoided by everyone this decade. He came to fight the best of the best right now, decisively controlled the fight throughout, beat Holyfield up and didn't get a decision. The slings and arrows ought to be aimed at those who denied him respect. I am ashamed as a boxing fan and an American who has seen this foreigner take so much stuff simply because he is not American. His great moment of glory was taken away from him.'

Naturally, no one was more angered by the latest fusillade of arrows than Violet Lewis. She cornered the wretched Holyfield in the ring and said, 'You know you were beaten – why don't you say so?' Later, she said, 'I think it was disgusting. Everyone knows that Lennox won the fight. But this is America. The result is a disgrace. I think it was all politics and I don't want to get involved in that. All I know is that my son won the fight. I don't know what fight the British judge was watching. It is for others to explain their decision and if they can live with it that is for them.' A mother would say such things, of course, especially one as proprietorial as Violet Lewis, but even Evander Holyfield could manage in response only a sickly smile.

I bellowed a question at King as we waited for Lewis and Holyfield to appear before us. I asked him how he could bear this disgraceful outcome to a promotion which he had described as his 'crowning glory', and did he not feel as sick as the rest of us, sick for Lewis and for boxing. You do not get much change out of King – ask the FBI – and this is especially so when he is pushed into a corner. I shouldn't have been surprised that he reached so adroitly for any available flotsam. He said, 'I cannot speak for the judges, they are human beings. It was significant that the British judge scored it 115–115. Who am I to be second-guessing the judges? When you have a man on the ropes you're supposed to finish him, not play chess with him. Evander has to face the great giant. Let's just get them back in the ring.' Yes, he would say that, wouldn't he, as surely as Violet Lewis would rage at the heavens on behalf of her son? Let's have a re-match, said King, let's go through it all again – let's push the credibility of the public a little further, let's see how much they will take, how tightly they can be squeezed.

When Lewis and Holyfield came to stand on either side of King you could see plainly the lunacy of the decision. Lewis's face was untouched but for two small strips of plasters, one star-shaped over the bridge of his nose, the other just above his left eye. He said both cuts had been caused by Holyfield's head. Holyfield looked old and distressed and repeatedly reached for the support of a table. Someone kept shouting, 'Take him to the hospital.' Whatever you thought of the treatment of Lewis, it was impossible not to feel for the condition of Holyfield. Both physically and psychologically, he was clearly in a terrible place. As King droned on, and the cry for Holyfield to be removed to the hospital kept coming in, hard and angry and in the most profound way humiliating, the beaten fighter – for how else could you see him, or describe him – yelped out in pain on several occasions, put a hand to his ribs and rolled his head in anguish. A debate in which he was not involved swirled over his battered head. This, you suspected, was the most hurtful thing. All these weeks the media had hung on his every word, however outlandish, but now it was as though he had never existed. He was suddenly a discredited myth, an idea of glory stranded, quite pathetically, beyond its time. Forget the nights he had thrilled us to our cores, the night our sports editors kept ringing from London to demand more copy on the sensation of the boxing age, the masterful defeat of Mike Tyson. Forget that he was boxing's ultimate warrior. Look at him now, battered, moaning softly in his pain, an embarrassment, a betrayer of the American belief that he was made of the Right Stuff and Lewis was some ersatz version of a champion, foreign and thus discountable right up to the moment he rammed your prejudice back down your throat.

Eventually, someone paid Holyfield the courtesy of a question. But when it came out, when it required him to break from his bleak reverie and address the world, it seemed not so much a kindness as another cruelty. He could scarcely speak and you had to listen closely to words that came out jerkily, almost disembodied, and were in danger of being lost in the roaring, scowling tumult. Holyfield said, 'I don't judge, I fight, but there ain't nothing like a man who, when he gets an opportunity, shines. The man [Lewis] really shined. I never said he wasn't tough. The man showed that he was tough. I'm not disappointed. I did all I could. The judges make the decision and I have to live with it. I can still get him. I guess I did the best I could. That's not my best, though.'

Then he left for treatment to his wounds and check-ups which said that no damage, at least no immediate damage, had been done beyond the inevitable effects of a beating so neatly tabulated by a computer: 187 jabs and 161 power punches received. Holyfield trailed wearily away, saying, 'I come in with God, I go out with God.' With Holyfield, and God, departed, the field was left to King. Yes, there would of course be a re-match. The public would demand it. The need for it would rise up in the blood of the people. Lewis shook his head and his manager Maloney, his voice hoarse from all the shouting, said, 'Lennox Lewis, the people's champion, is now leaving the building.' King shook his head and said, 'Not a smart move.'

But what was the smart move? Should Lewis really have taken the King money all those years ago? Had he done so, would tonight have panned out any differently? There were so many questions and the only one Lewis had the patience to confront would never be far from his lips over the next few days. It simply asked, 'How could they do this? How could they rob me?'

It was a question that was being thrown at the judges with great force now. O'Connell, looking stunned, bemused, kept insisting, 'I scored it as I saw it. I thought Lewis won the fight, but I scored it round by round. That's how I saw the fight round by round.' Eugenia Williams, whose financial affairs would be examined by the FBI in the next few days, and who would face the kind of grilling normally reserved for mobsters and female White House interns, had a special problem. Unlike O'Connell and Christodoulou, and probably every other person in Madison Square Garden, Williams had scored the fifth round for Holyfield. This was beyond reason. She said she wasn't interested in what television said. She didn't have the benefit of television when she scored the fight. She scored only the punches she saw and she saw Holyfield land more punches throughout the fight and, yes, in the fifth round. But then apparently her view was partly obscured by photographers – and a lot of the time she could see only Lewis's back. Hugh McIlvanney said that a reasonably competent judge could have scored such a one-sided fight with the help of pictures from a space satellite.

Perhaps the iciest verdict on the judging of Williams and O'Connell came from their colleague Christodoulou. He said, 'I don't want to comment on the scoring of my fellow judges, but I've been around boxing for a long time, 36 years, and I think I know how to score a fight. In my view Lewis won the fight.' Referee Arthur Mercante Junior, whose father had controlled the Ali–Frazier collision here 28 years earlier, was equally withering. He said, 'This is a crime for the sport I've been around all my life. Lewis won the fight easily. I'd have given Holyfield no more than three rounds. We should go back to the old days and let the referees score the fights.'

Lewis was offered some consoling cheers from scattered groups of fans and fight people as he walked away from the press conference and down to his limo. I joined him on his stroll into some of the bleaker landscapes of *déjà vu*. He carried the same weight of disbelief that came after the two McCall fights and the Akinwande fiasco. 'It hasn't sunk in yet,' he said. 'I suppose I'll wake up in the morning and say, "God, it's happened again. They've taken something away from me again, something that was mine." I just can't take it in right now. I can't talk about what I'll do in the future. It's just too soon. I'm so disappointed. It was my time to shine and they ripped me off. I'm the undisputed champion of the world and the whole world knows that. What happened there is what you call politics. I felt like I won the fight hands down. Holyfield should give me those belts. He knows they are mine.'

Back in the Garden conversations were still raw, edgy and if there were debates about the estimates of Lewis's victory very few argued that the result wasn't a travesty. It was that time of hoovering up the widest possible sweep of comment so that when you get back to your room, when the screen of the laptop blinks in emasculating reproach at the drift of the hours and the lack of meaningful action, you at least feel that you have covered most of the significant bases. This night, though, the comment was rooted on first base, from where the judgement was relentlessly consistent. Lewis had been mugged, bizarrely, and so shamelessly that for a while the cry for a re-match wouldn't seem so much an appeal for justice as a dangerous invitation to the possibilities of fresh outrage.

Steward, so critical of Lewis's refusal to step beyond his zone of comfort in the fifth round, had closed ranks now. 'Lennox and I are disgusted,' he said. 'I gave Evander three rounds at most. What I saw was Lennox working with a sparring partner, only we don't give sparring partners $20 million for their work. It was not even a close fight. This hurts boxing. It was daylight robbery.

164

Thieves came and took away Lennox's property. I don't take it lightly. I take it with disgust.'

Maloney was incandescent with rage. 'The look on 20,000 faces told the whole story. We were robbed. It's an absolute con. If I was Tony Blair I'd cut off all diplomatic relations with America. This result has sent boxing back into the dark ages.'

Classics of the We Wuz Robbed genre, you might say, but the indignation had spread like a forest fire beyond the Lewis camp. A large New York policeman said his assignment was to watch for pickpockets but the crime here, he decided, was Grand Larceny. Foreman, perhaps overstating the British royal family's fascination with the old game, declared, 'The Queen and all her subjects can be proud. Lennox Lewis proved he is undoubtedly the best heavyweight fighter in the world today. He should forget about tonight. It's over, just get up, dust your pants off, fight him again and knock him out next time.' Lou DiBella, vice-president of HBO, joined the tide of condemnation beating against the judges, saying, 'The scoring was shocking. I didn't see it as a close fight but even if I don't complain about the judge who made it a draw, how can anyone looking at the fight make Holyfield the winner by two rounds? It's impossible; that judge should not work again.' Lou Duva, Holyfield's former trainer, said, 'I think the decision was terrible. I had it 9–3 for Lewis.' Roy Jones, the world light-heavyweight champion from Pensacola, Florida, and widely considered to be the most gifted of current fighters, was appalled. 'I just feel ashamed about what happened tonight. I love Evander Holyfield but Lennox Lewis did not lose it.'

And so it went, all the way uptown to my hotel. The taxi driver noted my English accent but drove silently through the early-morning streets. When I got out of his cab he said, 'I saw the fight in a bar. Boy, did they do a number on your guy.' Indeed they did.

It was a long night of course and it was light when I filed my last piece to London and called up a bellboy to fax copies of the

165

scorecards, which would be displayed on Monday morning in all their raw and fascinating horror. But if it had been an arduous shift the hours had moved swiftly enough. The adrenaline of outrage is a good ally against fatigue and the words had moved briskly. Maybe a little too briskly, I couldn't really say, but certainly my main piece did not lack the irrigation of emotion felt as strongly as any that had come to me in more than 30 years on the road. I wrote, 'Lennox Lewis, who is not supposed to have passion, wept in the ring of Madison Square Garden. They were tears of rage and disbelief and if boxing has a shred of conscience it must also cry. Cry for truth. Cry for judgement. Cry for the scandal that after outfighting and outboxing Evander Holyfield Lewis is, officially at least, still a stride from the mountain top of being declared undisputed heavyweight champion of the world.'

Somewhat overwrought, you may say, but if you cared at all for Lewis and for boxing and the principle that talent and decency should, somewhere along the line, be recognised and celebrated rather than schemed against, I believed there was a case for indignation of an extreme order. Certainly no stretching or fakery was involved, and the night wasn't without its reassurances. When I handed over the scorecards for the fax, the bellboy handed me the morning papers. The *Daily News* and the *New York Post* revealed that surge of energy which used to be reserved for political corruption and mob slayings and after the low hum of the television in the corner of the room with its matter-of-fact reporting of 'a major fight scandal' it was agreeable to be reminded of the power of the printed word.

Veteran *Post* columnist Jack Newfield, who had been around the fights for 30 years, wrote beneath a huge front-page splash headline saying Robbery, 'It was the worst decision I have ever known in any championship. I watched every punch and had Lennox Lewis ahead by ten rounds to two. There is no shadow of doubt that he should have won. I believed the world heavyweight crown was sacred, but not any more. It's like the Vatican has been burgled. It was a disgusting decision. This was the crime of the century. Don King had everything to lose if Lewis won because he controls Evander Holyfield. Now he's looking for another payday when the re-match is staged.' Newfield's colleague Wally Matthews, a heavy critic of Lewis in the past, was no less biting. He wrote, 'The fight plan [Holyfield's] may have been drawn up by the Lord, but the scorecards bore the mark of the Devil. It was the night glory and honour was supposed to return to boxing; instead the stink returned to the air over the ring. Lennox Lewis beat Evander Holyfield from here to London – with stop-offs in Jamaica and Canada along the way.'

I read those first editions with a heart made lighter by the dawning recognition of a supreme irony. In his campaigning in America Lewis had been lacerated all the way from faint praise to the most savage dismissal. No one had quite matched the atrocity of the *Boston Globe's* Ron Borges's assertion that Lewis had a broad yellow streak running down his back, but the criticism had been relentless and heavy, as Larry Merchant pointed out so forcefully as the first shock waves swept through the Garden. Now, on his night of bitter disappointment, when the prize he had worked for so diligently had been stolen away from him, Lewis was getting notices which would have provoked an orgy of luvvy tears and hugs and the best French champange over a theatrical supper at Sardi's off Broadway.

I slept for a couple of hours, drank some more coffee and went off to see Lewis at his hotel suite in the New York Palace just a few blocks away across Fifth Avenue. The hotel lobby was filled with boxing types. Mickey Duff was still seething about events at the Garden; he was outraged on behalf of Lewis and his own lost bet, railing against the worst, and one of the most personally expensive, decisions he had ever seen. Richie Giachetti was still indignant but without prompting he made the point that had come to me back in the hotel room. 'Strange to say,' said Giachetti, 'but this could be the best thing that ever happened to Lennox Lewis in America. If he had got the decision he deserved a lot of guys out in the street would have shrugged and said, "Well, Holyfield is shot through now and Lewis just came along at the right time." Instead the American people will be behind Lennox a 100 per cent. They are already saying he's a talented guy who's been robbed. Boxing was supposed to be on the comeback here. This is really the home of big-time boxing in America. Now the people feel like Lennox. They believe they have been abused.'

Still, though, there was a catch, a worry and Giachetti – a hard and practical man – went to it as so many boxing men would in the next few months. 'The bottom line, though, is that Lennox really should have taken the matter out of the hands of the judges. He could and should have put Evander away.'

Up in his suite Lennox Lewis looked as he did in the Garden, fresh, untouched but for the small lattice work of plasters, and he continued to display a controlled anger. 'I still can't grasp how those judges could do that to me, but yes, I can see how it might work in my benefit down the next few months. I don't think anyone will really take boxing seriously if I don't get the chance to finish the job against Holyfield. At first when I heard the scoring of the judges I just couldn't believe it. It seemed like just another example of everything going wrong for me here. But now I can see how in the end it could turn out to be positive.'

Perhaps it could, but for Lewis there was no escaping the reality of boxing politics even in the great rush of American contrition, typically expressed by one New York radio station as an outright attack on Holyfield's hard-earned reputation as the nation's favourite fighter. 'If Evander Holyfield is really the Real Deal,' said the station, 'he will prove it by handing over his titles to Lennox Lewis, the People's Champion. Anything else and he will be part of a terrible injustice.' But of course the radio station, like so much of the city's media and political life, had picked up this boxing scandal quickly and riotously, and also in the knowledge that the story would run down quickly enough. Tomorrow an axe-wielding lunatic might go on the rampage down in the subway, a hair-trigger cop might shoot an honours student mistaken for a street punk and the riot police would be out in force and the mugging of Lennox Lewis, putative undisputed champion of the world, would be thrown back to the sports department soon enough. Meanwhile, there were the imperatives of boxing, the making of fights which would yield a profit and what else really mattered? Lewis was a martyr today but tomorrow he would be another fighter seeking his dues.

Lewis's American promoter Dino Duva was in the suite and he addressed the realities of boxing rather than the fleeting zeal of politicians and their desire for quick, cheap headlines. Said Duva, 'Anyone who knows Evander Holyfield will tell you that he came as close as he possibly could to admitting that he was thrashed by Lewis. It is just not in Evander's make-up to admit defeat, but I think he came close. I believe strongly that one of two things is going to happen in the next month. He is either going to quit or fight Lewis. I don't think anything else would square with his sense of honour. King will try to talk him into fighting people like Henry Akinwande in mandatory defences of the WBA and IBF titles. He will try to keep his hands on two of the three titles but he knows he's under tremendous pressure. This has turned into a public relations nightmare for him.'

For Lewis, for the moment at least, the opposite was true. Frank Maloney reported with some relish that the *Post*'s Wally Matthews had called the hotel that morning with what amounted to an apology. On the morning of the fight Matthews had gone along with Holyfield's prediction that he would knock Lewis out in the third round. Matthews said that Holyfield was so much more of a fighter than Lewis, more instinctive, more courageous, more of everything except size and weight. From Lewis's perspective it was routine

American comment. But Matthews told Maloney that he could now see that he had misjudged both the talent and the character of Lewis. He had proved himself more than a paper fighter.

Lewis shrugged and gave a frosty little smile when he heard of the Matthews conversion. He said, 'Wally Matthews is a clever writer, I enjoy a lot of his stuff, but as far as I'm concerned he has never dealt in reality. I gave up expecting a fair deal quite a long time ago.' Fair deal, raw deal, it all seemed a little academic up in the suite at the New York Palace Hotel. The overwhelming reality was that Lennox Lewis and his situation had become a very big deal indeed.

By Monday morning you might have thought the flames would be running a little lower in the sky, that the scandal of the fight would begin to ebb against some new sensation from the basketball court or a convulsion in the front office of the New York Giants or the Yankees. But, no, Lewis and Holyfield were still the news items of choice. On *Good Morning America*, the nation's top morning television show, Lewis and Holyfield were trading verbal blows. Lewis, turning to Holyfield, said, 'I feel I was robbed. He should be a man and admit it. I felt I won the fight hands down. I felt I was a much more superior boxer than Evander.' Holyfield countered, 'The fight was in the judges' hands. Once the fight is in the judges' hands that's where it stays. If Lennox knocks me out, then it wouldn't be no problem. The judges wouldn't be necessary. Unfortunately, when you have two good fighters, that's a matter of opinion.'

In all of this there was a perversity, and an irony, against which all the sermonising of those who would regulate boxing, codify its rules and its practices, appoint ombudsmen and safety commissions and drive a Don King back into the underworld from which he emerged, fabulously acquisitive and amoral, dwindles like an ebbing tide against the rocks. It is that if Lewis had been given justice, if his sheer volume of scoring punches had not disappeared so instantly from the consciousness of two of the judges, this fight would have been as cold as the Sunday joint by Monday morning. If he was lucky, Lewis would have received a few notes of praise for his superior technique in the American press, though nothing like the tribute bestowed upon him by Sri Senn of *The Times*, who wrote, 'Lennox Lewis answered every question his severest critics have asked of him. He beat Evander Holyfield out of sight. The decision was unjust and will only serve to confirm the belief that detractors of boxing have always held, that it is not so much a sport as a racket for keeping sleazy luminaries in business.' True enough, but maybe sleaze and outrage is the real oxygen of boxing. Of all the big fights I have covered in America, only one made its way to the front-page splash on Monday morning. It was the one in which Mike Tyson cannibalised the ears of Evander Holyfield.

Now, this morning in Manhattan, 36 hours after Jimmy Lennon announced the draw, you could flick on to any television channel and there it was all over again, Lewis indignant, Holyfield cowed as never before in the wake of a big fight, Emanuel Steward, eyes blazing, talking about grand larceny. The Governor of New York State, George Pataki, and the Mayor, Rudi 'zero tolerance' Giuliani, were running hard with the frenzy of it all. How could a politician lose on this one? Pataki fired off a memo to the New York Athletic Commission which said, 'Take a long hard look at the judging.' State Attorney-General Eliot Spitzer, already involved in a boxing task force, declared, 'The fight shows the judges were either guilty of tampering or incompetence.'

For Larry O'Connell, an engraver, and Eugenia Williams, a ledger clerk, it was going to be the weekend of their lives, a time when they brushed against celebrity and helped shape sporting history. But now, as the furies raged on every television channel and every front page, they could see the price they would have to pay.

171

A Crime of Folly

Tears had come to Larry O'Connell's eyes at the Starbuck's coffee house on the corner of 31st across the street from Madison Square Garden. His companion, Don Majeski, reckoned they were formed by a mixture of relief and exhilaration. Relief that he had survived an eccentric night's work as a judge at the big Oscar De La Hoya–Ike Quartey fight in Las Vegas the previous month. O'Connell was the only judge to score it for Quartey, a tough, gifted welterweight from Ghana but one who, it seemed to most of us in the Thomas and Mack Centre, had faded from contention against the sharper skills and stronger fighting personality of the Golden Boy from East Los Angeles.

'I thought that might have been the end of my judging in America,' O'Connell had told Majeski. 'Now I can hardly believe I'm doing the biggest fight of them all, Lewis versus Holyfield. It really is amazing.' Majeski had told O'Connell he probably owed his latest assignment to the policy of World Boxing Council chief José Sulaiman. 'José believes,' said Majeski, 'that if you have a good judge who has a bad night the best thing is to send him straight back into the action, like an infantryman who has been involved in a bad situation. The thinking is, "Get him back in there before he thinks about it too much and loses his nerve."'

O'Connell had been delighted to see Majeski when he walked into the Garden after checking in at the Pennsylvania Hotel, which in its more buoyant days was known as the Statler Hilton and included Glenn Miller and Muhammad Ali among its guests. Now the Pennsylvania is a big cheerless place and the sense of this had been exaggerated for O'Connell by some confusion over the booking of his room. He was going over to the Garden to check on the timing of the rules meeting and the details of his stay in New York. He had a few questions to ask Don King Productions. Was the cost of his room covered? Whom did he see for his per diem expenses? He was feeling a little neglected. There was no red carpet for him at JFK airport when he flew in from London.

Majeski is just the man to meet in such circumstances. He knows how everything works in boxing, where the bodies lie, how you conjure an opponent at the last moment, how you set up a fight card which will give some value for money whatever the budget at your disposal, and, most relevantly at this moment, how a fight judge gets to collect his food allowance. Majeski has been a fight man from his teens when he left his native New York and became an aide to the colourful, wise old Los Angeles promoter George Parnassus. He writes for boxing magazines. He is a confidant of Sulaiman and King and is currently retained by Lewis's promoter Panos Eliades. Get Majeski over a glass of red wine at his favourite East Side restaurant, Griffone, and he can tell you anything you want to know about the fight game, its nuances, its fables and its foibles, all of its characters in and out of the ring. He can tell you the names of Jack Johnson's girlfriends, the ones who caused so much trouble back when even black heavyweight champions of the world couldn't cross the colour line without risking the attention of a lynch mob. He can tell you about Louis and Marciano, Archie Moore and Hank Amstrong, Frankie Carbo, the mobster who ran boxing for a while. Want to know about Gunboat Smith, Jake La Motta, Charley Phil or Rosenburg? Majeski will have something on them back in his apartment, something buried under old copies of *Ring* magazines and posters for forgettable fights in forgettable towns. He can tell you where the old names hang out. Name a town, almost any town, in America and he'll tell you the right fight man to call. He can take you all the way from John L. Sullivan to Lennox Lewis. You name it, Majeski knows it. Naturally, the FBI talked to him about corruption at the IBF and the scoring of the Lewis–Holyfield fight.

Majeski told the Federal agents that they were wasting their time trying to make a case of corrupt scoring against Larry O'Connell. He didn't know Eugenia Williams, had met her once, briefly, when she struck him as a 'quiet, humble woman', but he could vouch for the honesty of O'Connell. So how did O'Connell get it so wrong, how did he shock even himself when the details of his scoring were boomed out across the bewildered Garden?

'My theory is that Larry O'Connell bent over backwards to be seen to be fair,' says Majeski. 'There he was, the British judge and he knew that if he scored it too generously for Lewis he would be written off as some guy who couldn't step away from his associations and do a job, just look at a fight and score it as he saw it. So I think Larry overcompensated. He desperately wanted do the right thing. He wanted to prove that he deserved the break he got after the De La Hoya fight. That obviously hung on him very heavily. You could see how important it was to him to get this one right.

'Looking back you can see an overwhelming case for having three neutral judges. I think in the cases of O'Connell and Williams we saw the problems you often get with judges who are not neutral. O'Connell went one way with the pressure of being associated with one of the fighters . . . and Williams went the other. In Williams's case the problem could have been com-pounded by sheer ignorance. Her scoring was just unbelievable, embarrassing. When I read her scorecard I just couldn't believe it, I didn't know what to say. Oh, man, how could anyone give Holyfield the fifth? It was just beyond reason. Now you look at Stanley Christodoulou and see that he didn't have any pressure. He was a South African, what did he care? So he scored the same fight most of us saw.'

Majeski saw O'Connell at a post-fight party at Bravo Gianni's, a club on East 62nd Street. It was an understandably sombre affair, and O'Connell would have added even more considerably to the gloom had he known that even as he sipped his drink a pack of British journalists, including myself, were scouring the Pennsylvania Hotel for a sight of him. Majeski recalls, 'O'Connell looked stunned. He kept saying, "I just handed in my slip after every round – and now I just don't know what to say. I scored the fight as I saw it but my overall impression was that Lennox had won." He looked to me like a guy who was going through quite a bit of agony.'

Initially, O'Connell struck a note of bemusement with more than a hint of contrition. He said to reporters, 'I feel very sorry for Lennox. I felt surprised I had given a draw. I felt it could have marginally gone to Lewis. I feel very sorry for him because he has done everything in the world you could have asked of him. I have been a referee for 23 years and this sort of situation doesn't happen often. If I have a message for Lennox Lewis it is that "you will be world champion" although he would probably turn to me now and say he already is. I thought Lennox had won it. My heart was with him but my head has to see it how it is. I'm an honest man. That's why they chose me to go there.' He added that the one thing he would have marked Lewis down for was not following through with his attacks. 'Lewis is a gentleman, but is he too much of a gentleman? I don't know. Remember he has hurt people before.' That was O'Connell in his Bravo Gianni's phase, when the night had come crushing in on him and he was still in the condition of a dazed fighter, his guard drooping, his defence unmustered.

But by the time he reached his home in the sleepy Kent village of Hartley his mood was beginning to harden. First he was nonplussed, now he was angry at the vehemence of the questions of reporters who, it seemed to him, had jumped from out of a bush screaming demands for an apology to both Lewis and the entire British nation. Certainly he was dismissive of the quote from British sports minister Tony Banks which was passed on by his Fleet Street welcoming party. Banks, O'Connell was told, had said the judgement was a disgrace. 'To hell with Tony Banks,' said O'Connell. 'I think they gave him the job to keep him quiet.'

But then the merest glances at newspapers on both sides of the Atlantic should have been enough to put O'Connell on his guard. Spike Lee, Hollywood film director, offered a quietly devastating quote, saying, 'Evander is my man but Lewis won that fight.' Tony Kornheiser wrote in the *Washington Post*, 'They [the judges] damaged the sport they love. They called the fight a draw when it was no such thing. It was like Three Blind Mice were scoring. Two Blind Mice anyway.' The perennially low-key *New York Times*, which bestowed upon a friend of mine a permanent nervous tic when they sacked him because they found his headlines a 'trifle dull', were shrill to the point of that sensationalism they despised so thoroughly in the New York tabloids. 'The decison,' said the *New York Times*, 'resembled a Brinks Trust heist perpetrated in front of 21,284 fans.' Perhaps most depressing of all for O'Connell was the reaction of John Morris, the British Boxing Board of Control's chief executive who had hoped for so much in Lake Tahoe when Lewis fought the pacific Henry Akinwande. Morris showed up in Lewis's suite the morning after the fight and urged reporters to refer to Lewis as the 'undisputed heavyweight champion of the world'. A few hours' sleep had not dimmed Morris's indignation. 'The reality is that Lennox Lewis won that fight,' said Morris. 'He deserved to take all those belts. He won them in the ring and out of it he had conducted himself brilliantly.'

By the end of the week the tide of criticism and abusive phone calls containing threats and vile language brought O'Connell near to breaking point. He was both anguished and angry, deeply resentful of the volume of the barbs being fired in his direction. He told Olga Craig of the *Sunday Telegraph* that he felt besieged in his own home. Craig reported that as he spoke he kept an 'anxious' eye on the ever-growing queue of cars jamming the road outside his house. Said O'Connell, 'Overnight, I went from being just an ordinary guy to Public Enemy Number One. I can understand passions running high. I can understand people's anger, but this . . . I've been yelled at down the phone, spat at during calls, sworn at. For being a fair man. It's beyond comprehension. I'm not a rapist, I'm not a murderer. I don't feel sorry. How can I when I scored it as I saw it? I have no regrets. If I did make a mistake, then it was an honest mistake. I accept that I'm in a minority but I was fair and honest in my scoring on the day. The moment the plane touched down I was relieved. I was exhausted and just wanted to go home. But the second I stepped out of my car a reporter and a photographer from a tabloid jumped out of the bushes across the road and began to demand to know why I had let Britian down. They wanted to know what I would do to redress my mistake. They kept wanting me to apologise. Yet I had done nothing wrong. When I got inside I found my wife Beryl in a dreadful state. The phone hadn't stopped all day, journalists had been battering on the door half the night.' Then, O'Connell told Craig, the abusive calls started. His phone line was choked with head-banging obscenity. 'It's unbelievable how vile people can be,' added O'Connell. 'They've accused me of taking bribes.'

O'Connell's worst experience was during a television interview in which he had pleaded his case of objectivity, of doing the right thing even if he got the wrong result. At one point his mind went 'blank' and he covered his head with his hands in a comic gesture of despair. Later that night he saw the footage and a commentary that said this was the moment when O'Connell said sorry.

The FBI file on Larry O'Connell is closed. He was questioned by telephone and his answers were deemed satisfactory. There was no smoking gun, no sinister brown envelope, as nothing in O'Connell's reputation or character had suggested there would be. But you only had to look at his face in those first days after the fight to know that he, in a different but no less profound way than Lennox Lewis, was a victim of that extraordinary night in Madison Square Garden.

He was caught in the passions which boxing can release like no other sport outside of football played in Latin America. Whether he tried, as Majeski believes he did, too hard to be the perfect arbiter of an imperfect world will be debated for as long as Gene Tunney's long count or Muhammad Ali's apparently slight punch which floored Sonny Liston in their second fight in Lewiston, Maine. Only one possibility can, I believe, be excluded. It is the one that he might have been on the take. A man on the take, for one thing, would not have been so glad to see Don Majeski at the artists' entrance to Madison Square Garden. He would have known who to see and what, precisely, were his dues.

Eugenia Williams is a stranger case, but one which, like that of O'Connell, was never likely to reach a courtroom. Certainly Sulaiman and the Lewis camp were able to raise valid questions about her suitability for the assignment at the Garden. A single mother of two, she had recently admitted to debts of $72,000. Her record as a professional judge stretched back ten years, during which she had worked 90 fights, but most of them were obscure and included a number of women's fights. There was nothing here to suggest her suitability for one of the biggest fights of the decade, one laden with huge significance both historically for Britain and generally for the public perception of the health of the game. As a young woman she had trained as a boxer, then changed to karate. Some said her elevation for Holyfield–Lewis was simply the result of IBF chairman Bob Lee doing a favour for a friend, though Williams was emphatic that their relationship was strictly 'professional'. One of the fragments of boxing administration, the British-based World Boxing Union, had already decided to 'rest' her from their list of potential officials, president Jon Robinson telling the *Sunday Times*, 'She is a local judge, not a world-title judge.' That assessment seemed to go to the heart of the problem.

Even so, the FBI put Williams under a lot of pressure. They were already deep into their investigation of the IBF and its chief Lee, who had appointed Williams over the protests of the Lewis camp. The controversy over the Lewis–Holyfield decision had simply put their enquiries under a sharply intensified spotlight. Whatever you felt about the validity of the outrage – and for me it would tingle long after the controversy had slid from the front pages – there was no question that a feeding frenzy had developed. O'Connell could complain legitimately about the concentrated agitation of a nation which had, overnight, become universally acquainted with the finer points of scoring a boxing match, but what he couldn't dispute was a deep sense that something shatteringly unfair had happened. Whether this justified a *Sunday Times* headline declaring 'Mafia's shadow on the big fight night' was an entirely different matter. The paper put its suspicions to Lee, who replied that he had never met Mob figures, adding, 'If the Gambinos were involved I think they would be going after something a little more lucrative than the fight game.' Mike Katz, waspish boxing writer for the *New York Daily News*, offered the English newspaper some of his typical piquant perspective, 'If you take away larceny you just get two guys beating the shit out of each other. Larceny gives the boxing game a little charm.'

Two facts, one of them emerging a few days later, would put Williams under immediate suspicion of wrong-doing. It was found that she had filed for voluntary bankruptcy at Camden, New Jersey on 25 January – seven weeks before the fight, and that a meeting of creditors had been set for early in May. Investigations later revealed that in her declaration of bankruptcy she had left undisclosed a bank account containing more than $20,000.

But despite her grilling by the FBI, there was no encouragement to place her case into the bulging IBF file, which contained dynamite evidence that Lee had received $100,000 from German promoter Wilfred Saurerland. The money was allegedly for a single purpose. It was to lift Saurerland's fighter Axel Schulz into the IBF rankings and thus qualify him for a lucrative title fight against George Foreman. Majeski's view on this particular situation does not show Foreman, the hugely popular Punchin' Preacher Foreman, in a good light. He says, 'What happened, I believe, was that Foreman, as usual, was looking for an easy opponent and the word went out that he needed a "stiff" – but a stiff who was ranked. What went wrong was that Schulz turned out to be a lot better than Foreman's people were led to believe.'

So much better, in fact, that the fight at the MGM Grand Casino in April 1995 created a controversy which occupied a rung just one below that of Lewis–Holyfield. As one reported from ringside at the finish, Foreman was still champion of the IBF's version of the world, but what kind of world? A world, you had to conclude, where every decision is accompanied by a dollar sign and natural justice has the shelf-life of one of Foreman's chocolate sundaes. At that fight Foreman was 46 years old but on those occasions when the tough young German, who came from a little town on the Polish border, moved in with rudimentary but strong combinations, the old fighter looked nearer 80. He kept his title and the theoretical chance of earning $50 million for fighting Mike Tyson, which given the rate of Tyson's current decline may re-appear as a possibility any day now, but little else. Certainly he lost the heroic aura of a timeless warrior shrugging off the years.

Schulz comprehensively ridiculed that illusion. He was supposed to be a random chopping block in another extension of the Foreman myth. But the big man knew the plan had misfired when he heard the cheers of sympathy for his 'beaten' opponent as he walked from the ring. What kind of a world was it? One in which a flood of callers to the MGM used the phrase which had become so familiar these last few days in New York, the one about being ashamed to be an American. Foreman retained his 'title' on a majority decision. Judge Chuck Giampa scored it a draw, 114–114, but his colleagues Jerry Roth and Keith Macdonald went for Foreman, both by two rounds.

Foreman said, 'He didn't show enough aggression to take my title away but he was tough and at one point in the fight I said, "Somebody better get me a baseball bat." I hit him so hard and expected him to fall but instead he was throwing punches at me. He was the toughest guy I ever fought.' Tougher than Ali, tougher than Smokin' Joe Frazier? Foreman shrugged away such comparisons. This was 1995, this was the world George Foreman had discovered one day when he looked at the television and saw ranked heavyweights he could smother and frustrate and almost certainly knock out while at the same time expanding his pension fund by many millions of dollars. George Foreman was the most popular 'geezer' in America and some said, with a straight face, that nothing would lift boxing's public appeal more than for him to step into the ring with the recidivist jailbird and convicted rapist Mike Tyson. Such was the world Lennox Lewis wished to conquer and, he insisted, straighten out a little.

At the time I rated the decision just behind the atrocities of Holmes–Spinks and Chavez–Whitaker but when the point was made to Foreman he absorbed it so easily it might have been a desperate, windmill flurry from one of the sad opponents who had come before Schulz and Michael Moorer, who had unaccountably lost the title to Foreman by standing in front of one of his slow but still crunching rights towards the end of a fight he had dominated utterly. Said Foreman, 'No way you can take a title the way this boy tried. He was a 26-year-old running from a grandpappy. I chased him and though he was tough and hit me so hard my teeth chattered, I never saw the fight as close. He never did enough to make it that.'

Foreman earned $10 million, Schulz $500,000 – and there was the $100,000 that went allegedly to the IBF for preferment which would, anyway, have been his in any other world than the one which the old fighter had come back to gouge. Foreman put on dark glasses almost at the sound of the last bell. He made one concession to the course of the fight, saying, 'I look like a junkyard dog and he looks like Elvis Presley.' Schulz flew off home and renewed membership of the forlorn legion of opponents, fighters who hoped for one, maybe even two nights in the glow of some big-name fighter. Poignantly, Schulz kept his post-fight comment brief. 'I know in my heart,' he said, 'that I won the fight.'

For Foreman there was the prospect of another big paycheque – maybe two or three. Apart from talk of Tyson, which was positively frightening at that time before the extent of his erosion could be properly calculated, there was mention of Lou Savresi, a handsome mediocrity with a certain following on the East Coast, and a plodding journeyman Northern American Indian named Joe Hipp. Foreman got an early flight home to Texas and was preaching in his church in Houston on Sunday night. He said his theme would be the value of friends, and he would have in his

183

mind those in the arena who had chanted 'USA . . . USA . . . USA' on his behalf. But of course the feeling back in sinful Vegas was that his real friends were a lot closer to the ring.

That by her actions Eugenia Williams made herself a friend of Evander Holyfield was a proposition about which there could be not much doubt, a point which the FBI, scenting blood, pressed upon with some force. But soon enough the spectre of incompetence was most pervasive. She performed dismally before the investigating New York Senate committee a few days after her grotesque interpretation of events in Madison Square Garden. Her main line of defence was that photographers had repeatedly blocked her view, that at one point her line of vision was so impaired she had hoisted herself on to a table to get a better sight of the action.

The committee invited her to review the film of the fifth round which she had scored to Holyfield. When she saw the replayed action, when she saw Lewis dominating the round so profoundly, at one point toying with Holyfield as a cat might with a cornered mouse, she said, 'From what I've now seen on television it looked like Lewis was the winner of that round. But what I saw on TV was not what I saw on the night. It viewed the bout from a different angle.'

Don King also appeared before the Senate committee. He said that there had been no financial inducements to any judge to bend the scoring. Eugenia Williams had received a standard fee – £3,260 – and the normal expenses. Yes, King said, Lewis had won the fifth round but, perhaps already thinking re-match and lines of extended controversy, he couldn't leave it at that. He added, 'If Lennox Lewis had been Ali or Joe Louis he would have knocked Holyfield out.'

José Sulaiman, the WBC chief, also gave evidence. He revealed that he had opposed the late appointment of Williams, but on grounds no more sinister than her lack of experience. The more you looked at Williams, the more you considered the critical extremity on which she had placed herself, the less likely appeared the possibility that she had come to the Garden with any mission more onerous than trying to keep up with events. As adroit criminals go, she would have resembled more Inspector Clouseau than the Jackal, and if the fifth round was the weakness of her position, in terms of her future as a professional judge of fighting, it was also her strength as a lady not yet above suspicion. Fixing this fight without repercussions would always have been difficult. Calling the fifth round for Holyfield dishonestly would have been seen only as a failure of professional duty, an invitation only to scorn and doubt. A dedicated, knowing fixer would have homed in on the rounds in which Lewis was most passive. In the fifth he was just one vital reflection away from outright rampage.

New York Governor Pataki stressed that Williams's financial situation warranted close examination and the New York Athletic Commission announced that this would also be an important aspect of their investigations. So the weight on Williams and King was, for the moment, still huge, and all of it exerted on behalf of Lennox Lewis. Having been drawn into the politics of boxing for so long he was, reasonably enough, not now prepared to stand back and allow them to take their usual course of fleeting outrage and swift reversion to the status quo. 'The way I feel now everything should be looked into,' he said. 'I've suffered at the hands of boxing for so long. People have ducked me, pushed me into corners and I've paid out millions in legal expenses just so that I could get my rights. But nothing has happened to me on this scale, not so out front where the whole world could see what was happening. There was something going on, some kind of conspiracy we don't know about. It has to be sorted out. Eventually, I assume I will get back in the ring and beat Evander Holyfield again. I'm prepared to do that, but it just shouldn't be necessary.'

Back home the tide was still rushing powerfully in the aggrieved Lewis's favour. From New York, Daniel Jeffreys filed an extraordinary indictment of all things American to his newspaper, the *Daily Mail*. Under a headline that screamed 'Can a Briton ever fight through the sleaze to beat America in its own backyard?' Jeffreys wrote, 'America has sunk to many new lows in the last year, but none has been more spectacular than the disgraceful decision to deny Lennox Lewis the heavyweight boxing championship of the world. Few independent observers could avoid the conclusion that the Holyfield–Lewis fight was fixed. And no one took more evident pleasure from the extraordinary result than Don King, the ex-convict who stands to make millions from the re-match. A country that can acquit Bill Clinton of perjury is not one where truth seems to have much value, but sport is supposed to be above the sleazy backroom deals that bailed out the President.'

One could only wonder which sport Jeffreys had in mind? The Olympian one of track and field, where every world record is overlaid with huge doubt about the fuelling of the athlete concerned? The venerable game of cricket, where the stars of Pakistan and Australia had been sucked into a huge bribery scandal? Not horse racing, surely, where race-fixing allegations were endemic and perhaps not even football, the world game, where unresolved bent referee stories stretched back to the sixties? And what on earth had persuaded him to think the best of boxing?

There was, though, a formidable head of indignation building on both sides of the Atlantic. Reg Bullock, a New York lawyer, went to cheer Evander Holyfield but he came back into the street saying, 'Lennox Lewis got that special American shaft, the one with the American flag wrapped around it.' Somewhere the truth lay buried beneath the mountain of headlines and the television footage and the outrage of people who just couldn't let it fade away. A fight is a fight, undoubtedly, but this one had taken us beyond the usual waves of cynicism. It had a shelf-life which, surely, would run all the way to a re-match.

'I shouldn't even have to consider the idea of getting back in the ring with Holyfield,' sighed Lewis. 'It should be done, over and we all should be moving on. But you can't spend a lot of your life trying to achieve something and then just sit down when somebody takes it away from you. That cuts deeply. It's like being mugged in the street and not lifting a finger. Some things you just can't let happen. As far as I'm concerned this is one of them.'

For whatever motives, this was for a while the urgent priority of law enforcement agencies, the executive heads of one of the greatest states of the Union, the fabled city of New York, the New York Athletic Commission, the Manhattan district attorney, the sports minister of Britain and any number of New York state and US Senators and Congressman.

However, the charge of dishonesty against Eugenia Williams and Larry O'Connell was for some, myself included, never a serious runner. A member of the Manhattan district attorney's staff put it best, saying, 'We could be looking at tampering or illegal payments. Then again, maye we're looking at lousy judging, which is not a crime.' Not unless, perhaps, you just happened to be Lennox Lewis.

King Flies Again

At first the idea of a re-match was appalling. It would be like re-sitting an exam which had plagued you for so long with the idea and the importance of it and then, when it had been experienced and suffered, caused you to be told, sorry, you'll have to go through all of that again – all of those fears, all that adrenaline and angst. And for what? The possibility that some other adjudicators would for one reason or another prove not to be up to the job. The truth was that after that first surge of rage in Madison Square Garden there came a terrible feeling of weariness.

We had all been here before. We had seen Holmes's face up in the suite at the Sahara. We had seen Whitaker in San Antonio, Schulz in Las Vegas. Join the club, Lennox. We knew where all the inquiries would lead. We knew how quickly the politicians and the news editors would tire of these particular pickings.

One of the biggest players of all, Seth Abraham, the urbane head of Home Box Office, the man who holds Lewis's television contract and, like his counterpart at the rival Showtime, Jay

Larkin, is effectively the paymaster of big-time boxing, certainly initially leaned against the instant fix of a re-match. Lewis should get on with his life and his career, Abraham first concluded. The public had seen the fight, which wasn't so distinguished, another factor which worked against the re-match, sales had been excellent, more than a million and a ranking third in the all-time list behind Holyfield–Tyson I and Holyfield–Foreman, and Abraham's instinct was that the drama was played out. Whatever the assessment of the margin by individuals, the consensus was overwhelming. Lennox was bigger and younger and of the two fighters palpably had a much deeper well of resources.

The classic appeal of a re-match, a stupendous first fight which had left some questions unanswered, or at least the possibility that the beaten man had left some shots unfired, that he had within him the power of resurrection, seemed to be missing from the prospectus of a Holyfield–Lewis II. Ali–Frazier II, Leonard–Duran II, Bowe–Holyfield II and Leonard–Hearns II all fulfilled the promise of either the development of an intriguing story or the continuation of a war. What could Lewis–Holyfield II offer? Not much more, you had to conclude as you surveyed the wreckage of Evander Holyfield, than the correction of an appalling administrative lapse; good for the peace of mind of Lennox Lewis perhaps, but not necessarily compelling box office.

When I spoke with Abraham in his midtown Manhattan office on the Monday afternoon after the fight his responses were less animated than usual. Like his rival Larkin, Abraham is very much a man of the world, superbly literate and giving off a strong sense of life beyond the rumpled neighbourhood of boxing, a place where values that were not entirely subordinate to the need to turn a buck or two lived and even prospered. It was as though Abraham had wearied, at least for the moment, of the whole boxing show. Larkin, who for so long had had to deal with the tumultuous vagaries of Mike Tyson, would generate the same mood later in the year when the fighter's first engagement after being released from Maryland prison, for which he was being paid $10 million, ended after one round as he drove his left hand into Orlin Norris's face clearly, a few-runs proved beyond any doubt, after the sound of the bell. 'How long will the public put up with this, where will it end?' asked Larkin with a weary shrug.

Implicitly, Abraham was asking the same question. 'It has always seemed to me that boxing operates in the state of having a permanent cold – and that when the decision came in on Lewis–Holyfield it was simply more like a bad case of the flu. I don't want to get involved in the controversy by more than saying that on my card Lewis was ahead.' But then Abraham did not question for a second the force of the performance of his broadcasting team. 'We look for professionalism in our broadcasters,' he said, 'and with that goes editorial freedom.'

It was, the more you thought about it, an extraordinary performance by the HBO crew. In an age of television sports salesmanship, when 'analysis' is another way of selling the product, their reaction had the effect of a fresh breeze in a sewer, and if Larry O'Connell could fairly protest about the bombardment of his personal life and the harassment of his family, he could scarcely complain when gut emotions were expressed by those whose duty it was to produce honest reaction. Lewis–Holyfield was the HBO product but their frontman Lampley said it had been rendered a fraud. No public relations waffle here. Just maybe an underpinning of the long-held view by Abraham and his colleague, HBO vice-president Lou DiBella, that the three main sanctioning bodies had been living for too long on borrowed time and that now, perhaps, their credit had been exhausted by the blundering at ringside.

In the past Abraham and DiBella had openly questioned the value of the belts for which Lennox Lewis still pined. 'Out of self-interest, the sanctioning bodies have put all of boxing at risk,' said

191

DiBella after the Lake Tahoe travesty of a title fight between Lewis and Akinwande. Now that debate was certain of a new airing, and in a climate which, as rarely before, was utterly hostile to any possibility of another collective shrug of the shoulders.

Both Lewis and his trainer Emanuel Steward also seemed besieged with concern about the potential futility of a re-match. Steward's preferred course was a push to overturn the verdict, which was something of a reach for such a worldly boxing man, even with the widespread disgust which seemed to be sweeping into every corner of the press and television. Said Steward, 'I never thought Evander should have taken the fight with Lennox in the first place. He looked like a slow, old, bald man. He should be man enough to say Lennox beat him. The injustice should not stop here because I heard on that television that the public gave Holyfield only one round. That's decent, intelligent people. The fifth round should be the core of the investigation.'

Lewis was sceptical about Holyfield's willingness to take a re-match, and for reasons quite separate from the fact that his own promoter Panos Eliades had already made clear that if it was to happen he would demand a straight split of the $28 million purse. Lewis said, 'I don't think Evander is going to want a re-match. He was feeling disappointed at the end of the fight. He never even held up his hand. I held up my hand. I went over to him to say sorry and he said, 'That's the way it goes.' There is no doubt he lost. He looked bad after the fight, like a hurt man, like an old man and there was a lot of despair on his face. Physically, he looked beat up. It seemed that he was a man living in a fantasy world who had just woken up. When someone asked whether he wanted a re-match he wasn't quick to answer and Don King jumped in. Holyfield should realise that a re-match could put him in some physical danger. He should start thinking about the health aspect. He claimed he was suffering cramps after the fight. I heard a whisper that it was his ribs. Next time I'll knock him out.'

But despite all appearances, the fact was that when the first pain receded, when the throbbing of his face and the ache of his ribs began to relent, Holyfield was beset with another affliction – for him, the most serious one that could be anticipated this side of the grave. His pride was beginning to hurt. As Don King knew it would.

King was in his Manhattan apartment that Monday afternoon. He was feeling about as abashed as a buccaneer with the scent of booty in his nostrils. 'They try to hang me for everything,' he told me, 'but, man, they're barking up the wrong tree this time. My conscience is clear. I had breakfast with Evander this morning and he wants to fight again. He's not happy with this situation at all. He has lived by vindication and he will be vindicated again. He said to me, "Get the re-match on" and I'll be honoured to do so. I'm used to being the target when anything goes wrong in boxing. I just push it all on one side. I'm going to make this fight happen again. There is too much unfinished business. And you know, I don't go where the wild goose goes. I go where the money goes.'

King was talking re-match, in very clear tones, and where does the money go? In boxing it goes to Las Vegas. Even with the bullets whistling over the parapet, it was the same old King, inflamed by the roar of controversy, thrilled by his sure knowledge of what it meant. It meant, sooner or later, when the investigations had run their course, when the nag of Holyfield's pride and Lewis's deep need to get his hands on all three heavy-weight belts, and with no slivers of doubt, official or otherwise, became insistent enough, there would be a re-match. There would again be a call of the blood, Lewis's, Holyfield's and that of all those who found in boxing something that stirred them to the very core of their beings.

Wherever King looked, to the television screen, the front pages, the placards on the street, he saw thrillingly that there was a captured audience, some of it declared, some of it furtive, which was far wider and deeper than all those 'naysayers' had ever believed. King knew the people, he was saying. He knew their darkest yearnings. He understood their fascination with the monstrous possibilities of Tyson, he knew their liking for the hubbub of controversy. A truly boxing-orientated audience? Perhaps not. But an audience hooked on the intrigues and the violence and the random sensations of the ring? Undoubtedly. Why were the politicians falling over each other to issue statements? Why were first editions flying off the newstands in New York City, a place where the old game was supposedly dead, laughed out of town and to its grave? Because it still had a pull. Atavistic, perhaps, offensive to any sense of gentility or care for humanity, maybe. But a pull without question, a claim that went to the very entrails of a society which, for all its liberal manifestations, sold Saturday special handguns as naturally as it dispensed fast food and Class A drugs.

No, there was no doubt, a re-match would happen. Lewis would have to do it again and in America there would, yet again, be speculation about the ability of Evander Holyfield to re-make himself. The re-match would rise like a new mountain in the eye of a climber. It was simply there. It would be climbed and within days we had confirmation that once again the grappling irons were being reached for in Las Vegas.

Marc Ratner, executive director of the Nevada State Athletic Commission, a college gridiron football referee who in less than a year had been obliged to steer his way through wave upon wave of controversy following the Tyson ear-biting, the McCall nervous breakdown, the Akinwande surrender, said, 'We would love to have the re-match here, unequivocally. We believe there was no corruption shown in the judging of the first fight and don't believe that any corruption will be shown to have occurred in the inquiries. I have no misgivings about the re-match. I wanted the first fight here. I want the second fight here . . . I have no worries about whoever promotes it, and that includes Don King.'

But there, of course, was the rub, and the nub of it all was that HBO were not happy with King, nor was Panos Eliades and, as ever, his fighter Lewis. The problem went beyond Lewis's conspiracy theories and the HBO belief that a new promotion association with King would be deeply, and probably irreparably, flawed in the minds of the public. Already the battle lines had been drawn. HBO were still raw about the fact that King went into the first fight with a low-risk deal which had yielded him an estimated profit of $14 million while they had got the thin end, even after guaranteeing the purse of $32 million. The digestion of this reality had not been improved for HBO by the fact that it was reported that at one stage in the build-up to the New York fight King had threatened to pull out Holyfield if all the details of his negotiated advantages were not made watertight. DiBella confirmed the bruised feelings in the executive suite in midtown Manhatten. 'We did a deal which was not a very good economic deal for us. Others made money out of it, and we didn't. There could be a problem selling the next fight with Don King up front, even if he had nothing to do with any wrong-doing – and I don't think he did. But it's not Don's style to walk away.'

King was also under fire from Eliades – and his long-time promotional rival Bob Arum, the Harvard-educated lawyer who served on the anti-racketeering staff of the late Robert F. Kennedy. There is an old joke about King and Arum. It goes like this, 'Don King and Bob Arum were caught in a leaky sampan when a typhoon struck in the China Sea. Who was saved?' Answer: boxing. Traditionally, when one or the other of these promotional heavyweights hits stormy weather, the boot is administered instantly and with great relish. Now Arum weighed in with typical force, saying, 'According to a poll in the *New York Post*, 55 per cent of the public think boxing is fixed. For Don King to be talking about re-matches before an inquiry is properly conducted is plain wrong.'

Eliades took up the same theme. He said, 'HBO should know that I can put up $35 million to stage this fight tomorrow. I don't believe HBO want King and Lennox certainly doesn't. Don King has controlled heavyweight boxing for a long time and now the public is losing confidence. It is time for a change.'

When HBO offered King a reported $10 million to step away from the promotion they were, predictably, rebuffed. For most men picking up $10 million with no greater demand than that you make yourself scarce for a little while, perhaps spend a little time in a health clinic, get the blood pressure down, would have been a proposition mailed from Fantasy Island. But not for King. For him it was an arrow aimed at the very heart of his own self-belief. You couldn't have a fight guaranteed huge media attention, with his rights spelled out in legally enforceable detail, and have King skulking in the shadows. Ten million dollars was no price for such a torment of the spirit.

So negotiations would drag into the summer. Though King was reporting by late May that the fight was a 'done deal' – and that a contract had been made with Las Vegas casinos led by the Hilton – Eliades was refusing to go along with the optimism. Indeed, he virtually hosed away all the King talk of a breakthrough. Said Eliades, 'If Don's done a deal he's on his own. I'm the joint promoter and I can assure you I know nothing about this. It isn't even agreed that King will be allowed to promote this fight. If King is indicted for fight-fixing, and that could still happen, HBO would want nothing to do with him. But this is normal King practice. He's just done this deal, which means nothing, to put pressure on and make everybody think the fight cannot go ahead without his involvement. And that is simply not the case. King won't want to step down but I believe there is a big possibility that I could still wind up promoting this fight on my own. If people believe his involvement could damage pay-per-view sales, then he may have to step back.'

196

A week later Eliades was reporting on his efforts to apply pressure to Holyfield, perhaps drive a wedge between the fighter and King. If King proved too obdurate, said Eliades, Holyfield needed to know that he was legally entitled to find another promoter. 'We expect to hear from Holyfield in the next 48 hours,' added Eliades. 'We will see if he is serious about facing Lennox again. As HBO definitely don't want King if he is indicted, it seems that if Holyfield can't swing it, the fight is off. I have spoken to Don and asked him to agree to HBO's terms. He has categorically refused.'

It was at this time that the plot began to thicken to the point of breakdown. DiBella made the point that Eliades's fight with King was probably more significant than his own and HBO's reservations about staying with the man who, for all his negative aspects, was still widely regarded as a promoter of genius, evil or otherwise. In fact HBO, reasonably enough when you considered their past investment, began to apply a little pressure of their own – on all parties. In June they made it clear that they saw a Lewis defence of his WBC title against Michael Grant, who is widely considered the best of a new generation of heavyweights, as a viable alternative to the re-match and at the same time gave another tweak to the pride of Holyfield.

DiBella, who hinted that the Grant fight had already moved off the list of mere possibilities for a future date beyond a re-match, said, 'In any build-up to a Grant fight we would be calling Lennox the undisputed heavyweight champion of the world. No disrespect to Evander, but there really isn't any doubt about who won the first fight. Lennox Lewis is the best heavyweight in the world – and that is beyond doubt. All the ratings organisations like IBF, WBA and WBC are in dispute and cannot say who is top dog. But the world knows it because Lennox beat Evander fair and square. He is top of all the rankings in all the latest magazines at a time when there is a Grand Jury sitting on the IBF and there's a Federal investigation into the ratings organisations and their relationships with the promoters. Lennox will enter the ring announced as the heavyweight champion of the world. There may be no initials after his name to indicate that, but everyone watching around the world will be left in no doubt that he deserves the accolade.'

At the very least this was another nudge by HBO in the direction of a fight scene stripped of the tyranny of alphabet soup boxing politics. It was also a clear word that it was time for King and Eliades to thrash out a deal if there was going to be a re-match. Lewis flew to New York with his trainer Steward and his manager Frank Maloney to take a look at Grant, who was fighting Lou Savarese in Madison Square Garden. It was a wretched fight, Grant winning on points and Steward leaving after three rounds, telling his fighter, 'I don't think we need to lose any sleep over Michael Grant.' Later in the year, Grant would win a little more respect for the way he got up to beat Andrew Golota in Atlantic City despite suffering two early knock-downs. But Grant, the Savarese fight announced, had still a lot of work to do if he was to project himself as a serious alternative to Holyfield and a re-match guaranteed the momentum of media fuel stored up in the spring.

By now, Holyfield had produced a large, fresh deposit. His attitude had changed sharply since that desperate night in the Garden. He now accused Lewis of milking the opinion of the mob, of 'behaving like a kid'. Said Holyfield, 'I've been seeing the video of the fight over the last few weeks and one thing I know is that I didn't lose. People who didn't know anything about boxing were affected by the biased TV commentators who were saying stuff like I never won a round. I was wrong to predict I would finish him in the third, but if he won how was it that he was going away from me all the time?

'How was it he never really hurt me? I won't give him back his belts. If he wants them he has to earn them. He was behaving like a kid who couldn't get his way. We'll do it again in the rematch and sort it out then. That's how boxers do it. Sure, everyone says he hit me more than I hit him. But he's six foot five and 246 pounds and he was hitting a 215-pound fighter, but his punches weren't effective. He kept moving away from me all the time. He kept jabbing and moving away. If he wants to be the champion, he's got to move out of the comfort zone, he's got to risk getting knocked out to have the chance of knocking me out. I've looked at it and, no, it wasn't an interesting or exciting fight. I wasn't moving properly because of cramps in my leg and so I was too slow moving inside, and even when I did my hook was falling short because he was moving away. I got some lumps and bumps but if I didn't get them I would have lost. But I took a chance and got the draw. He didn't take a chance and he got a draw too.

'Next time I hope we both try to knock each other out. That way the judges won't have to make a decision. I didn't do my job properly last time. If I had, the judges wouldn't have had to make a decision then, either. It's a shame that the fight has created such a lot of controversy. I blame the commentators and the media; people who do not know much about boxing have been listening to them and being influenced by them. The trouble with boxing is that there are so many people involved in the sport – not the boxers themselves but writers and others – who always seem to be criticising it and tearing it down and giving it a bad name. Sure, Mike Tyson should not have bitten my ear in 1997 but it was the first time he had done such a thing – and he got punished for it. But that was one guy – what Mike Tyson does doesn't make the whole sport rotten, as people are trying to say.

'I love the sport and it got me out of the ghetto, for a start. And it's given me money and fame and everything else. Yet I love the boxing itself; the months of training and talking about it, though for years I was scared of the actual fighting itself. Now through prayer, and God's help, I've overcome that fear and even love the boxing. I've always said I'll retire as undisputed champion of the world, and I will.'

There, it was back again in Holyfield, the old rage to fight, the old need for another challenge, another shot at redemption. Holyfield may have been in denial, he may have hated to see the evidence of the film that indeed he had slipped back to a point where his form against Bowe, even that against Tyson two years earlier, was beyond recovery but in his case it seemed still true that to be seeing was not necessarily to be believing. If your philandering can qualify you as at least an apprentice Casanova, while concurrently declaiming the gospel to a point of ecstasy, there is a good chance that fantasy and reality will merge at some point. From a distance, Holyfield's Atlanta Declaration seemed to be the moment. But the critics had scoffed no less forcibly when he returned after his epic first fight with Bowe to say that he would turn things around. Against Tyson, he was received as a dangerously exposed shell of a man. But he fought masterfully at the limits of his last possibilities. Could he do it again against Lewis in the fall? No, of course he couldn't. You wrote that with absolute conviction. And then thought about all the times Evander Holyfield had marched through stronger logic than your own.

About one thing you could be sure beyond a doubt. Holyfield had already launched some powerful themes for the re-match, ones that the American media, for all their *mea culpas* in Madison Square Garden, would sooner or later run with strongly enough. Holyfield, in a sliver of time when set in the context of a fight build-up, would have back his status as the fighter who broke all the rules of probability. No matter that Lewis, in the classic phrase of Sri Sen, had 'boxed his ears off', or that Holyfield finished that night in a pitiful condition both mentally and physically, his sheer presence would blur the outline of the night he was over-whelmed.

Something else, you could be certain, would happen. Lewis would also suffer something of a role reversal. The strengths he exhibited in the Garden, control, a tightly defined and pretty much flawlessly executed fight plan, and an absolute refusal to put at risk all his advantages, would be transferred into weaknesses. Lewis's position of moral superiority would erode, we could be sure.

It left just one final question. Would there be a re-match? Would King stay afloat in his leaky sampan long enough to confirm the deal that he trumpeted at the end of May? Would he move and shake his way past the discouragements of Eliades and HBO and the pinpricks of the FBI? We might as fruitfully have queried the likelihood of the sun rising over the Nevadan desert. Or the casino money cage retaining a profit.

Five weeks after Panos Eliades professed ignorance of King's deal with the Las Vegas Hilton, it had come to pass. There would, it is true, be certain modifications to King's ideal scenario, but like Lewis, in his way, he had got there in the end. He had fought doggedly for the right to promote the fight even as the IBF was hit by the 52-page indictment alleging corrupt practices, including the selling of rankings, and rumours each day grew stronger that he would be dragged into the mess. He argued fiercely for his belief in the sanctity of 'due process', yelled down every available airwave that it was a fundamental part of the American way that a man was innocent until proven guilty. He lashed out against his arch-critic Arum, a man who, said King, thought he could 'hunt with the hounds and run with the hares'. He made sport with Eliades's passing difficulties with Scotland Yard. When HBO's Abraham was asked about the Eliades situation, his arrest and charge of 'defrauding' the government, he said, 'It has no effect on the re-match. Nevada Main Events is Lewis's promoter of record for this fight. This situation has nothing to do with boxing, but it is ironic, isn't it?'

King was gleefully on the offensive now, saying, 'I take no pleasure in another man's misfortunes but ain't that a bitch? This guy was always talking about how there would be no fight because I was going to get indicted and how everyone in boxing was crooked but him. He created problems for this promotion that didn't exist. They wanted me at risk of getting thrown out of the promotion if the government indicted me. Now what are they gonna do about Panos? A man is entitled to be considered innocent until proven guilty and I would fight for that right, so I hope they don't do anything. But that didn't apply to Don King.'

In the end, and inevitably, there was compromise. Nothing brings peace in boxing so swiftly as the certainty of profit. The second fight might not go so well as the first, but it would sell all right. The fight would go on, on 13 November in Las Vegas under the aegis of a consortium of casino hotels, the Hilton, Caesar's Palace and the latest extravaganza, the Mandalay Bay, as King said it would – and Lou DiBella had quietly predicted when negotiations had reached their least promising point. 'The more you think about it, the more you conclude it has to happen,' DiBella had said. 'There always has to be a reason for a big fight, and there is a big reason for this one. There is controversy that it is still alive and there is a need for an undisputed heavyweight championship of the world to be declared officially and without any question marks.'

King and Eliades would make another uneasy alliance, and there would be niggles and sparring all the way to the first bell, but an issue did have to be resolved and HBO were happy to sell to the public the right to see it happening in the Thomas and Mack Centre in Las Vegas.

King's necessary concession was that he would cover Holyfield's 50 per cent, $15 million share of the purse. He would have preferred to have avoided such risk, but he knew it was nominal. He knew he had something real to sell and he would do it with his usual vigour. He considered the risk eminently worth taking. His name would again be in lights; he would be flying again, as he insisted he would in New York, not in the company of the wild goose but with his old companion, the one made of gold.

12

The Honest Nave

Three weeks before the re-match I discovered, with both shock and revulsion, that there would be an empty seat at ringside at the Thomas and Mack Center. No, that's not quite right. It wouldn't be empty. It would be improperly occupied.

The seat would go to Ms Amy Ayoub, a political worker who had helped in the election campaign of Nevada Governor Kenny Guinn. She was newly appointed to the Nevada State Athletic Commission and would join the chairman of the commission, Dr Elias Ghanem, a general practitioner, and fellow members Luther Mack, a hamburger franchise multi-millionaire, and Glen Carano and Lorenzo Feritta, big men in the casino industry, among the movie stars and the high-rollers seated close to the ring.

Royce Feour, the boxing writer of the *Las Vegas Review Journal* who covers his beat so exhaustively Bob Arum once referred out-of-town reporters to his column as the most reliable smoke signal west of the Mississippi, said that Ayoub's appointment was a surprise. She had no boxing background that he knew of. He had 'occasionally' seen her at the fights. But her arrival meant there would be no place at ringside for Jim Nave, a 55-year-old veterinary surgeon who runs the animal hospital out on Tropicana Boulevard. Nave had been fired as a commissioner by the Governor. In a brief phone call, Nave was told that he had done a great job but that it was over now. He would be out of office two weeks before the re-match.

One of his last duties as a commissioner was to talk to Pat English, a lawyer for Lewis's American promoters Main Events. Nave told English that his man would get a fair deal in Las Vegas, and the lawyer was immediately reassured. Lewis's camp would waive their right to demand that there would be no more than one American judge and they would accept three local nominees. There are few things you can take for granted in boxing but Nave's word is one of them. So why was he fired?

It's a long story but it needs telling, especially in the context of Lennox Lewis's gruelling battle to prove that a decent man, fighting rather than playing politics or titillating his audience with gratuitous badness, might just finish up winning the game's greatest prize, and it can be summarised neatly enough. Jim Nave is the man who said no to Mike Tyson.

Nave's dismissal provoked disbelief – and a flood of tributes. They came in from everywhere, from the street and the local gyms, from politicians in Washington and at home in Nevada, and from major fight figures. Everybody said the same. Jim Nave really cared about boxing, he was a genuine fan and he had always fought for its good name. A typical testament to Nave's impact on boxing was delivered by John McCain, US Senator for Arizona, a Republican presidential candidate and a powerful campaigner for government-enforced regulation of the sport. Said Senator McCain, 'All boxing fans across America can be grateful for Jim Nave's distinguished service. He was dedicated to making boxing a better, more honourable sport on behalf of both the boxers and the fans. Dr Nave's personal efforts were vital to the US Senate passing several reform measures.'

We can pick up the story of Jim Nave, an extremely private man, one day late in November 1997. After several days of entreaties, he had finally agreed to see me and my colleague, New York photographer Michael Brennan. It was a time when the drumbeats were sounding again for a return to the Vegas ring by Mike Tyson. Out-of-town drug-pushers and hookers had marked down a date late in January, 1998. Meanwhile, business was as usual at the Tropicana animal hospital. A team of vets treated a stream of domestic pets. A young girl sat in the waiting-room nursing her cat. On the wall a beseeching note offered a reward for the lost 'Lollipop' – a two-year-old Lhasa Apso. It was a scene you might have encountered anywhere in America, in a sleepy Midwest town or a suburb of one of the great cities.

Certainly it could have been a thousand miles or more from the glitter of The Strip rather than a ten-minute taxi ride and perhaps this was one of the keys to why Jim Nave, a poor farm boy from Missouri who served in Vietnam before setting up shop across the street from Ricardo's Mexican restaurant, had become only the second man to stand up to Tyson outside the boxing ring.

The first was Teddy Atlas, the trainer who made that brave but futile stand against the early rampaging of Tyson. Nave became the second when, after being taken from his hospital bed, where he lay seriously ill, he was the only Nevada State Athletic Commissioner to vote against the return of Tyson's boxing licence. Nave said he did it after days of 'rassling' with his conscience. Now he was talking for the first time about what some were saying was one of the bravest acts in the history of fight administration. Nave said he did not expect to be sacked as a commissioner for his defiance of the majority view that Tyson should be allowed back into the ring 18 months after cannibalising the ears of Evander Holyfield. Indeed, he was still proud of a commission which he insisted acted in the best interests of boxing.

'I do not doubt the motives of my fellow commissioners,' said Nave. 'Those who say this was an economic decision overestimate the impact of one fight on this city – even a Mike Tyson fight. I would not have spent ten years of my life working with people capable of making such a decision simply for reasons of money, for one night's profits. People sneer at Las Vegas all the time. I'm used to it. It just rolls off me. The casinos are one thing, yet there is another side to this city. But the point is I had my own position on Tyson. I turned him down on three points which I thought were too important to ignore. He didn't speak to me after the hearing, but there was a good reason for that. I went straight back to hospital. I was quite seriously sick. I don't know how he'll treat me when I next see him. You know, it is something that hasn't even crossed my mind. My job is to administer boxing – not socialise with boxers. I admire almost all of them. I admire their courage and their character. But in my position you have to be a little detached.

'I got disconnected from those tubes and left the hospital for the hearing [he had two operations just a few days before the final session] because I did feel there was an important job to do – for boxing and for the state which had appointed me to the commission. All the commissioners came to that hearing with different instincts but I believe everyone had an open mind. There wasn't any other agenda but whether Tyson was mentally fit to return to the ring.'

Here lay the great irony of Nave's exposed position as the one man who ultimately challenged the idea that because Tyson was such a raucous, and economically valuable, part of Las Vegas's image of danger and controversy and general wildness, his re-licensing as a fighter was really a formality. Nave had been

appalled by the quality of psychological evidence produced by
Tyson's lawyers at the original hearing in September and was
visibly exasperated when one witness said that the root of the
problem was that the fighter was a victim of society with a deep
need to be touched and to be loved. The psychiatrist said that the
problem had been addressed and he felt quite confident in
pronouncing Tyson sound for a return to the ring. At this point,
Nave leaned forward and asked how much time the doctor had
spent in Tyson's company. The psychiatrist looked as if he had
been hit by a well-thrown left hook. 'Several hours,' he spluttered.
Nave immediately moved that the hearing be suspended and that
Tyson be sent to a leading psychiatric institution for an
independent evaluation.

The new report, compiled by a team in Boston, suggested that
Tyson was probably fit to fight again, but qualified that verdict
with a list of his psychological problems. It was certainly not the
profile of a man with whom you would choose to share a
hazardous mission – or casually look at in the wrong way. But it
was good enough for Dr Ghanem, the chairman. When the votes
were called he said, 'Aye.' So did the burger man, Luther Mack. So
did the casino guys Feritta and Carano. Nave said nay.

He told me, 'The main reason I said no to Tyson was that I
couldn't get one question out of my head. Why had all his
counselling and pyschiatric help come so late? What had been
happening for the 15 months since the Holyfield incident? Of
course that cast doubt in my mind about Tyson's remorse. Did he
not think he had a problem? That was my second concern. There
was also the question of premeditation in the act of biting
Holyfield's ears. Was he truly sorry for what happened? Then
there was the business in Maryland.'

As we spoke the Maryland matter was still unresolved. Tyson
had admitted he lost control when he was involved in a three-car
collision in the Washington suburbs. He told the commission that

he had been preoccupied by the idea of buying a Harley-Davidson motor bike. He had been angered by the incident, conceded that he had used obscenities. But he denied he had kicked and punched two middle-aged men. His lawyers were still working on the matter and they assured the commission that the matter would be cleared up soon enough after a little negotiation. Nave's concerns were not appeased by the arguments of Tyson's lawyer – nor two character witnesses who came from the top drawer of celebrity. Muhammad Ali came to the hearing and had a statement read on Tyson's behalf. Marvin 'Magic' Johnson, the demi-god basketball player, said that he hoped to promote the fighter. Both Ali and Johnson spoke of the power of redemption and Tyson's determination to build a new life and a new career.

Nave remained underwhelmed. 'However impressed you are with individual witnesses – and of course I have the highest respect for such men – you have to look at the relevance of their evidence to your decision. I was far from sure that Magic Johnson would emerge as Tyson's promoter – and that has proved to be the case. I was also unmoved by the appeals of Tyson's lawyers for a quick decision. They said how important such a decision was for his finances but I thought, "Why are you saying this now when you wasted three months by applying to the New Jersey Commission?"'

That move imploded when Tyson, needled by questioning, erupted into a show of anger and the uttering of an obscenity. It was a brief lapse but this was a fighter who in the full view of the world had torn at the ears of an opponent with his teeth and was now asking for the right to perform again in public something that had driven him to the point of madness. His task was to show true contrition and a resolve that such savagery would never happen again. The fragile image of a penitent shattered in a hundred pieces and the Tyson camp folded their tents and headed for Nevada. They had done rather better along Las Vegas

Boulevard, despite the intransigence of Jim Nave. Before the original hearing opened, Tyson and his manager Shelly Finkel appeared at a boxing reception attended by commission members in a banqueting suite at Caesar's Palace. Tyson was amiability itself. He posed for pictures with chairman Ghanem and his wife and other officials. Jim Nave, as was his custom, kept his distance.

'It came down to a basic question for me,' Nave told me. 'Is this right? Can I agree to the return of his licence without serious doubts. I decided I couldn't. I have to say it wasn't the hardest question of my life. Indeed, I've worried more about the reinstatement of some four-round fighter no one has heard of. In those situations you worry because this is someone who is desperate to fight but you know you might have his life in your hands. Thank God, I've never had to pay that price. I agonised over the reinstatement of Evander Holyfield when it was reported that he had a heart condition. We sent Holyfield to the Mayo clinic. All the time you thought, "If we let this great fighter back in the ring are we putting him at risk?" I hold no bad feelings towards Mike Tyson. In fact I like him in many ways and now I pray he will grow after these experiences and find real peace in his life. I know what it is to grow up in a poor place. I know what it's like down there and I suppose that's one reason I've loved boxing since I was a little bitty-boy back in Missouri.

'Boxing gets a lot of bad publicity but look at the opportunity it presents to poor folks to improve their lot in life. Look at all the great people it has produced. Look at a champion like Muhammad Ali or somebody like Oscar De La Hoya, who is promising such excitement. You can worry a lot about boxing but in the end you have to say it is a very basic part of life. It's such a big step up from the streets. It demands courage and character and this is why I've always thought it was worth the devotion of a lot of my time. No, I didn't think of resigning after my fellow commissioners voted to let Tyson back. I didn't agree with it but we all had the chance to examine the question and reach our own decisions. I think, or at least I hope, Tyson knows now that he cannot step over certain limits again. If he does, well, it's over. He has been punished quite severely for his mistake. He has been out of boxing for 18 months at a vital time in his earning capacity, he was fined $3 million and new legislation means that we can fine a fighter much more in the future. I like to think the whole episode has taught boxing a lot about what it has to do to protect its image.'

He rolled his eyes when he thought back to the night when Tyson went mad before the eyes of the world, biting Holyfield's ear and spitting a piece of it away, and then, when referee Mills Lane finally disqualified him, charging around the ring, scattering officials and security men and police like some enraged bull spreading havoc along Estefata street in Pamplona at the time of the fiesta. The crowd howled and booed him out of the MGM arena and, demented, he cried that he was fighting for the rights of his children and, really, what was the difference between biting an ear or, as he charged Holyfield, slamming your head into the face of your opponent. It was the time when the fragile conventions of boxing were consumed by the imperatives of the street.

'I didn't feel so much shock and disgust as absolute, total sadness,' said Nave. 'Here was potentially the greatest of boxing nights – a great, historic fight was unfolding before our eyes. It was so great for this sport and this city which I love. And then it happened and I don't think I've ever felt so sad about an opportunity lost. Now that my colleagues have voted to give him another chance I will be at his fight in January – and I will go there with an open mind.'

It was extraordinary that on the weekend of the leaking of the news of Nave's sacking Tyson had for the second time in ten months just extravagantly confirmed the wisdom of the fallen commissioner's stand. In his January fight against South Africa's Francois Botha, Tyson had come close to triggering another riot when he ignored the bell signalling the end of the first round. He also admitted that he had attempted to break Botha's arm. It was a travesty of a comeback redeemed only by the latest evidence that the last asset of a fighter is the power of his punch. He produced a devastating right hand in the fifth to demolish the South African, who had been made cocky and careless by the ease with which he had carried the first four rounds.

Now, after his second comeback fight – which came after he had served another prison sentence in Maryland for the crime which his lawyers had assured the Nevada commission was the most trivial of hiccups – against the mediocre Orlin Norris, Tyson had crossed into anarchy yet again. The fight was declared no-contest after he had knocked Norris down with a short left hook after the bell for the end of the first round. Norris complained that he injured his right knee when he fell to the canvas. Some charged Norris with the sharp practice of taking his money – $800,000 against Tyson's $10 million – and running. Whatever the truth of that allegation – and the commission doctor Flip Homansky announced that a scan showed that he had indeed aggravated an old gridiron injury – the fact was that Tyson had behaved not like Caesar's wife but again as some abandoned creature of the night.

Nave flew straight from the fight to a veterinary conference in Washington DC – he is the president-elect of the American Association of Veterinarians – from where he confirmed to me that he had been dismissed by the Governor. He had a week left to serve, and he added, 'Yes, I saw the fight before flying here and I formed a few opinions, which I will put to my colleagues if I get the chance before I leave. The Governor has told me I'm finished on the commission after next weekend. All I can say now is that I don't regret a second of my time on the commission. I have always loved boxing – and I know I always will.'

Nave agreed to join me for breakfast a few days before the re-match. He was far from down and there was a deliciously ironic part-explanation for this. A few days earlier – and just a week or so after the announcement of his dismissal from the Nevada commission – the federal judge in New Jersey who was probing the International Boxing Federation had called to ask if he would be prepared, if necessary, to take over the running of the indicted organisation. Nave told the judge that he might consider the invitation – 'if I could do it my way'.

So Nave, the man whom some in boxing thought was too honest for his own good, had been pulled back into what seemed to many the death writhings of the sport he loved. He told me, 'I made it clear I would only tackle the job if I had real power to make decisions. It had to be my way.' His way is not that of so many men who profit so hugely from the sport. It is the way of a devotee, a purist who fills a room of his house with videos of all the fights that have touched him so deeply. It is the way of a farm boy from Missouri who helped his mother bring up three other children after their father was murdered. 'He was shot, coldly, in the chest five times and after that life was quite hard,' Nave said over breakfast. He worked on the farm, paid his way through college, qualified as a vet and then volunteered for service in Vietnam. Before leaving for that unpopular war – 'I thought my country needed me' – he was stationed in New Jersey and spent all his leave walking around New York City. For a country boy it was the most wondrous of places to see. He had barely the funds to ride the subway but he didn't really need money. He could walk and he could look and on one occasion he went into the restaurant of the great Jack Dempsey and shook hands with him.

'Boxing has always been my inspiration and I want the best for it, as much now as ever. People ask me if I'm bitter but I ask them, "Why should I be?" I had 12 great years doing something I loved and my feeling for the sport was never conditioned by the

214

privileges it gave me. Sometimes I think of boxing as an alcoholic. It has to go right down before it can heal itself. It has to kiss the concrete and it is pretty close now. There have been so many blows, so many scandals. I don't say "I told you so" when I discuss the Tyson affair. I just did what I thought was right at the time. If it hadn't been proved that he assaulted those motorists, if he didn't go to prison, if he didn't behave the way he did in the Botha and Norris fights, I would still believe I made the right decision. When you are dealing with a situation like that you have just one option. You do the best you can with the facts you have.'

Nave was in New York for Lewis–Holyfield I. He took his daughter to Madison Square Garden and they sat some way from the action. When, at the finish, his daughter said, 'Lewis won that easily,' he trained his opera glasses on the ring and then, after a moment or two, shook his head. 'No,' he said. 'I think there is a problem.' He saw José Sulaiman, chief of the WBC, with his head in his hands. Nave turned to his daughter and said, 'I think they're going to call it a draw.'

He was reluctant to discuss his part in the negotiations which had brought the re-match to Las Vegas, but he did say, 'I can't remember when boxing was ever in bigger need of great fights and undisputed champions, men who are looked up to right across their sport and in the wider world. We really need those great fights. We need for people to be reminded of how great boxing can be. We can't keep having one scandal after another. I read this morning that this fight might not make a million pay-per-view sales. If this is so, it is the most serious warning. We are definitely in a crisis if the best fight out there cannot make a million sales. There is a hard core of fight fans out there but they are no longer captive. They have options. Maybe a guy has three choices: he can buy the fight for $49; he can watch a nice movie; or he can really please his wife by taking her out to dinner. With the kind of fights we have been seeing recently, it's getting harder to convince the fight fan that he should make the first choice. I find this tragic.' Tragic, certainly, for a man who has never found a better metaphor for the challenge of life than the demand of the square ring.

Nave has watched one of his fight films at least a hundred times. It is the one of Marvin Hagler and Tommy Hearns, the one which for those of us who happened by the grace of God to be there to see it on a warm desert night can never be forgotten. Nave wasn't a commissioner when he took his seat in the outdoor stadium at the back of Caesar's Palace. He was what he has always been, a boxing fan, pure and simple and open to all the emotions that come with the condition.

He knew that night he would always be a boxing fan, however relentless the sport's slide into sleazy rankings and kickbacks, because he knew there would always be the seeds of redemption. They would always be there in the spirit of a Hagler or a Hearns.

As the breakfast waitress served another cup of coffee, Nave was there 14 years back as Hearns and Hagler tore at the night and made thunder. He said, 'As long as I live I will remember the moment Hearns hit Hagler with a perfect shot. It was everything Hearns wanted it to be. It hit Hagler flush in the face as he was coming in. Hagler stopped, momentarily, and then he kept on coming. What a lesson in life, in determination, in taking a shot that went into your bones and questioned every ounce of your resolve. The fight didn't last a full three rounds but it was extraordinary. It was the greatest fighting I have ever seen and when it was over I just sat in my seat for so long thinking about all of it, all the brilliance of Hearns and all the resolution of Hagler. They were cleaning up the arena when I walked out.' Nave said that the memory of that fight, and other great ones, was his covenant with a sport that was in danger of dying of greed and chicanery and an abandonment of the rules of genuine competition.

'Boxing,' he said, 'has given me so much in life I would always be ready to serve it. I was stunned when I was invited on to the commission and of course I will miss that involvement, but you know some former commissioners never come near a fight now. I don't understand that. Who are they hurting but themselves?' He suggested that everything depended on what you brought to a sport. He agreed that boxing faced tough odds. But why would he want to surrender to them? If he was ever tempted he would just think of Marvin Hagler.

When Jim Nave returned to his animal hospital out on Tropicana, I took a little sun at the artificial beach of the Mandalay Bay. On the way I collided with another boxing man, Mickey Duff, the doyen of the British fight scene, the handler of 20 world champions, a fighter in his youth and with the profile to prove it, a manager, a promoter, a gambler, a boy refugee from the pogroms of his native Poland. A very different boxing man from Jim Nave, no doubt; more worldy, more cynical, but not without an ideal or two. Duff gave me a copy of his recently published autobiography, *Twenty and Out*, and as he went off into the lobby of the big casino happy in the knowledge that he would inevitably collide with some old friend or foe and they would go off to the coffee shop and talk about the old days, and no doubt the coming fight, I flicked through the pages of his life's story.

I found a page which contained the intriguing question, 'How would I like to be remembered by boxing people?' Duff wrote, 'I would like to be remembered as a man who knew his business, as a tough but fair negotiator, as someone who always acted in what he thought were the best interests of his boxers as a good manager and matchmaker. I don't expect to be remembered as a man who only made life-and-death matches. Hopefully, I will be remembered as a man who made matches in the best interests of the boxers I was representing, but at all times with regard for the public who were paying money to watch. And I hope, more often than not, that I succeeded.'

What was it about this sport, you had to wonder, that could so enslave the imaginations of a rabbi's grandson from Poland and a farm boy from Missouri, men from utterly different worlds but who shared the common ground of fascination with a violent and so often unprincipled sport and who met in such a clear understanding of what was required for its survival?

And what was that elixir? Something very basic, as it happened. A sense of value from the product, of respect for the consumer and a grasp of how reckless boxing had been in its toleration of the cheap and the opportunistic. No, you couldn't take the sleaze out of boxing, no more than you could yeast from bread or grape from the wine. You couldn't divert all the morbid but lucrative interest in Tyson's capacity for public self-immolation and channel it all to worthier figures like Lennox Lewis and Evander Holyfield. You couldn't keep Don King's fingers out of the cookie jar. But you could hold the line at a certain point. You could say that there were lines that could not be crossed, as Jim Nave did in his brave and lonely fashion, and you could hope not to be fired for saying so.

The Nave business was shocking, as was that of the scoring at Madison Square Garden. Generally speaking, Seth Abraham's first instinct was probably right. The Garden had been sold out and pay-per-view sales had rocketed because of the hunger to see not who was the most anarchic heavyweight in the world, who had the most riveting hype, but who was the best? Lennox Lewis had to the satisfaction of almost all but the ringside judges answered that question, so now some of the drama of the first fight was inevitably missing. Still, Lennox Lewis had an understandably enduring desire to be officially declared the undisputed heavyweight champion of the world.

That kind of unanswerable vindication had already come to the man who had given his word that Lennox Lewis would get a fair deal. Less than a week after the Governor of Nevada told Jim Nave he was gone, Mike Tyson was advised that his next fight would not be welcome in Las Vegas.

218

One Last Step

If you were a believer in Lennox Lewis, if you came to Las Vegas convinced that justice this time had to be in his corner, you had an excuse to make a little noise. Reasonably, you could assume the bearing of a retainer of a long disinherited son who had been restored to his proper ranking. You could contemplate with some confidence a slice or two of the fatted calf.

Unfortunately some of the Lewis supporters who made it to the weigh-in, where their fighter announced his serious intent by coming in at 17st 4lb, four pounds lighter than in the Garden, belonged to that school of British sports travelling which hands out a pair of blinkers with every passport. This turns anywhere the bearer happens to be in the world temporarily into a backstreet of Millwall or Cardiff. At the Mandalay Bay, the Lewis fans made a horrible noise in the big ballroom, created a strange desire for decorum even among time-worn denizens of the raucous, fevered Strip and, most inexcusably, they booed Evander Holyfield.

It was not much of a shock to those of us who had so many times been obliged to witness the great piazzas of Europe disgorging English football fans with the help of paddy wagons and riot police. But it was, all the same, depressing and inappropriate and you had to question the point of officiously striving to re-activate the warrior instincts of a three-time world heavyweight champion who already had more to prove than at any time in his extraordinary career.

Certainly Holyfield's eyes narrowed perceptibly when the tide of disdain washed over him. Could he pull off the old trick one last time? Could he send home these beery Britishers stunned into silence by the sheer redemptive power of a fighter who refused to acknowledge boundaries of age and power? Could he re-make himself yet again? A surprising number of Americans believed he could. Wally Matthews, so appalled by the New York decision he had volunteered to present an unofficial world title trophy to Lewis at a Manhattan dinner thrown by the American boxing writers, was back in the Holyfield column. 'I didn't think Evander was quite right in the first fight, mentally or physically, and he is really up for this,' said Matthews at the weigh-in. 'He has done it so many times and I think he will do it again. I'm going for Evander – by a decison.' Ron Borges, who had written of the big yellow streak running down Lewis's back and didn't argue with the decision at Madison Square Garden, naturally agreed. So did Bert Randolph Sugar, the flamboyant editor-in-chief of the magazine *Fight Game* and former boss of the boxing bible *The Ring*. 'Evander had a bad night in the Garden,' said Sugar. 'But he doesn't ever have two in a row. Lennox has a lot of talent, but Holyfield is just more of a fighter.'

Holyfield had changed the pattern of his preparation. He worked in the evening now, so that his body would not be expecting rest rather than fighting when he walked into the ring at the Thomas and Mack Center around 8 p.m. local time. I went

220

straight from the airport to the Las Vegas Hilton to watch his Monday night work-out. It was at a different time but the same routine. Same religious muzak, same crooning, swooning Holyfield, and his preparation for a brief work-out in the hot room seemed to a weary traveller to be impinging upon eternity. Paul Hayward of the *Daily Telegraph* was quoted in the *Revue Journal* for his dry aside, 'Evander Holyfield is the undisputed champion of stretching excercises.' But after Holyfield worked on the pads, a little languidly it seemed to me, a crushing verdict came in from Floyd Mayweather Senior, a respected American trainer. 'The game's over for Evander,' said Mayweather as he walked out of the room. 'He's old, he's tired, he's finished.'

Of course Holyfield dismissed such a bleak theory. He had had time to re-charge himself, to go back to the basics of his game – speed, movement, aggression and, no, there would be no reckless naming of a round this time. 'I have a tough fight, no doubt,' he said. 'Maybe I didn't give him enough respect in New York, maybe I took too many things for granted. And he was good. He worked his jab very well and he gave me a lot of problems there. But if he was good, I was bad – and, man, you better believe I'm going to be a whole lot better here.'

There were just two points of genuine intrigue for the re-match of a fight Lewis had dominated in every important area except finishing aggression and Holyfield had touched on one of them. How much could he improve from New York, what could he do now that he didn't do back then? 'Maybe nothing, but I can do it so much better,' said Holyfield. 'I can have more belief, more determination and I know I will feel better. I felt bad in Madison Square Garden.'

But more important than anything, it seemed to me, was the unresolved question about Lewis's willingness to cast aside his respect for Holyfield as a classic guerrilla fighter, a man who could hit you square between the eyes just when you thought the battle

221

was over. Like many others, I believed the result of the fight was a formality and that a bigger question had emerged. Yes, Lewis would win, barring some atrocious act of God or official incompetence, and claim his rights but with what style, with what authority?

The case for the prosecution was certainly put well by Richard Hoffer of *Sports Illustrated*, who wrote, 'Like Holyfield, Lewis can be childishly competitive. Holyfield's camp remembers going bowling with him and not being allowed to return until Holyfield won. Similarly, Lewis's friends are never stunned when, in the midst of losing a chess match, he rises and accidentally upsets the board. For all his qualities, however, there is not in Lewis the usual heavyweight recklessness. There isn't that certain kind of foolhardiness that, with big men in a small space, sometimes causes spectacle. There isn't that wild and senseless conflagration of spirit that generates history or, at the very least, a great fight. Lewis might never produce that. He may be too smart to produce that. He will win because he hates to lose. But he will not give anyone any more than is necessary to do just that. The rest he keeps to himself, selfish beyond regret, safe in his own skin.'

Safe in his own skin? It was a biting phrase but was it true? In his Poconos training camp before coming down to Vegas, Lewis engaged the question – at least to a degree. He was insulted by suggestions that he lacked courage. How could that be the problem? 'For me, for most fighters,' he told me, 'it is not a question of courage, that's just not part of it. You prove your courage every time you step into the ring. If you didn't have courage, you wouldn't go in the ring, full stop. Once you're in the ring you have decisions to make, and the most important one, I'll always believe, is to do with how you're going to win the fight. Knock-outs, how good you look, all that stuff, may be important for your profile with the public, it might affect you're next paycheque, but first you win. So how do you go about it?

What's the best way? I was very sure about what I was going to do in the Garden. And I did it. I wasn't going to go inside, at least not in the early stages, because that's what Riddick Bowe did the one time he lost to Holyfield. Evander wants you to go inside, he wants you to come to him, that's his game – hey, against someone like me or Bowe, with our build, our weapons, it's his only game.

'So there I was fighting for the undisputed heavyweight championship of the world, the thing for which I had suffered all those trials and tribulations, and was I going to give Holyfield any advantages, was I going to play his game? Why would I do that? My job wasn't to play hero, be a spectacular loser. It was to win. Just to win.

'People keep telling me I should have finished off Holyfield when I appeared to have him beaten in the fifth round. But they weren't in the ring. They didn't have all their life's hopes at stake, and they didn't know how completely in command I felt.

'Maybe in the second fight I will be less cautious, more assertive when I know I have hurt him, but basically I still believe I was right in the Garden. People hadn't studied Holyfield's past fights as closely as I had. Perhaps they didn't weigh properly what he had done in his last big fight, when Michael Moorer seemed on course to beat him a second time. Remember that? Moorer was confident that he had him, was piling on the pressure and taking chances and then Holyfield jumped off the ropes and put an end to him. You have to respect a fighter like Holyfield more than most. He is a warrior, a very cunning and ruthless one, and since the fight he has admitted to me that he was trying to draw me in and then deliver the sucker punch. Anyone who thinks he wasn't capable of that doesn't really understand boxing.

'I'm more confident now than I was before the first fight. I know now what he can do – and what he can't do – because I was in there with him, and I saw what I did to him, physically and mentally. At the end of the fight he knew he was beaten. Everybody knew who had won the fight, except the judges. I'm not so bitter now about those verdicts. I just put it down to being the victim of the lower echelon of judges – and even in boxing I don't really think that could happen a second time.'

Certainly not at this time, you had to believe. The decision in Madison Square had been manna for all those who believed that boxing had become rotten to the core. The call to Jim Nave from the federal judge was just one example of the widespread conviction that boxing had to be saved from itself. King was using the stage of the re-match to pour scorn on the reformers. He claimed that he had become the bogeyman for white America; he compared the harassment he claimed he had always received with the easy ride given his chief rival Arum. But you knew his arguments well enough. You also thought you knew the outcome of this fight, this hangover from an old dispute, this clearing up of business essentially done.

Despite a certain amount of 'revisionism' in some areas of the American media, the majority still favoured Lewis's chances; he was a clear favourite in the sports 'books' at the casinos and most of the speculation concerned the quality of the fight. Everyone agreed it would be better than the first one because Holyfield had to make it so. He had to go into the mouth of Lewis's cannons. If his challenge faded as it did in New York, his career was over and with it much of his self-respect. Each day Holyfield hammered at the point that for various reasons he had not been himself in the Garden. 'Man, I've looked at that film so many times and the guy fighting Lewis just isn't me. The real Evander Holyfield fights any circumstances he finds in front of him. The guy fighting Lewis in New York didn't do that.'

It was not the least of Lewis's irritations, this suggestion that he had morally beaten some imposter in New York, a Holyfield lookalike who had the same bald head but not the fighting heart.

As the fight came closer Lewis, by his own amiable standards, had become downright peevish. Two days before the fight his manager Maloney had a particularly careworn expression. 'Lennox is in a terrible mood,' he confided. Sky Television, who hold Lewis's broadcasting rights in Britain, had requested a late interview and the fighter had 'gone potty'. But it was understandable enough. Fighters get meaner the closer they come to the fight. It is in the natural order of things and Lewis's trainer Steward was not about to complain. He hated Lewis in his chess mode. He liked him edgy, mean. All trainers like to see their fighters that way. In Steward's situation this was particularly so at this time. He was looking for something more than Lewis had shown in New York. Yes, of course, said Steward, he won hands down. But he could do so much better. He could consume Holyfield. Perhaps this widely held sentiment was also gnawing at the big man.

By the eve of the fight Lewis was being accused of sending mixed messages, and it is true that under a barrage of questioning over the course of a few days he said different things at different times. The conflicting quotes on which he was now being impaled were, 'Maybe I was a bit cautious in the first fight – I will be less so this time' and 'I'm not going to try to knock him out in the first, second or third rounds. I'm going to build up to it.' So there was some doubt. Maybe he would charge Holyfield in the way that he had Ruddock and Golota. Or then maybe he would do it the way he had in New York, this time buttressed by the certainty that the judging of a big fight would never have been so carefully scrutinised. He was floating the two possibilities, no doubt, while Steward seemed obsessed with the belief that something extraordinary, and very violent, would happen in the opening rounds. 'Usually,' said Steward, 'I have a dream, a vision of a fight – I can see it very clearly, but not this time. I just have this strong feeling that there will be some kind of sensation, maybe something like Hagler and Hearns, something wild, off the graph.'

Safe in his own skin? Or wildly off the graph? Here was the theme of the re-match, and maybe another indicator of how profoundly Lewis had dominated the first fight. Holyfield was required to claim that he had fought the first fight by proxy and been grievously misrepresented, and Lewis to defend a performance which had been generally accepted as so superior to that of his oppenent that the verdict of a draw was considered to be one of the most outrageous in the history of the sport. So Lewis was at times a little tetchy. It shouldn't, when you thought about it, have been so amazing.

After working in a small oven of a room at the Mandalay Bay, Lewis was briefly softened by the speech of a Mexican girl, who declared, 'You have a lot of British fans here in town but I want you to know that a lot of people across the world already see you as the world champion. You behave well and with great dignity – you are a true champion.' Lewis almost shyly accepted the tribute, but when he stepped down from the ring and into a cluster of writers, who were sweating but grateful for a respite from one of Don King's more convoluted monologues on the checks and balances of the American constitution, his fighting face was back in place.

He said, 'People keep saying I didn't fight the real Evander in New York, but who really knows the real Evander now? I think I do. I was in the ring with him for 12 rounds and I think I know what he can do. More importantly, I know what he can't do. He can't match me in any area. I don't doubt his courage and I know he is cunning. I know Tyson was right, he uses his head very dangerously and I would be foolish to give him any chances. Evander says he's going to be better. Well, so am I – about 30 per cent better. I don't have to take chances. It is all in my hands. I can apply pressure on my own terms.' It was hard to argue with Lewis; much harder, certainly, than picking holes in Holyfield's assertion that he was a fighter re-made and that the proxy man of

226

the Garden had been banished. Holyfield said, 'Lennox Lewis had his chance and he missed it. Sometimes in life you only get one shot at something and if you miss it, well, it's gone forever. When that happens a man can suffer a lot of heartbreak and I'm afraid that's what Lennox is heading for now. He's gonna have a lot of time to regret he didn't take me when he had the chance. I know what I have to do now. I didn't understand that properly before the first fight.'

On other lips these words would have seemed impossibly glib but Holyfield had crossed that line in boxing which separates myth and reality, as Muhammad Ali had done when he fought Larry Holmes a little way down The Strip 19 years earlier. Some of us still believed in Ali even then when he had been forced to shed pounds not on the road and in the gym but with diuretics which turned him not into a fighting machine but a beautiful shell. It was silly to believe that it could be otherwise, and it was the most flagrant breach of Red Smith's rule on the importance of separating the dictates of your head and those of your heart. For seven rounds Holmes punished Ali for his folly, and it was hard to get that out of your mind when you came to make a final assessment of the prospects in Holyfield–Lewis II.

As always, you trawled the full range of opinion. You couldn't quite detach the knowledge that the conviction of Mickey Duff, one of the shrewdest readers of a fight the game has ever seen, was maybe reinforced by the fact that he was determined to win back his New York losses with another thumping bet on Lewis. But then nor could you ignore the fact that for most Americans even the evidence of their own eyes was not enough to budge from the belief that the idea of a foreign heavyweight champion was utterly implausible.

Always you delay the moment of commitment, the grim tryst with the laptop waiting amid the chaos of old newspapers, coffee cups and ashtrays. I had a coffee beside the Mandalay 'beach' and considered all the big fights I had seen and how this one was somehow different. There was a sadness to it that wasn't so easy to put into words. The sadness of Holyfield's diminished aura was one thing; the idea that so late in a career which had been marked by so many glories, so many points at which he could have walked away, rich beyond any boyhood dreams and into the pantheon of champions, he should be fighting now not so much for a realistic chance of returning to the mountain top but for a degree of redemption. I thought of all the great careers that had gone this way: of Roberto Duran, fat and penniless, fighting on, hopelessly, into his forties; of Sugar Ray Leonard, still fabulously rich by most men's standards, explaining on a snowy afternoon in New York City why he had to go, long after his prime, to face the pitiless fists of the much younger Terry Norris; and, above everything, the chill that came to the spirit when Ali sighed and submitted to dispatch by Holmes. I thought of how Lewis's career had been mired in so much frustration, and now he had to go into the ring and do something he had done before, with all the attendant risks, just to get that which in truth was already his and arguably should have been in his possession long before, when we were all quite a bit younger and Tyson, Bowe and Holyfield were at their most vibrant. It was not the way it should have been. I thought of all of this and then I went up to my room and picked Lewis to win in six.

I believed I saw in him an edge of conviction, a certain coldness, that had not been so apparent in New York. Also the phrase of Floyd Mayweather Senior jangled in my head. *The game is over*. That seemed to be the measure of it. Holyfield said he would be better, but why wouldn't he be worse? He had last looked good in the first Tyson fight three years earlier. That surely was the last sustained statement of a glorious fighting will. The consensus was that he would have prevailed in the second fight, even if Tyson hadn't gone to pieces, and indeed it was, went the theory, the latter's dawning sense that he was heading for a second defeat which provoked the outrage. But then what was Tyson now? Holyfield had beaten Moorer, certainly, but then so had George Foreman, and in rather similar fashion; one punch had unhinged the resolve of the younger man in both fights, in the one with Foreman in a disabling instant and in the other under a tide of punches which had been set flowing, as Lewis had constantly pointed out, when Moorer had been drawn into a Holyfield trap at the ropes. Against Vaughn Bean Holyfield seemed to be fighting from memory, a poor one, even though his home town of Atlanta had filled the big stadium as a tribute to his career rather than out of compulsion to see him dispense with a mediocrity few in the crowd had heard of before the fight was made.

Lewis, I argued, was required to do something more than beat again a man called Holyfield for the right to be called undisputed champion of the world. He had to destroy a myth. He had to avoid the motivational quicksand of making something bigger than it really was. He had to deal not in the fable of yesterday but the reality of today. He had to put away Holyfield and I said, against the advice of an observer as acute as Duff – he insisted it would be Lewis by a decison – he would do it in the sixth. Even after New York it was not so easy to say. It was difficult because Holyfield had enjoyed more revivals than anyone since George Gershwin and Irving Berlin. Also because Lewis was as stubborn as any man alive. He knew he had beaten Holyfield once, beaten him his way, and why should he change just because he had been set new targets of achievement by those who had never been in the ring with Holyfield? And all the time he hadn't lost sight of the fact that his mission, the one he had always been told was impossible, was simply to beat the best man around, within the rules of boxing and his own capacity to shut down all possibility of defeat.

Lewis, a 2–1 on favourite now, issued one last statement of intent before he grumpily entered that time of isolation and foreboding and reactions so hair-trigger a boxer's people know they often have to think more than twice before uttering the simplest sentence. It is an ambience of omens and emotional nitroglycerine. He told me, 'I will beat Evander Holyfield and then show myself to be the champion boxing needs right now. I'll be the one and only heavyweight champion and that's how it should be in all divisions. I love boxing and it has given me so much but anyone can see that it has big problems now. There are people out there who do need indicting. There are lots of them. By unifying the world title I will set the right pattern for boxing. It has always been by mission. Most of the trouble in boxing concerns ranking lists and how they shape the fights. There should be one champion at every weight, one standard. It is what the fans want.'

Even Don King, who might just have been one of Lennox Lewis's candidates for indictment, agreed that the fight game was at a pivotal phase of its tortuous history. He said, 'Boxing is the greatest of sports and in my heart I believe it will always survive. It is too strong to go under, because there will always be great champions around the corner, men who will excite the people, oh yes. But there is no doubt boxing needs a little redemption now. It needs a great fight and we are going to see one here.'

A great fight? Perhaps, perhaps not. But a fight to shape the rest of Lennox Lewis's life? There could be no doubt, certainly not in the minds of anyone heading for the Thomas and Mack Center on Saturday night, and least of all those whose job it was to tiptoe about their duties in the big suite of Lennox Lewis as he looked out over the desert and wondered if, truly, he had passed the point where anything more could go wrong.

A Kind of Justice

Lennox Lewis lost the toss of the coin to decide who would enter the ring last, and carry the aura of being *the man*, but he merely shrugged and said, 'It doesn't worry me. I'll be waiting for him to come into the ring and when he does, when the American crowd cheer for him, I'll just be thinking, "Enjoy this, Evander, because it's the last time you'll hear that kind of cheering. It is my time now."'

His confidence seemed unfeigned but who knew about the demons of the ring? That night in the restaurant just down the road from this arena Bruce Seldon was serenity itself. Then, 48 hours later, he dissolved in the minutes before Mike Tyson threw his first, inaccurate punch. But Seldon was stepping into the unknown. Lewis believed he knew what was before him. He knew he faced a good, brave fighter – but one on whom the curtain of age had surely fallen. Lewis looked solemn but relaxed in the ring. Holyfield bobbed his head and pounded his gloves together as the Four Tops, grey but still tuneful, sang the 'Stars

231

and Stripes'. There was still an edge to this fight, even if the atmosphere was different from Madison Square Garden, more workaday in its tension, less overlaid with a sense of history. The intrigue lay mainly, I believed, in the ability of Holyfield to make something of a fight of it. He had strong support in the arena. For every cry of Lewis's name from the British fans up in the cheap seats, there was a strong counter swell of 'Holyfield, Holyfield' from nearer the ring.

Andre Agassi, the local boy who used to valet park cars at the casinos, came to ringside holding hands with Steffi Graff. They looked as if they were going on a high school date; and as if the pain of Graff's injuries and her father's maverick life, and imprisonment, and Agassi's collisions with such American princesses of celebrity as Barbra Streisand and Brooke Shields had happened on another, more careworn planet. Elizabeth Murdoch, daughter of Rupert and head of Sky Television, managed to look both tough and glamorous in her leather trousers. Her father, surprisingly, was a little further away from the action, beyond the fenced off ringside section.

One of my immediate companions was a huge black man in a white suit who didn't have a ticket, a fact which security men half his size seemed disinclined to investigate. He was jammed into the right side of my workplace. A few places away was Tommy 'Hitman' Hearns, a friend of both fighters and still an electric presence among the fight fans, if not the rubberneckers crazed by the close real-life presence of so much fame and fortune. Richard Williams of *The Independent* was on my left. Williams and I had had a lively discussion at Madison Square Garden. No, that's not quite accurate. I ranted at him when he told me he had no serious quarrel with the judges' decison. I eventually apologised. This night, I swore to myself, I would keep off the soapbox.

The trouble with a soapbox is that there is always a danger of falling off it, a possibility I was reminded of when I came to score the first round. It was close but I gave it to Holyfield. In New York

232

Lewis had taken him in hand in the first round, jabbing him almost with disdain and launching crisply controlled right hands, but now even though Lewis awaited the first bell in the middle of the ring and started aggressively, it was Holyfield who was the first to get inside and score with a good combination. Holyfield harried Lewis into a corner and when Lewis responded with a big right hand it missed. He rectified the mistake with a good right to Holyfield's chin but there was no encouragement in the victim's reaction. He took the punch without a hint of a wobble and came boring in. Holyfield looked better than he did in New York. Disturbingly so.

There was an old, sickening feeling at the pit of my stomach. The one that sometimes announces, beyond any logical assessment of the facts, that something you want very much will always be elusive. Now the fear was that Lewis had lived too long with the assumption that if the re-match happened it was his right to win it. He had been assured that the judges, familiar names at the top of big fight scorecards – Jerry Roth, Chuck Giampa and Bill Graham – would dutifully note every scoring jab and right cross, every long right and hook and every uppercut; there would be plenty of uppercuts. But had the weight of Lewis's confidence somehow congealed? Had the moment come and gone and taken residence with all those other hopes and dreams good men are required to shed under the weight of discouraging fate? Was Lewis about to be ambushed in his own glowingly healthy skin?

Well, perhaps not. You might not have thought so from the bellowing to my right, but Lewis won the second round handily enough. Holyfield was still lively, still recognisably a Holyfield who hadn't looked into the future and seen only a skull, but Lewis repulsed him comfortably with a triple jab that brought a brief, reflective silence at my right shoulder. Holyfield landed a right to Lewis's ribs but was almost instantly punished as Lewis responded with a perfectly launched uppercut. It was a textbook punch, though, that should really have at least disturbed Holyfield's balance but there was no sign of disruption to his aggressive intent and the big man in the white suit believed he had seen a decisive moment. 'Woooooow,' he screamed. 'You took his best punch, Evander . . . it's going to be easy, champ.' Holyfield confirmed that he remained on course with a good jab and a right-left combination to the body. But as the fighters clinched and wrestled at the bell, there was no doubt that Lewis had produced a little more authority and scored the more freely.

He resumed the pattern at the start of the third, keeping Holyfield away with the jab and scoring with another well thrown uppercut. It was, for the first time, possible to believe we were back in the Garden. But not for so long. My big neighbour was suddenly on his feet as Holyfield, responding to restive noises in the crowd as Lewis dominated with his jab, delivered an overhand right to Lewis's head. It was a real punch and Lewis couldn't conceal the fact as he took a hard right hand shot to the body and was driven back into the ropes. Lewis, no doubt, was ruffled as the bell sounded. Holyfield was back in front on my card, which didn't mean that much in the context of a 12-round fight in which Lewis carried heavier weapons and a jab that was again in good working order, but it meant everything, you could be sure, to the way Evander Holyfield thought about himself and his prospects of redefining himself as a warrior. As always, he had a big structure of ambition and at its base was the desperate need to win back the self-respect lost in New York. Now it was evident to everyone, not just the big man in the white suit, that he was off first base. His dogs of war were running again.

The fourth was close but I shaded it for Lewis. The middle of the round was mostly passive, but around the clinches Holyfield was the busier and just before the bell he landed a right cross. But I noted the frequency of Lewis's jab and his uppercut, and I believed he had scored the more cleanly, and so I scored it with that in mind. But a bad feeling persisted, a sense that Holyfield was alive again in his aura and his myth.

The fifth was untidy but it started fiercely enough. Holyfield doubled up on the hook to the head and the body and as Lewis responded with a big right Holyfield was warned by referee Mitch Halpern for using his head. For some time a great tide of advice for Holyfield had been flowing from the right of me, and at this point I had suggested to its source that there had been little need to coach his man on the illegal employment of his head. I worried, instantly, about the rashness of inviting debate with such a large and ferociously partisan customer but I had no need to worry. He looked down benignly and said, 'You got that right, little brother.' Lewis was cut alongside his right eye and the Americans in the crowd, excited by a sniff of blood, began to chant 'USA! USA!' Lewis was provoked into heightened action and landed a big overhand right but the result was no more dramatic than some frantic grappling as Lewis fell on top of Holyfield and teetered at the point of falling out of the ring. I gave the round to Lewis but even with the presumption of the fairest of deals for him in Las Vegas I did it with no great confidence.

The sixth round was mostly quiet but even though the blood had stopped trickling from the cut beside Lewis's eye the spasmodic action was not so reassuring. His jab continued to work, but it wasn't nullifying Holyfield as it had at the Garden. After an exchange of short rights, Holyfield landed a left hook on Lewis's chin and followed it up with a good, solid uppercut. As Lewis clinched, he complained to the referee about Holyfield's head. Holyfield had the round – and the momentum.

The seventh was the best round of the fight. It was the action we had hoped for in New York. It was Holyfield doing what he had said he would all those times back in Miami and the House of Pain and in the gym down by the Bowery in New York. It was Holyfield dancing and punching in the mouth of the cannon. And it was also Lewis fulfilling some of his own promises. Jabbing with power. Unleashing hooks and big right hands. It was proper fighting and it had echoes of some of the best of the Holyfield–Bowe series, when Lewis was becalmed and frustrated and, in his pursuit of justice, making almost as many court appearances as an old lag.

The problem was that Holyfield won this round too. The first phase went overwhelmingly to Lewis. He was increasing the tempo, shoving Holyfield around. He landed an overhead right and a good solid shot to the body. After referee Halpern warned both fighters that they should remember the rules, Lewis connected with two left hooks and another uppercut. There was just time enough to wonder if, finally, this was the point of Lewis's breakthrough, the moment when he rose up to his full height and took hold of his destiny, before Holyfield hit him with a punch that threatened to change everything. Lewis went back on his heels with a look of deep concern crossing his face and Holyfield followed up, landing a big right-left combination which brought the crowd to its feet. Lewis was having to ransack his vulnerable skin for resistance now. He checked Holyfield with a short right hand but was hit by two more big punches. At this point salvation might have been Lewis's chief ambition but just before the bell sounded he got off a big pounding right which stopped Holyfield's charge. It would prove a vital punch. Holyfield may have initiated the most dramatic action of the fight, he may done more in three minutes than he did in 12 rounds in Madison Square Garden, but his walk back to the corner was not so much triumphant as reflective. He had made the fight close, he led on almost all unofficial scorecards but at the end of his brilliant offensive effort, Lewis was still capable of producing a punch that shook all his bones. It was a good battle to win but it wasn't, Lewis's punch said, the war.

The eighth round was almost too close to call. It was pale

compared to the furious tides of the seventh. Both men were taking stock of their resources. Towards the end of the round they exchanged uppercuts, but mostly they clinched and wrestled and then, right at the bell, they erupted with a flurry of punches. It was not hard to see the round going to Holyfield on the official cards. For Lewis, you feared, a full-scale nightmare might just be unfolding.

As the big man in the white suit – now joined by acolytes who had infiltrated ringside – chanted Holyfield's cause, you thought of all that Lewis had said about his hopes of crossing that final territory of ambition, of leaping through small windows of opportunity, of fighting through the 'vacant ground' of will and experience, and making it home to his promised land. You knew he had some tough ground to cover and he had to do it quickly. He had to quell Holyfield. Though some of the rounds had been close and though Lewis was again throwing more and landing more, though much less obviously so than in New York, I concluded nervously that it was entirely possible Holyfield was leading by five rounds to three with four rounds left.

It was thus a relief to score the ninth, tenth and eleventh in Lewis's favour. The action in the ninth was again spasmodic but it seemed to me that Lewis's punches were more telling and he was uppercutting almost at will. One such punch stunned Holyfield after he had stretched himself with a right and missed. Lewis was emboldened by this success and threatened to take over the fight, but this time it was Holyfield's turn to respond under pressure and he got through with a left hook just before the bell. But it had been a clear round for Lewis and he had the base to build some new momentum. He did, dominating a tenth round of slight action and much circling which was punctuated sparsely but significantly by Lewis's jab and a few hooks. In the eleventh you felt your own tension draining away, or perhaps moving over one place to the right, as Lewis brushed aside a Holyfield assault,

237

which had been fuelled by a new chorus of 'USA! USA!', and drove him back towards the ropes with a combination of four punches, all of which scored solidly.

It was not as Lewis, or Emanuel Steward, had wanted it. It was not an imperious final stride to the peak of boxing. It was an edgy, probing investigation of unexpected resistance from Holyfield. Surprisingly, it required as much fortitude as authority, especially in that seventh round when Holyfield was whipped along again by the force which so often had come to him at the most critical moments. But Lewis had come close to the shore now. He weathered the last blow of the Holyfield storm and all he had to do, as far as I was concerned, was keep hold of the fight and he would have, at last, all the belts and the all glory. The problem was he didn't win the last round. At least not on my card.

The crowd, so roused by the violence of the seventh round but almost silent at points when the action trailed away, yelled now and mostly for Holyfield. He was dredging resistance up from the well once more and if his attack was not devastating it was more visible than Lewis's and early in the round he caught Lewis with a good combination of left and right – as he was cautioned again by the referee for dangerous use of his head. Holyfield remained the busier through the round and when the bell sounded Lewis, ritualistically, raised his hands, but with less conviction than in the Garden. In New York, Holyfield had turned wearily towards his corner. Again he looked exhausted, but this time his face was less bleak. He made a small, tight smile which might have said that he gave himself a chance of gaining the verdict – or at least that this time he hadn't allowed himself to drift out of the fight, outreached, outgunned, outwilled.

You sat there at ringside, edgy and angst-filled once more. Big white suit, naturally, called it for Holyfield. Richard Williams found no argument, or tirade, this time when he said it was very close. Behind me, Tom Archdeacon held up his arms and said he thought it was Holyfield. I had it a draw but, if there is such a thing, perhaps a Larry O'Connell draw, a defensively scored draw which, when counted up, surprised its perpetrator. Certainly my overall sense was that Lewis had landed more punches, scored more points, but when it came to rounds, my notebook said Holyfield six, Lewis six. In the ring King's face gave nothing away, no more than that of a tense Steward. But, suddenly, Frank Maloney's did. He had seen the scores as they were handed to announcer Jimmy Lennon and he looked like the Artful Dodger at a moment of great professional satisfaction. He raised his thumb. Lewis was home and the scoring was only marginally less outrageous than in New York, at least in the case of 83-year-old Bill Graham.

Graham gave it to Lewis by six rounds. Chuck Giampa's margin was four rounds and Jerry Roth's was two. Lennox Lewis was, by unanimous decision, the undisputed heavyweight champion of the world. Six weeks from the end of it, he was the century's first British holder of the title of Jack Johnson and Joe Louis, Jack Dempsey and Gene Tunney, Rocky Marciano and Mike Tyson, and – it was the lure which had drawn him on most compulsively – of Muhammad Ali. Lewis had made it all the way and you had to say there was a justice to this which flew beyond the black and white of another set of dubious scorecards. Not perfect justice perhaps, not a single arrow into the heart of all those who questioned the legitimacy of the outrage which followed the first fight, but justice all the same because for all of its apparent inexactitude it reflected a truth which the fierce ringside debate would not touch. Lewis had won in New York and, whatever you thought of his second performance, he had not lost in Las Vegas.

He agreed that it had been a lot more difficult than he had anticipated. He said, 'It was a lot tougher than in New York but deep down I expected that. He got a lot closer to me and obviously he had watched a lot of film on that first fight. He

239

trained up for me and he fought as you would expect a warrior. But I've come through a lot of trials and tribulations – in the ring tonight and over the years. I know I am the best heavyweight in the world. I know I deserve this tonight. I went to win all the belts in New York and they were stolen from me there.'

He said that in the same room where seven years earlier Riddick Bowe had delivered his stream of insults but he was in no mood for any deep re-examination of the past. He had the moment to savour and it would not be soured by some hostile questioning by several American journalists who, absurdly enough, were in the mood to equate what happened in the Thomas and Mack Center with the scandal of Madison Square Garden. Holyfield headed off that line of questioning with a dignity that reminded you that when he was taken away from the quicksand of living with both declaratory religion and an apparently inexhaustible libido, and placed squarely in his natural habitat of the ring, he had instincts which indeed ennobled a game too often tragically cheapened by opportunism and avarice and the playing to the gallery. Said Holyfield, 'You fight, you do your best and then it is handed to the judges. I just thank God now that I was able to put in a good performance, make a fight of it. Lennox Lewis is a good man and a good fighter and I congratulate him.'

That should have meant more to Lewis than the irritation of having in his possession only two of the three belts he had won in the ring. The third, that of the International Boxing Federation besieged by a criminal investigation, was spirited out of the ring minutes before the first bell. It had been taken away by the IBF fight supervisor Walter Stone under the orders of the indicted federation president Bob Lee. In the hours before the fight Lewis's American lawyer Pat English believed he had a deal with Stone over the question of to whom the IBF sanctioning fee of $300,000 should be paid. English had proposed that the fee be placed in a holding account until the tangled affairs of the IBF were unravelled, and at one point Stone had agreed. But a phone call from Lee scotched the deal and threatened that if the money wasn't received, whole and unhindered, by week's end the IBF title would be declared vacant. English and Lewis's promoter Panos Eliades made the principled argument in the face of a barrage of questions, but you could see on Lewis's face the expression of a young boy who had been promised a certain birthday present and had been somewhat betrayed. 'I came for three belts and that's what I want,' he declared. Within the week he had them all, the IBF buckling, for once, under the weight of a champion's indignation.

Several hours after the fight, Emanuel Steward swept through the lobby of the Mandalay Bay on his way to a celebration party. But how deep would be the celebration? 'Oh, deep enough,' he said. 'It wasn't the fight or the performance from Lennox that I wanted, but he won the fight all right and he deserves to be called the undisputed heavyweight champion of the world. He's a good man and an intelligent fighter and no one could have worked harder than he has over the last few years. He had a lot of work to do and he did it, and he didn't complain. I love him like a son and I think he loves me and we can go on from here and we can do a few things. We can do more – a lot more.'

A week or so later, back in his office in Detroit, Steward returned to his theme with an extraordinary force. Yes, he wanted more from Lennox Lewis. He wanted 50 per cent more. He wanted Lewis finally to put flesh on the bones of his own often derided belief, the one Steward shared with Mickey Duff, that Lewis was indeed the most talented heavyweight boxer since the rise of Muhammad Ali.

'I want Lennox to go to the limits of his talent,' said Steward, 'because after working with him for four years I can tell you it is just amazing talent. Some people think I'm a little hard on him but I reject that because I know what he can do. I've seen it in the gym and when he does it, I think, 'That's unbelievable, this guy is the most amazing athlete I have ever seen.' When I talk about my dislike of Lennox playing chess some think it's a joke, some strange obsession I have, but I mean it as much as I've ever meant anything in boxing. I want him to stop seeing boxing as a series of clever moves. I want him to just take control. Just go for it, just understand how much better he is than the other guy across the ring. If he did that, believe me, he would be awesome. The reason I was disappointed Lennox didn't blow Holyfield away is that I know how much better equipped he is than Evander. I think I know that more clearly than anyone because I've worked with both fighters and I know their potential. I know Evander has had a great career because he has always fought pretty much to the edge of his potential. I don't believe Lennox has come anywhere close to his.

'Lennox has at least 50 per cent more than Evander. There are sparring partners out there I wouldn't put in with Evander because, frankly, I might worry that they would be too big and rough and they would wear him out before a big fight. On the other hand there are sparring partners I wouldn't put in with Lennox because I would worry about them. That's the difference in their capacities to do damage. Lennox has a few years left to prove he is one of the greatest heavyweights there has ever been.'

But against whom would he do it? John Ruiz, Henry Akinwande and David Tua, the mandatory challengers of the WBC,WBA and the bedraggled IBF? In themselves they did not exactly stir the blood, but perhaps they might provide a measure of Lewis's growth from the experience of disposing of one of the two last significant names of the era which had consigned him to the margins as Tyson, when not incarcerated or on the rampage, Bowe, Holyfield, Foreman and Moorer dominated the market. There was also Michael Grant, a serious contender in the minds of some American writers despite the brusque dismissal of his potential by Steward, and he seemed to be the early favourite to be first to challenge the new undisputed heavyweight champion. Of course there was still Tyson, ramshackle and wild, indentifying more and more with the sullen martyr Sonny Liston, but still, in the right setting against a good opponent, surefire box office. By the end of January, when Tyson, after weeks of huge publicity, wrecked the hopelessly overmatched British champion Julius Francis, that prospect had come into fine, lucrative focus. First Lewis would defend against Grant in New York on 29 April. Then Tyson would be pencilled in for later in the year.

Lewis has always liked the idea of fighting Tyson, ever since the time when as teenagers they sparred for several days in the gym over the Fire Station in Catskill, New York, where Cus D'Amato was grooming his last contender for a run at the world heavyweight title. Lewis's first trainer, the beloved Arnie Boehm, who ran the boxing club in the police gym in Kitchener, Ontario, was inclined to end the exercise when the more physically mature Tyson had got the better of it. But Lewis reacted strongly to the idea. He would go back to the gym and re-engage this bullock of a kid from Brownsville. He did so, successfully. 'That was so typical of Lennox,' Boehm recalls. 'He was a young man of tremendous pride and determination, and quite fearless. I remember how some kids came to the gym causing trouble and Lennox just knocked one of them down, just like that. I had to give him a good talking to about the need for discipline, but you couldn't help being drawn to a boy who had a strong idea of what was right and what was wrong and who was always ready to work for what he wanted. I remember his impatience to drive. He got in a car once and he didn't really know how to drive it, but he was so set on the idea, and I looked at him with his hands clenched on the steering wheel so tightly and I could imagine him driving clear across Canada in one go.'

Now, so long after that first furious encounter with the young man who would, one way or another, dominate boxing for nearly two decades, Lewis still liked the idea of getting in the ring with Tyson. 'I want to fight in England at some point and I want to have serious fights,' said Lewis, 'but you know in boxing a lot of decisions are made with money in mind. I've come to live with these kinds of decisions. Fighting Tyson now would not be the same as it would have been ten years ago, but it still interests me. It would be the fight to end an era, I suppose.'

Of course in boxing you can never be sure when one era ends and another starts. In 1910 the 35-year-old Jeffries was brought out of retirement to stop the march of Jack Johnson. He hadn't fought for five years, weighed around 22 stone and was reported to have a $12,000 gambling debt. But he was seen as the white hope to bring down the 'uppity nigger' Johnson, and the old champion 'Gentleman Jim' Corbett assured a largely racist fight crowd that 'the black boy has a yellow streak and Jim Jeffries will find it'. He didn't, he was beaten near to pulp over 15 rounds and there were 11 deaths in the subsequent race riots. Joe Louis and Archie Moore were clubbed to defeat by Rocky Marciano and for both these old, great men the imperative was neither glory (they had so much of that to spare) nor consideration of race, but money, simply money.

Such would be the impetus of Lewis versus Tyson. When Tyson's handlers made a fight with Julius Francis, an inflated sparring partner, in Manchester in January 2000, they were addressing again their fighter's still mountainous debts. Tyson was due around $6 million for the Francis fight. They knew they could get at least four times, maybe five times that amount for a Lewis fight, but first Tyson had to bring his life into some kind of order.

It was as Lewis said, 'Down the years Tyson has done some terrible things, he has been a great embarrassment to boxing and sometimes, along with everybody else, I've criticised him, but if I

did too much of that I would be a hypocrite. Because all the time
Tyson was going in and out of jail, all the times he seemed to have
lost the plot completely, I couldn't help noticing that the fans kept
wanting to see him fight, whoever he was fighting. And of course
that interested me from my own point of view. Fighting Tyson
would mean a lot of money – and a lot of attention. Boxing feeds
on that, doesn't it? That's what keeps it going, public interest. My
fight in New York became so huge when something bad
happened. Yes, a fight with Tyson has to be in my plans, and not
too far down the road. It is really just a question of him keeping
out of trouble for a while, looking up and realising what is at
stake. I hope he feels strongly the need to earn $30 million and is
prepared to make sure it happens. A good start would be staying
out of jail.'

As the latest big fight camp folded its garish tents in Las Vegas,
as Lennox Lewis flew off to Los Angeles and then New York for
the top TV shows and the celebrity circus, as Evander Holyfield
headed back home to Georgia and his horses and his children and
his litigious womenfolk to peer again into the future, it could be
said that boxing also had a huge need to stay out of jail.

In many cases, as the FBI pressed on with its work, this might
not have been entirely possible, but the game itself had received
something of a stay of execution. If Lewis–Holyfield II had failed
to light up the desert sky, if some still complained that Lewis was
too complacent in the luxury of his own skin, boxing did have an
unchallenged heavyweight champion of the world. It also
happened that he was a good man, with no police record and with
a dignity that was unforced and as natural as his gangling
boyhood strides in the streets of east London. Who could say in
all the circumstances that this wasn't something of a miracle?

15

Standing with Ali

It is a few weeks after the re-match and I'm travelling along Marylebone Road in a cab when my mobile phone rings. 'Who's that?' demands a voice I recognise immediately as that of Lennox Lewis. I announce myself and say, 'Is that the undisputed heavyweight champion of the world?' and I am told, 'Yes, and it don't come any bigger than that.'

There is the lightest chuckle in Lewis's voice and it reminds me all over again why I had allowed myself to be so caught up in his cause from that first moment I saw him disengage Gary Mason from the fiction that he had an earthly chance of finishing up on top of the heavyweight heap. I believed right then in Lennox Lewis, in the way that persuaded me to make a saving bet on Lester Piggott in the last race at Kempton Park and to have a flutter on Mike Atherton at 14–1 to make a century after a lean run in New Zealand. I won on Piggott and lost on Atherton, though the batsman did make 92 flawless runs and fell to a freak catch. The point is that of all my habits the one I least despise is a willingness to invest a little in class for its own sake. You know where you are with class, however lightly formed, and that, it seems to me, is always more important than the win and loss column of any particular day's work. Class goes marching beyond the imposter's triumph and defeat.

If at any point in this book I have given an impression of great familiarity with Lewis, I formally withdraw it. For it would be false. He has always been unfailingly courteous and helpful within the pressures of his life and his job and it is true that when I once took my youngest daughter, Hannah, to lunch with him, at a difficult time in her life when she had just tragically lost a close friend, he behaved with that type of unfussy kindness which can never be forced. I have also seen the reaction of East End kids who had fallen through the net of society when he visited the trade school he helped to set up in Hackney. They saw him not as some celebrity figure but a big, amiable young man who cared about them, and perhaps in a way that had not been exhibited before. But all this is by the by.

The professional appeal of Lewis for me has always been a competitive integrity which I have seen as especially splendid at a time when both boxing and the wider world of sport seemed to be slipping into a value system underpinned chiefly by compromise and the need to make money. Of course Lewis has made money, vast amounts of it, and sometimes he has been a little slow to recognise that often its most generous source, for one reason or another and doubtless not all distinguished by the pure flame of altruism, has been Don King. It is maybe not true that Confucius said that if you walk on the mountainside you can't always be on the level, but if he had been around boxing he might have done. However, Lennox Lewis has been careful not to cast himself too thoroughly in the role of boxing's knight of honour, and we have seen recent evidence of this in his appraisal of the appeal of a Tyson fight in the dog days of an era which gave us

Foreman and any number of refugees from the graveyard and paid Tyson $30 million for fighting the wretched Pete McNeely. Some are critical of Lewis's decision to take step-aside money from Tyson, but by then he was weary of the courts and it was Tyson who paid to avoid the fight, not Lewis.

Lewis called me, and broke into my climactic discussion with the cab driver on the affairs of Arsenal football club, not out of whim or to discuss the turn of the world but because I had sent a message that I needed to speak with him. I wanted from him a brief postcript to his Mission Impossible, a little reflection after a few weeks on what it meant to have achieved his goal, to have fought his way through the politics and the sleaze and from that bleak night in Wembley Arena when Oliver McCall threw the punch from hell and all the potential ambushes that had intervened before the moment it was declared, offically, that he had beaten Evander Holyfield and become the one true champion of the world.

Lewis told me, 'It took a few days to sink in. You know, it would suddenly come to me out of the blue that I had got there, that all those nightmares were in the past. Whatever happened now, I could say that once I was the one and only heavyweight champion of the world. That goes beyond money or anything else. It's what I was chasing and now I've got it I know it was all worthwhile, and that I was right to carry on after the first McCall fight. I made the right decision when I was in the mountains in Jamaica and thought it all through. I was right to put up with all the legal action when I knew I had enough money that I never had to really worry about it for the rest of my life. Now I'm asked what I want to give to boxing and the world as heavyweight champion. Well, all I can do is give myself. I can't give what Muhammad Ali did, or Holyfield or Tyson. We are all different. I just hope what I have is worth something to the people who support boxing, who have made every champion rich.

249

'I like to think I can give the people something they expect in a champion of the world. That I won't let them down. I'll never quit. I'll get the job done in the best way I can. That may not please everyone, I realise that now. Ali was always my idol, I looked up to him and he never disappointed me. If some kid can say that about me in 20 years' time, well, I'll be very proud. I will have done my duty as a champion.'

At the end of our last conversation before this piece was finished, he said, 'I'll see you on Monday.' But he didn't make it to the special lunch the British Boxing Writers Association threw to celebrate his triumph. His manager Frank Maloney sheepishly admitted to the writers, who were naturally disgruntled, that their guest of honour was nursing a fairly serious hangover. It was perhaps not the toughest task of communication, explaining to a group of journalists that sometimes in life the need to celebrate can impinge on the best-ordered business agenda.

Lewis had taken champagne with the players of Manchester United after the BBC Sports Personality of the Year ceremonies, at which they had been given the team award for the extraordinary treble success of Premiership, FA Cup and European Cup, and he had collected the individual prize. He had won it on an overwhelming vote of the public and it was for him the most beautifully rounded moment of triumph. If he was undoubtedly the British sports personality of the year after his historic achievement, there was, equally, no question about the right of Muhammad Ali to steal some of his glory. The great man stood shaking from the effects of Parkinson's disease and too many blows in the ring but defiant and so warm in his humour and his humanity he could have substituted for the National Grid as he received his trophy as sportsman of the century.

It was a moment, perhaps, for a little measuring of the glory. In so many ways the life and the career of Lennox Lewis could not compete with that of Muhammad Ali. Lennox Lewis never had to run the vicious gauntlet of racism in the southern states of America. He never had to overwhelm the fighting psychology of the ogre Sonny Liston, who made Floyd Patterson's blood run cold. He never had to stand against the white political establish-ment of the most powerful nation in the world with the simple statement that he had no quarrel with 'them Viet Cong'. He never had to overcome Joe Frazier in a fight which brought both men close to death. He didn't have to send a seismic shock around with the world with a defeat of George Foreman.

But he did have to do a few considerable things. He had to stand up for what he believed sport should be all about – a degree of honesty, of decency, and the need for true competition where the public saw real fights between the best men available. He also had to build himself up again from the devastation of shocking defeat. He met all these challenges and at the end of a sporting millennium he stood, proudly, shoulder to shoulder with the greatest fighter, and one of the greatest men, who ever lived. It was indeed somewhere to be and who could say that Lennox Lewis didn't deserve his place in the history of the land of his birth and the whole world of sport?